CLIFFS NOTES

on

THE BIBLE

> **Summaries and Commentaries
> about both the Old Testament
> and the New Testament**

Cliffs Notes

INCORPORATED

LINCOLN, NEBRASKA 68501

Editor

Gary Carey, M.A.
University of Colorado

Consulting Editor

James L. Roberts, Ph.D.
Department of English
University of Nebraska

ISBN 0-8220-0236-1

The Old Testament Notes © Copyright 1965; The New Testament
Notes © Copyright 1965 by Cliffs Notes, Inc.

ACKNOWLEDGEMENT
The author of Cliffs Notes on the Old Testament
and Cliffs Notes on the New Testament is
Charles H. Patterson, Ph.D., Professor of
Philosophy, University of Nebraska-Lincoln.

Cliffs Notes, Inc.   Lincoln, Nebraska

THE OLD TESTAMENT

INTRODUCTION TO THE OLD TESTAMENT

Although the Old Testament is often referred to as a book, it is really a collection of many books, or separate manuscripts, produced by different individuals over a long period of time. These individual books were not written for the same purpose, nor were they considered to be of equal importance at the times when they were written. Many were in existence in some form long before they were assembled into a single collection and given the status of Scripture, or sacred writing. Not until the sixth and fifth centuries B.C. was any portion of the Old Testament writings arranged in the form in which we have them today. During this period, they came to be regarded as authoritative documents for declaring the word of the deity to the people of Israel. At later times, other writings were added to the original collection, but not until near the close of the first century A.D. was general agreement reached concerning all of the books that are now included in the canon of the Old Testament.

The importance of the Old Testament as reflected in the influence it has had through the centuries can scarcely be overestimated. Its religious significance is indicated primarily by the fact that it is recognized as a part of the inspired sacred literature of three of the major religions of the world. First of all, it was the sacred Bible of Judaism and is so regarded at the present time. Along with the New Testament, it is included in the Bible of Christianity, and it holds a similar place in the religion of Islam, for the followers of Mohammed accept its teachings along with those of the Koran. But the influence of the Old Testament has not been confined to the adherents of these three religions: It has permeated the cultures of many countries of the world and has been one of the main sources of the moral and political ideals that have played so vital a role in the history of Western nations. The ideas of democracy, individual worth, freedom in its various forms, the rights of humans, divine purpose in the world, human destiny—all find their origin, in part, in the literature of the Old Testament. The influence of this book is also reflected in the great literatures of Europe and America. Allusions to passages in the Old Testament are so frequent that many of the great books in English and

American literature cannot be read intelligently without some familiarity with the context from which these passages are taken.

To understand the writings included in the Old Testament, we must bear in mind that they are predominantly an expression of the religious life of the ancient Hebrew people. In this respect, they must be distinguished from writings that are primarily scientific or historical in the secular sense in which these terms are used. Modern scientists and historians have as their main objective an accurate description of the way in which events occur. Whether these events are related to some divine purpose or merely illustrate the sequence of their occurrence is not for historians to say; they neither deny nor affirm any divine activity. But this passive stance is not true of the Old Testament authors, who begin with the assumption of a divine being whose character and purpose are disclosed, at least to some extent, in the course of human events. With this assumption, they write for the specific purpose of pointing out the divine element as they see it illustrated in the historical process. In this respect, the real significance of their writings is to be understood, and to judge the value of the Old Testament account of events on the sole basis of either scientific or historical accuracy is a mistake. The individual books of the Old Testament were written with a different objective in mind, which does not mean that the narratives in the Old Testament have no historical value at all. They are recognized, even by secular historians, as one of the most reliable sources available for reconstructing the history of the Hebrew people. But as source materials, they must be evaluated in the same way as any other source material. The greatness of the writings lies in another area: in the disclosure, or revelation, of the divine element in history, along with the moral and religious lessons that are derived from it.

It has long been customary to regard the books of the Bible as the revealed word of God. Speaking of them in this way is justified provided that one understands the meaning of revelation. Important to remember in this connection is that revelation is always and necessarily a two-way process that involves both a giving and a receiving. We may appropriately think of the giving as the divine element and the receiving as the human element. However perfect the source of divine revelation may be, the human understanding of it is necessarily limited and subject to error, which is not to say that divine wisdom can never be imparted to human beings at all, but it does mean that the reception of this wisdom must take into account the limitations that belong to human understanding.

THE HISTORICAL BACKGROUND OF THE OLD TESTAMENT

To understand the Old Testament, it is necessary to have some familiarity with the history of the people who wrote it. Judaism is a historical religion, which means that the ideas associated with it were disclosed to the Hebrew people through the concrete events that occurred in that part of the world where they lived during the centuries in which the Old Testament was in the making. A detailed account of the entire history of the Hebrew people would go far beyond the scope of this present study; however, a brief outline of some of the major high points in that history will be sufficient for our purpose.

While it is true that the books of the Old Testament begin with an account of the creation of the world, we must bear in mind that the narratives dealing with such topics as the Creation, the Garden of Eden, the Fall, the Great Flood, and other events related in the Book of Genesis were never intended to be regarded as an accurate historical account of the entire world process. None of these accounts appeared in written form until *after* the Hebrews had settled in the land of Canaan, west of the Jordan River, which did not take place prior to the ninth century B.C. Obviously, the stories that one finds in the early chapters of the Book of Genesis, as well as those that have to do with the activities of the patriarchs, who were believed to have lived before the time of the Exodus from Egypt, were not written by eyewitnesses of the events that were recorded. Neither were they written by people who lived during the times about which they wrote. Not until after the men who eventually wrote the narratives had reflected on the events connected with the history of their people was any attempt made to record these events or to set forth their meanings. When this recording was done, the interpretations necessarily reflected the perspective from which they were written.

The beginnings of Hebrew history are obscure and cannot be known with certainty. It is generally believed that the people from whom the Old Testament eventually emerged came from a group of Semitic tribes known as the Habiru. These tribes inhabited the region referred to as the Fertile Crescent, a strip of land lying between the Tigris and Euphrates rivers and stretching southward for some distance in the direction of Egypt and the Nile River. They are known to have moved about in this territory as early as 2000 B.C. Eventually, some of these tribes migrated to Egypt and lived there for some time, probably for three or four centuries. Apparently, they were initially welcomed by the Egyptians, for the Hebrew colony grew and prospered. But their numbers increased to the extent that the Egyptians became alarmed lest their own security become endangered. An Egyptian pharaoh, in order to protect his people against any further advances on the part of the Hebrews, inaugurated a program of harsh measures toward the newcomers, forcing them into a condition of servitude and slavery. This situation is referred to in the Old Testament as the period of Egyptian bondage. In connection with this period of oppression, we first learn of Moses and his role in bringing about the deliverance of his people. Under his guidance and leadership, the Hebrews were able to leave the land of Egypt—the Exodus—and journey to new territory, where they were to make their home.

The Exodus from the land of Egypt, usually dated as 1250 B.C., marked the turning point in the history of the Hebrew people and enabled them to become a separate nation. It was to this event that the great prophets and teachers of later generations always referred when they recounted the way in which their god—known to them as Yahweh—so graciously dealt with them. The Exodus was followed by a period of wandering in the wilderness, after which the various tribes now known as the Israelites established themselves in the land of Canaan. Those who had emerged from bondage in Egypt were then united with other tribes that had not been involved in the Egyptian oppression, and together they formed the nucleus from which the Hebrew state came into existence.

Although the literature that is now included in the Old Testament did not begin to appear until after the settlement in the land of Canaan, it was only natural that the history of the people should be projected back into the period that preceded the migration into Egypt, for a relatively large number of stories and legends had been handed down orally from one generation to another. Although there are good reasons for believing that these stories grew out of actual experiences, the narratives cannot be regarded as authentic history, nor can we place the same reliance on them as we do on the accounts of events that occurred after the settlement in Canaan. Accordingly, biblical scholars customarily refer to the period that preceded the migration to Egypt as the Age of the Patriarchs, or the prehistoric era of the Hebrew people.

After leaving Egypt, the Hebrews are said to have spent forty years wandering in the wilderness prior to their entrance into the land of Canaan. The number forty is generally understood to represent a relatively long period of time rather than an exact number of years. Although the settlement in Canaan is described in two widely differing accounts, we can be fairly certain that it required a considerable number of years before the new settlers obtained full possession of the land. During this time, the various tribes were organized into a confederacy, and judges were appointed to rule over the people. In theory at least, these judges were governed by Yahweh, who communicated directly with them. This theocratic government came to an end when the people demanded a king, and Saul was chosen to head the newly formed monarchy. He was succeeded by David, and after David, Solomon, who was the last ruler of the united kingdom. After Solomon's death, the kingdom was divided. Ten tribes revolted and formed what came to be known as the northern kingdom, or the Israelite nation. Because the tribe of Ephraim was the largest and most influential of this ten-tribe group, the new unit of government was frequently referred to as the Ephraimite kingdom. The two tribes that did not revolt became the southern, or Judean, kingdom.

The two separate kingdoms existed until about the year 722 B.C., when the northern kingdom was overrun by the Assyrian empire. The people were taken into captivity, and their national existence came to an end. The southern kingdom continued until 586 B.C., when it was conquered by the Babylonians, and a large portion of the Hebrew people were forced to live in exile. The Babylonian exile lasted for more than a century but finally came to an end when permission was given to the Hebrews to return to their own land. The Hebrews rebuilt the city of Jerusalem, restored the Temple and its services, and organized their state along lines that had been laid down by the prophets and priests of the exile. But the restored state never enjoyed the peace and prosperity that was anticipated. Internal difficulties arose, the land was troubled with drought and pestilence, and the danger of attack from surrounding states never diminished.

The close of the Persian period and the death of Alexander the Great brought about a new set of circumstances most unfavorable to the Hebrews. Egypt and Syria were two rival powers, each struggling for supremacy over the other, and the Jewish nation became a buffer state between them. Toward the latter part of the second century B.C., the Maccabean wars, launched by Antiochus of Syria, brought extreme suffering to the Jews and threatened complete destruction of their state. Fortunately, the Jews were able to survive this crisis. Under the leadership of Judas Maccabeus and his successors, they were able to regain the land that was taken from them and once again become free and independent. However, this situation did not last very long, for the Roman government ultimately conquered the region.

Some of the more important events and accomplishments in these successive periods of Hebrew history may be summarized briefly as follows:

The Prehistoric Period.   This period is recounted in the stories and legends preserved by the Hebrews as a vital part of their cultural heritage. Narratives concerning the Hebrew ancestors enabled later generations to establish continuity with the great traditions of the past. To what extent these stories record actual events that took place we have no way of knowing, nor does it matter a great deal. The important thing about them is the way in which the ideals of a later age are reflected in them. Because the historical period of Hebrew activities begins with the Exodus from Egypt, we can say only that the stories about what happened prior to the Exodus provide a record of what later generations believed to have taken place, although we do have good reasons for thinking that these accounts were originally based on actual events.

In these stories, the beginnings of Hebrew history are traced back to Abraham, who, according to the record, was called out of the land of Ur of the Chaldeans; to him, it was promised that his seed would become a great nation and inherit the land of Canaan. This promise seemed impossible to fulfill because both Abraham and his wife, Sarah, were old and childless. However, Yahweh intervened, and in due time Isaac was born to the couple. Isaac's two sons, Esau and Jacob, were the ancestors of the Edomites and the Israelites, respectively. Jacob's twelve sons were the progenitors of the twelve tribes of Israel. Because of a severe famine in Canaan, Jacob's sons went to Egypt to buy food. One of the sons, Joseph, who had been sold into slavery at an earlier time, was now a prominent official in the Egyptian government. He had charge of the food supplies, and when his brothers came to make their purchase, they had to deal with him. His identity was concealed from them for a time, but eventually he made himself known. As a result of these meetings, it was arranged that Jacob and all of his sons and their families should move to Egypt, where they were peaceably settled in the district known as Goshen. Here they remained until the Egyptian pharaoh of the oppression ascended the throne and began a policy of hostilities toward them.

The Wilderness Journey. The journey into the wilderness following the Exodus from Egypt was marked by two important, closely related events: the proclamation of a code of laws that, according to the tradition, Yahweh revealed to Moses on Mount Sinai, and the establishment of a covenant, or contract, between Yahweh and the people of Israel. The basis of the covenant was the body of laws that Yahweh had given and that the people had agreed to obey. Yahweh's part of the contract consisted of his promise to care for the people, supplying for their needs and protecting them against attacks by their enemies.

This covenant relationship between Yahweh and his people, one of the dominant ideas throughout the entire Old Testament, served to distinguish Yahweh from the gods of the surrounding nations. Generally, these other gods were believed to be related to their peoples by the natural ties of physical descent. In other words, they were bound to their people by ties that were not dependent on any contractual agreement or on any type of moral qualification. Consequently, they could not abandon their people because of any moral transgression by the people. But this was not true of Yahweh in his relation to the Hebrew people. His promise to remain as their god was conditional on their living up to the terms of the agreement. Whenever they failed to obey the laws he had given to them, he was no longer bound to protect them or even to claim them as his own people. The prophets of later generations would call attention to this fact and thus remind their contemporaries that security for the nation could not be expected so long as people failed to fulfill the requirements of the covenant to which they had committed themselves.

The content of the law code—the Law—on which the covenant relationship between Yahweh and the Hebrew people was based is recorded in what is now known as the Book of the Covenant, in Exodus 20:23-23:19. The famous Decalogue, or Ten Commandments, found in the first seventeen verses of Chapter 20, may have been included in the law code given by Moses, although certainly it was not given in the exact form in which we have it today. Both Jewish and Christian traditions have for many centuries regarded Moses as the great lawgiver of the Hebrews and, accordingly, as the author of all the laws contained in the first five books of the Old Testament—the Pentateuch.

Modern scholarship has produced ample evidence to indicate that many of these laws were not known until long after Moses' own death. That these same laws were attributed to Moses was not intended to deceive anyone concerning the time of their origin; rather, these laws were in harmony with the ones given by Moses and were added to his for the purpose of continuing the work he had begun. How many of the laws contained in the five books known as the Pentateuch were actually given by Moses is not known. However, a reasonable assumption is that the ones contained in the Book of the Covenant were first enunciated by Moses since these laws are appropriate to the age in which he lived. The similarity of this law code to the older Babylonian code of Hammurabi has led many scholars to believe that the Mosaic code was modeled after the Babylonian one. However this may be, unique elements in the Mosaic code may rightly be regarded as a distinctive Hebrew contribution.

The Settlement in Canaan. The accounts of the settlement in Canaan, described in the Old Testament books of Joshua and Judges, were evidently derived from different sources since there are significant differences between them. The conquest of

Canaan required a considerable period of time and was attended by some important changes in the daily lives of the Hebrew people, including a change from a nomadic or shepherd type of living to a permanent settlement and an agricultural mode of securing a livelihood. This new way of life called for a different type of organization among the various tribes, which is why a great assembly was called at Shechem. Under the leadership of Joshua, steps were taken to unite the tribes into a kind of confederacy, an organization similar in many respects to what has been known in other cultures as an amphictyony. The newly formed community was predominantly religious rather than political. Membership in the community consisted mainly of Hebrews but was not limited by racial qualifications. Anyone who chose to worship Yahweh and who promised to obey the Law that Yahweh had given was accepted as a full member of the community. It was this body of people that came to be known as the twelve tribes of Israel.

The government of the new community was placed in the hands of judges, who were believed to receive instructions directly from Yahweh through dreams, visions, and other forms of charismatic experience. Deborah, for example, was one of these judges. She was the judge who sent out a call to the scattered tribes to come to the aid of those who were being attacked by the Canaanites. The call was sent out in the name of Yahweh, whose intervention at a crucial moment enabled the Israelites to defeat their enemies in a battle that was fought on the plains of Megiddo. Gideon, whose band of three hundred warriors achieved another important victory, was also a judge of Israel. Because of his success, some of the people wanted to proclaim him king, the chief reason being the need for a stronger type of organization to resist attacks from surrounding nations. Gideon refused to be king. However, after his death, his son Abimelech yielded to the temptation, and an attempt was made to have him reign as king over Israel. The attempt failed, but the demand for a monarchal type of government continued, and finally Samuel, who was the last of the judges, anointed Saul to be the first king of Israel.

The United Kingdom. Beginning with the reign of Saul, the united kingdom was continued under David and Solomon. In some respects, Saul was an able ruler and a competent warrior who spent much of his time battling the Philistines. His military successes won for him the praises and admiration of the people. He was not an arbitrary ruler but one who tried to follow the charismatic directions that had been in vogue during the period of the judges. During the latter part of his reign, he was subject to prolonged periods of melancholy, which he interpreted to mean that Yahweh no longer communicated with him. He was rebuked by the prophet Samuel for the way in which he conducted the war against the Amalekites, and his career ended in disaster when he died on the hills of Gilboa in the midst of conflict with the Philistines.

David's reign marks the high point in the history of the united kingdom. David was idealized by later generations as Israel's greatest king, and excuses were made for the unfortunate things that happened while he was king. Nevertheless, he was a great king who accomplished much for the nation he served, including successfully uniting the northern and southern tribes under one centralized government, with its headquarters at Jerusalem. His plans for the building of the Temple were carried out after his son Solomon ascended the throne. David's reign was not altogether peaceful, for it was marred by external conflict and internal dissension and revolt. In spite of these difficulties, however, the nation grew and prospered. Centuries later, no higher compliment could be bestowed on an Israelite king than to say he was like King David.

Solomon, too, was idealized by later generations but not in the same way as his father, David. Solomon's greatest accomplishment was the building of the Temple at Jerusalem. In order to extend the power and influence of Israel among surrounding nations, Solomon contracted a number of foreign marriages. The wives whom he brought to Jerusalem were permitted to worship their native gods, and thus idolatry was introduced and encouraged alongside the worship of Yahweh. Solomon's building operations were made possible by heavy taxation, along with other burdens that the people were forced to bear. Solomon was so strongly resented that when the question of who should succeed him on the throne was raised, people inquired of Solomon's son Rehoboam about his attitude concerning the oppressive measures of his father. When Rehoboam replied that he would not only continue these policies but would be even more severe, ten of the tribes revolted and set up a new government of their own.

The Divided Kingdom. The schism began with the death of King Solomon and lasted until the fall of Samaria in 722 B.C., at which time the northern kingdom ended and its people were taken into captivity by the Assyrians. The southern kingdom continued until 586 B.C., when Jerusalem was destroyed and the Babylonian captivity began. The histories of these two kingdoms are recorded in 1 and 2 Kings, whose author evidently belonged to the southern kingdom, for his account indicates a strong bias in that direction. Concerning each of the kings who reigned in the north, the Kings author uses the same statement: "He did evil in the eyes of the Lord." Although some of the southern kings were evil too, the Kings author was usually able to find some excuse for the things that they did. Because there was no fixed system of chronology for recording the dates when things happened, the events in the reign of each king were synchronized with what took place in the other kingdom.

The northern kingdom, known as Israel, had a very difficult time during the first century of its existence. The tribes were frequently at war with neighboring states, and peace was obtained on more than one occasion only by making large concessions to the enemy. Later, the tribes' fortunes changed as they were able to regain most of what they had previously lost. Under the leadership of King Jeroboam II, who reigned for more than half a century, Israel enjoyed a period of unprecedented prosperity. With the death of this king, a period of decline set in, and conditions went from bad to worse. Moral decay led to political weakness, and soon the nation became an easy prey for the advancing Assyrian armies. During the years that preceded the collapse of the northern kingdom, the prophets Elijah, Amos, and Hosea carried on their work.

The southern kingdom, known as Judah, lasted for more than a century after the fall of Israel. It occupied less territory than the northern kingdom and, for the most part, led a more peaceful existence. All of the kings of Judah were direct descendants in the line of David, which was of particular significance because it was believed that some day the Messiah would come from this line and that under the Messiah's leadership the full realization of the divine purpose in the history of the Hebrew people would be realized.

The most prosperous period in the life of the southern kingdom came during the reign of Uzziah. After his death, the country was invaded by the Assyrian army, and for some time it looked as though Judah would suffer the same fate as Israel. Then, suddenly, the Assyrian army withdrew, and the nation was spared. However, for the remainder of their existence as an independent nation, the Judeans were forced to make concessions, including an enormous tribute to the Assyrian rulers. Likewise, after the fall of the Assyrian empire, they were subservient first to the Egyptians and later to the Babylonians. During the decline of the southern kingdom, many of the great prophets delivered their messages, including Isaiah, Micah, Zephaniah, Jeremiah, and Habakkuk.

The Exile and After.   When Jerusalem was captured by the armies of Nebuchadnezzar and the inhabitants of Judah were deported to Babylon, the worshipers of Yahweh were put to a severe test. To many, it must have appeared that the gods of Babylon had triumphed over the god of the Hebrews. If Yahweh still retained his power, he must have forsaken his people, for they were now subject to a foreign government. The survival of the Hebrews' religion was due in no small measure to the work of the two great prophets of the exile, Ezekiel and Deutero-Isaiah, who provided an interpretation of the captivity that accorded with their understanding of the nature of Yahweh. They kept alive the hope of a return to the Hebrews' own land and the prospects for a glorious future of the restored state.

The captivity lasted for a long time. Eventually, the Babylonian empire was overthrown by the Persians, who exhibited a more tolerant attitude toward the Jews. Cyrus, the head of the new empire, granted the captives permission to return to their own land, and he even aided them in their preparations for the journey back. But the return of the exiles did not prove to be the happy event that they had anticipated. They found the Temple in ruins, and the country was desolate; the land was plagued with drought and pestilence; their neighbors were often hostile; and, in many respects, their lot was now more difficult than it had been while they were in captivity. Prophets offered explanations for the way things were and did their best to encourage the people to look for a brighter future. Priests were especially active, and a new emphasis was given to the ritualistic aspect of their religion. Literary productions were numerous, and legalism became dominant in the religion of Judaism.

Politically, the affairs of the restored state grew steadily worse. The Persian empire was overthrown by the Grecian armies under the leadership of Alexander the Great, whose conquests included Palestine. He was tolerant of the Jews, allowing them to continue their religious activities so long as they did not interfere with his political ambitions. After Alexander's death, the Jews experienced some of the most severe persecutions they had ever known, for Antiochus, the ruler of Syria, tried to obliterate completely the long-established customs and traditions of the Jewish faith. Antiochus' efforts sparked the Maccabean wars. When these wars were finally over, the Jews enjoyed a brief period of political independence, but ultimately they became subjects of the Roman government.

A CHRONOLOGICAL ORDER OF OLD TESTAMENT WRITINGS

The history of the Hebrew people is reflected in nearly all of the literature found in the Old Testament. Sometimes it is the history of the people as a whole; other times, it is that of a smaller group or even the experiences of a particular individual. The writers of the Old Testament believed that Yahweh revealed himself through history in much the same way that we think a person's character is disclosed through that person's actions. For this reason, some familiarity with the historical setting of each of the writings is prerequisite to an understanding of them.

The exact order in which the contents of the Old Testament were initially placed is not known. The literature as we have it today contains many fragments that appear to have existed separately at one time. They have been combined, copied, edited, supplemented, and arranged so many times that not even the most expert scholars are in complete agreement about the order in which they first appeared. This confusion does not mean that we are unable to know anything concerning the Old Testament or that we cannot be reasonably certain about the approximate time when the various parts of the literature were produced. On the other hand, our conclusions should be reached with considerable caution, and we must always be ready to revise them in consideration of new evidence. Our purpose here is merely to outline the approximate order of the writings in accordance with generally recognized Old Testament scholarship.

The oldest writings are now included as parts of historical narratives that did not reach their final form until a relatively late date. Many of them can be located with a fair degree of accuracy in the books of the Pentateuch, the first five books of the Old Testament. Other early fragments are found in Joshua, Judges, and those portions of the Old Testament that deal with the early history of the Hebrew nation. Some of these writings are as old as the conquest of Canaan, and some even older than that. Not all of the early literature of the Hebrews has been preserved in the Old Testament—for example, the Book of the Wars of Yahweh, the Book of Yashur the Upright, the Book of the Acts of Solomon, the "Royal Annals," and the "Temple Annals"—but we know of their existence because of Old Testament references to them. In several instances, extracts have been taken from them and included in other Old Testament writings.

An exhaustive account of these early writings cannot be attempted here, but their general character is indicated by the following examples. Poems were written in commemoration of significant events. For example, "The Song of Deborah," recorded in Judges 5, was written in celebration of a victory over the Canaanites. "The Fable of the Trees," found in Judges 9, discusses the abortive attempt of Abimelech to become king over Israel. "The Blessing of Jacob," part of Genesis 49, recalls Jacob's last meeting with his sons. "The Oracles of Balaam," recorded in Numbers 23 and 24, describe an experience that occurred during the wilderness march. "David's Lament," which commemorates the deaths of Saul and Jonathan, is found in 2 Samuel 1:19-27, and a song celebrating a victory over the Amorites is recorded in Numbers 21:27-30. One of the oldest of these poems is Lamech's "Song of Revenge," found in Genesis 4:23-24. Miriam's "Song of Deliverance," in Exodus 15:21, may be as old as the time of Moses.

Among the early narratives that were used as source materials for later histories are such documents as "The Story of the Founding of the Kingdom." Written by an ardent admirer of King

David, it presents the story of David's kingship in a most favorable light. The writer believed in the monarchy and describes in considerable detail the events that led to its establishment. He begins with an account of Israel's oppression by the Philistines, which, he argues, clearly shows the need for a strong and capable leader. The prophet Samuel sees the proper qualifications in Saul and promptly anoints him to be the first king of Israel. The writer tells of important events in Saul's reign, but the real hero of his story is David. The reader is impressed with the charm of David's personality and the accomplishments of his reign. Although David was proclaimed king at Hebron, located in the southern kingdom, he was able to win the loyalty and support of the northern tribes as well. As a means of further unification, he made the city of Jerusalem, located midway between the northern and southern kingdoms, the capital of the newly formed state. The story concludes with an account of the succession to the throne of David's son Solomon.

Two other narratives that furnished valuable information for later historians are the Book of the Acts of Solomon and "The Rise and Fall of the House of Omri." The first of these tells of King Solomon and the events that took place during the early years of his reign. Solomon's prayer at the dedication of the Temple, his request for wisdom to guide his people, and the grandeur of his building operations are given particular emphasis. The other narrative concerns the reign of Omri, who was one of the more important rulers of the northern kingdom. Only parts of this narrative were used by the author of 1 Kings, for some of the material did not serve the purpose for which that author wrote. The reign of King Ahab, Omri's son, is described at considerable length. The account is especially important because it helps to correct some of the unfavorable impressions of King Ahab conveyed by other narratives.

Stories concerning the work of the prophet Elijah and his successor, Elisha, are also part of the early narratives produced in the northern kingdom. Of these stories that have been preserved, those having to do with Elijah are by far the most significant. They indicate a conception of Yahweh that is far more advanced than previously held beliefs, whereas the Elisha stories are of a somewhat lower level of religious development.

No account of the early fragments that ultimately became parts of the Old Testament would be complete without mention of the laws that were designed to regulate human conduct. Probably the oldest of these laws are those contained in the Book of the Covenant. Although we do not know when they first appeared in written form, there are good reasons for believing that these laws were known as early as the time of Moses, but they were not put in writing until a much later date. We do know that new laws were added from time to time as the need for them arose. Later, all of the laws were placed in a historical framework and, along with the early poems and narratives, were incorporated in the lengthy historical documents that constitute a relatively late but significant portion of the literature of the Old Testament.

The first books of the Old Testament to appear in the approximate form in which we have them today are the ones attributed to the prophets. It would be a mistake to suppose that all of the contents found in the Old Testament books that bear the names of prophets were written by the persons for whom the books are named. Actually, the work of the prophets themselves constitutes only the main basis or essential core of the books. Editors, copyists, and redactors added materials that they regarded as appropriate, and these additions were preserved along with the original materials.

Amos and Hosea are the only prophetic books that belong to the literature of the northern kingdom. Both books were produced during the eighth century B.C., and both concern conditions that existed in Israel prior to that nation's collapse. The Book of Isaiah (Chapters 1-39) and the Book of Micah come from the same century and are addressed to the people of Judah, or the southern kingdom.

From the seventh century B.C., or the era that preceded the Babylonian captivity, we have the prophecies of Zephaniah, Nahum, Habakkuk, and Jeremiah. Of these four, the Book of Jeremiah, who in many respects is regarded as the greatest of the Old Testament prophets, is not only the longest but also the most important. Ezekiel and Deutero-Isaiah (Chapters 40-55 in the Book of Isaiah) are especially significant. They came out of the period of the exile and greatly influenced the development of religious ideals in the centuries that followed. The prophets of the post-exilic period—Haggai, Zechariah, Malachi, Joel, and Obadiah—are usually classified among the so-called minor prophets. The books in which their messages have been preserved are relatively small, and their contents indicate that their authors were men of lesser stature than the ones who appeared earlier.

The historical writings that make up approximately one-third of the Old Testament—the Pentateuch, or what is often referred to as the five books of Moses; Joshua; Judges; 1 and 2 Samuel; 1 and 2 Kings; 1 and 2 Chronicles; Ezra; and Nehemiah—cannot be dated or arranged as definitely or with the same degree of accuracy as the prophetic writings, the chief reason being that they were in the process of being written and amended over long periods of time. Whether they are to be regarded as early or late will depend on one's point of view. If we have in mind the source materials that were used, they are among the earliest of the writings, but if we consider the final form of these narratives, they will be relatively late but not the latest of the writings to be included in the entire Old Testament.

A complete analysis of the contents of the Old Testament books is a very complex and difficult task, one in which there is no universal agreement among competent scholars. However, some conclusions have found general and widespread acceptance. For example, few people would question that the Pentateuch is composed of documents written by different persons who were widely separated both in time and in point of view. The hypothesis of four separate and distinct narratives, known respectively as *J, E, D,* and *P,* has been widely publicized. Although many corrections and modifications have been made since this hypothesis was first proposed, its main thesis is still relevant. Recent investigations merely indicate that the Pentateuch literature is even more complex and requires a larger number of documents to account for all the materials found in these books. In their final form, the historical writings are presented in a manner that is designed to account for the laws and institutions peculiar to the Hebrew people from the time of creation to the post-exilic period. Thus we find the laws of Deuteronomy, as well as those that belong to the so-called Holiness Code and the relatively late ones known as the Priests Code, included in historical narratives that attribute all of the laws to Moses.

During the post-exilic period, it was considered necessary to attach great significance to those religious institutions that were unique among the Hebrew people, and one of the most effective means for doing this was to indicate their ancient origins. Events belonging to the distant past were presented in a manner that would reflect the interpretation given to them at the times when the historical narratives were written. For example, the belief that the increasing sinfulness of man has shortened his life span is reflected in the accounts concerning the large number of years that the early patriarchs lived. And the sordid events so numerous in the Book of Judges reflect the sentiment of those who held that conditions that preceded the establishment of the religious monarchy were intolerable since they permitted everyone to "do that which was right in [their] own eyes."

The sacred writings of the Old Testament include not only the prophets and the historical narratives but also a collection of miscellaneous books, which are sometimes referred to as the Hagiographa. These writings cannot be dated with precise accuracy, nor can they be placed in the exact chronological order in which they were produced. Concerning this group of writings as a whole, they are relatively late and belong for the most part to the post-exilic period. Three of these books—Proverbs, Ecclesiastes, and Job—are known as wisdom literature. Characterized by features that sharply distinguish them from the writings of the prophets, they address problems of a universal nature rather than problems peculiar to the Hebrew people. Their appeal is to essential reasonableness instead of the "Thus saith Yahweh" of the prophets. The topics that they consider are ones that pertain to the practical affairs of everyday living.

The Book of Daniel, one of the latest to be included in the Old Testament, represents a different literary type known as *apocalyptic.* As such, Daniel stands in sharp contrast with the prophetic writings. Produced during a period of crisis that occurred in connection with the Maccabean wars, it was designed to strengthen and encourage those who were suffering extreme persecution. The Book of Psalms is a collection of hymns, prayers, and poems reflecting both individual and group experiences of the Hebrew people from almost every period of their national history. A part of this collection was used as the hymn book of the restored Temple after the people's return from the Babylonian captivity. "Short stories" is an appropriate title for three books produced during the post-exilic years: Jonah, which is a classic protest against narrow-minded nationalism on the part of the Jews; Ruth, written in protest against the law forbidding international marriages; and Esther, which provides an account of events leading to the origin of the Feast of Purim. The book called Lamentations portrays some of the bitter experiences that followed King Zedekiah's flight from the city of Jerusalem at the time of the Babylonian conquest. The Song of Songs is a love poem that came to be included in the sacred writings because of the allegorical interpretation given to it.

CRITICAL COMMENTARIES

THE PROPHETIC BOOKS

AMOS

Summary

The Book of Amos, which is the earliest of the prophetic writings to be preserved in book form, consists of nine chapters. Not all of the material found in these chapters came from Amos himself. Editors and copyists added comments to the prophet's original oracles that they deemed appropriate in light of events that occurred after his death. Whether Amos' words constitute a series of speeches or belong to one single address is unknown. The theme that runs through all of the material is one of protest against the social injustices that prevailed in northern Israel during the reign of Jeroboam II. Along with this protest is the warning that Yahweh will surely punish the nation for violating the demands of justice. The punishment will be nothing short of captivity by a foreign power and the end of Israel's national existence.

Amos was a shepherd who lived in the region of Tekoa, not many miles from the city of Jerusalem. He made his living by raising sheep and taking care of sycamore trees. When his produce was ready for market, he went to the towns and villages of Israel. His journeys took him through the country districts, where he observed the hardships imposed on the working class of people by the wealthy landowners who lived in the towns or cities in the midst of comparative luxury. While in the cities, Amos was deeply troubled not only by the contrast between the rich and the poor but by the way in which the political and religious leaders tried to justify this disparity. These leaders insisted that Yahweh materially rewards those who are faithful in the performance of their ritualistic obligations to him. Hence they interpreted their own prosperity and that of the nation as a whole as evidence that the divine favor rests on them and will continue to do so for all time to come. At the same time, they reasoned that poor people deserve their hard lot in life because they do not regularly participate in the sacrifices and other religious activities practiced at the established places of worship. Amos was not impressed by this kind of argument. He was raised in an environment where it was understood that loyalty to Yahweh involves fair dealings among people rather than observance of religious rites and ceremonies.

As Amos pondered the situation that prevailed in northern Israel, he began to have dreams and visions, three of which he recorded. In one of them, Amos sees a man with a plumb line measuring a wall that is about to fall. The man is told that the bulging wall is none other than the house of Israel: Just as a wall of this kind will soon collapse, so the nation that it represents will surely go into captivity. In a second vision, Amos sees a basket of summer fruit that represents the people of Israel, whose material prosperity is like the fully ripe fruit. But ripe fruit lasts only a little while and then rots and decays. So the peaceful years of the Israelite nation are about to come to an end. The third vision is one in which Amos sees a swarm of locusts about to devour the produce of the land. This vision is also interpreted as a warning of the evil days that lie ahead.

After a time, Amos reaches the point where he can no longer keep quiet about his dreams. Addressing a group of people who have gathered at the place of worship known as the Bethel sanctuary, he declares that Yahweh has this to say to them:

> I hate, I despise your feasts; I cannot stand your assemblies. Even though you bring me burnt offerings and grain offerings, I will not accept them. . . . Away with the noise

of your songs! I will not listen to the music of your harps. But let justice roll on like a river, righteousness like a never-failing stream! Did you bring to me sacrifices and offerings forty years in the desert, O house of Israel?

Amos' statements are daring for him to make because they directly challenge the generally accepted religious practices of his time. Strong opposition to Amos developed at once when Amaziah, a priest, sent word to King Jeroboam that Amos was a dangerous character and should be expelled from the land. Although Amos insisted that he spoke only the words that Yahweh told him to proclaim, Amaziah told him to leave the country and never to prophesy again in the land of Israel.

The coming downfall and the utter collapse of the northern kingdom are two major themes in the Book of Amos. The basis for these predictions is not the rise in power of the Assyrian empire, with its threat of invasion from the north, but rather the immorality expressed in the political, economic, and religious life of Amos' contemporaries. Amos is convinced that Yahweh is a god of justice; Yahweh's power over the nations of the earth is evidenced by the fact that transgression of the principles of justice and social righteousness will inevitably be followed by ruin and decay. This cause-and-effect is illustrated in the book's first two chapters, which record oracles concerning Damascus, Gaza, Tyre, Edom, Judah, and Israel. The first four of these oracles tell of calamities that have fallen upon the respective kingdoms because of their utter disregard for what is just and right. The last two indicate that both Judah and Israel are subject to the same kind of treatment.

The nation of Israel, because it "sells the righteous for silver, and the needy for a pair of sandals," and because of the many other instances in which it violated the principles of justice, is doomed. The luxurious homes of the rich will be spoiled, the women who have spent their time in idleness and pleasure will be dragged away into exile, and the entire country will be laid waste, a point about which Amos is especially emphatic. He insists that the coming captivity is a certainty and will mean final and complete destruction. He declares, "Fallen is Virgin Israel, never to rise again." Whatever remnants remain after the approaching invasion from the north will be insufficient for rebuilding the nation. These remnants will be comparable to "only two leg bones or a piece of an ear" that a shepherd rescues from a sheep that has been torn to pieces by a lion or a bear.

According to Amos, Israel's fate is fully deserved. That its religious and political leaders have overconfidently believed that their manner of worshiping Yahweh will bring them continued peace and prosperity avails them nothing at all. They had the opportunity to learn from the experiences of the past that Yahweh's relationship to them is conditional on their obedience to his moral requirements. Because their opportunities in this respect have been greater than those of other nations, they must bear the greater responsibility. Yahweh, no longer obligated to protect them, will not be influenced by their prayers, offerings, or solemn assemblies.

Amos interprets the coming of the Day of Yahweh—God's kingdom on earth—in sharp contrast to what generally was accepted by the priests and other contemporary rulers of the land, in whose opinion the coming Day of Yahweh will be a triumphant day of gladness for the people of Israel, a time when their enemies will be subdued and their own peace and prosperity made permanently secure; these acts will be the final realization of the divine purpose that from the very beginning has guided the destiny of Israel. But for Amos, the coming Day of Yahweh means nothing of this kind. If Yahweh is indeed the god of justice, he cannot show special favor to the Israelites by allowing them to escape the type of punishment that he brought down upon other peoples for exhibiting the same kind of irreverent and disrespectful conduct. The Day of Yahweh will, therefore, be a dark day for the Israelites: "Woe to you who long for the day of the Lord. . . . That day will be darkness, not light." The nation's captivity will not mean the overthrow of the god of Israel but rather the supremacy of the god of justice.

Commentary

The prophecies of Amos mark an important point in the development of the religion of the Old Testament. The prophet was indeed a spokesman for Yahweh. That he was not speaking for himself or trying to please his listeners is made clear by the content of the message he delivered. Critics have often maintained that the Old Testament prophets created the god of whom they spoke out of their own imaginations. However, had these prophets done so, it does not seem at all likely that Yahweh would have spoken so critically of what was being done by the prophets' own people.

In the ancient world, each nation customarily had its own god, a deity whose power and influence were limited by the boundaries of the country over which it presided. Evidence indicates that Yahweh was so conceived by the Hebrew people. But for Amos, Yahweh is not subject to these limitations. As a god of justice, Yahweh's demands are universal and consequently affect all nations alike. Israel is no exception. Dishonesty and transgression of the rights of people will bring about the destruction of this nation just as surely as they did in the cases of Tyre, Moab, Damascus, and Gaza. The implication is clear enough that Yahweh is the god of all nations. If Amos is not to be regarded as a pure monotheist, we can at least say that his thought is moving in that direction.

The opposition of the priests toward Amos can be understood in light of what Amos says concerning the solemn assemblies, sacrifices, public prayers, and other ritualistic observances. One function of the priests was to ensure that these activities were maintained; Amos insists that these rituals are worthless and should be abolished entirely. His position appears to be extreme, for properly used ritual can be an aid toward spiritual ends. On the other hand, when observance of ritual becomes a substitute for morality, nothing less than its total abolition seems to be appropriate—undoubtedly the case with Amos.

Several passages in the Book of Amos, especially in the last chapter, indicate that the Israelites will return from captivity and will be happy and prosperous in their own land. Whether these passages are from Amos or were added to the original by persons who lived at a later time is a question concerning which there is some difference of opinion. However, the weight of the evidence seems to indicate that such passages are later additions. As the manuscripts were copied from time to time, Amos' message inevitably was viewed from the perspective of later events; naturally, insertions were made in order to bring his message into harmony with such subsequent events. Furthermore, the type of restoration that is indicated in the closing chapter of the book is not the kind that one would expect from Amos since it indicates material prosperity rather than a moral transformation.

HOSEA

Summary

Like the Book of Amos, the Book of Hosea is addressed to the people of the northern kingdom—Israel. Its fourteen chapters contain both a warning concerning future events and an interpretation of these events' meanings. Throughout the book, the prophet speaks to the people of Israel about the critical situation that developed during the years that immediately followed the death of Jeroboam II. When Amos prophesied the disaster that would befall the nation, he was promptly repudiated by those who were "at ease in Zion" and who were confident that no evil would ever come upon their land. However, when Hosea came on the scene only a few years later, these attitudes had changed. Events had occurred that shook the confidence of even the most optimistic persons. No longer was there a stable government on which the people could rely. The line of kings changed rapidly, and often the change was attended by violence. With invasion by the Assyrian armies imminent, Israel kept the peace only by paying an enormous tribute to the Assyrian rulers.

To raise this tribute, it was necessary to impose a policy of taxation that placed a difficult burden on the people, but there were always those who resented paying tribute to a foreign power. At times, this resentment led to open revolt. The Israelite king would be murdered and his assassin would take over the reins of government. The situation was chaotic, and no one seemed to know what to do. In their desperation, the priests increased the number of sacrifices, offered more prayers, and called more solemn assemblies, but none of these measures stemmed the downward tide. Under these strained and trying circumstances, Hosea performed his mission as a spokesman for Yahweh.

The first part of Hosea records the tragic story of the prophet's unhappy marital experiences. Hosea's wife, Gomer, whom he married in good faith, proved to be an adulterous woman. Three children were born to her, but they were not Hosea's. Because of Gomer's unfaithfulness, the prophet divorced his wife and lived apart from her. Following her separation from the home, Gomer continued her adulterous life and eventually was scarcely different from an ordinary slave. But Hosea still loved her in spite of her unfaithfulness. To rescue her from her lovers, he sought her out and purchased her freedom.

Whether this story is to be regarded as a parable or as a record of actual experiences in Hosea's home life is a question concerning which there are different opinions. The material found in the book's third chapter suggests what Hosea regards as the meaning of his experiences in relation to Yahweh's dealings with the people of Israel. Yahweh chose Israel and entered into a covenant relationship with it, but Israel has been unfaithful to the covenant; it has forsaken the one to whom its loyalty was pledged and now serves other gods. The licentious practices followed by the worshipers of the Canaanite Baal gods have become a part of the religious life of the Israelites, and even their professed worship of Yahweh has been contaminated with the ideas and ceremonial rites of Baal worship. Because of this unfaithfulness on the part of Israel, Yahweh will permit the Assyrians to overrun the land and carry the people into captivity. But unlike Amos, for whom the coming captivity would be final, Hosea views the captivity as a means for bringing the Israelites to their right senses: After they have learned their lesson, they will return to their own land, and a king who is like King David will reign over them.

As this lesson, which comes out of his own bitter marital experiences, becomes more clear to Hosea, he records it from the perspective of his later years. Understanding that his own relationship to Gomer parallels the relationship between Yahweh and Israel, he realizes that Yahweh used this lesson to communicate his will and purpose to those who claim to be his people. From this point of view, we can understand Hosea's statement that Yahweh instructed him to marry an adulterous woman and later directed him to make provisions for her moral restoration.

The remainder of the Book of Hosea consists of a collection of miscellaneous statements expressing Hosea's convictions concerning the character of Yahweh and Yahweh's relation to the people of Israel. Hosea appears to have had the temperament of a poet; his thoughts are usually expressed in terms of strong analogies and striking figures of speech. But it is not always easy to understand what he is saying, for his statements are not arranged in chronological order, nor do they indicate the time or circumstances under which they were delivered. In spite of these difficulties, the materials contained in these chapters reveal some remarkable insights that contributed in no small way to the development of Israel's religious ideals.

Anyone who reads the Book of Hosea will be impressed by Hosea's conception of the deity. For Amos, as well as for most of his predecessors, Yahweh is conceived primarily as a god of justice. He gave laws for his people to obey, and disobedience of these laws must inevitably bring punishment sufficient to atone for the wrongdoing. But for Hosea, Yahweh is a god of love and mercy. Our best understanding of Yahweh's nature can be grasped by means of analogies drawn from family relationships. The love of a husband for his wife and the love of a father for his children are appropriate symbols for indicating the character of the deity. Speaking for Yahweh, Hosea declares, "When Israel was a child, I loved him, and out of Egypt I called my son." And again, "How can I give you up, Ephraim? How can I hand you over, Israel? I will not carry out my fierce anger, nor will I turn and devastate Ephraim."

Punishment for wrongdoing is indeed necessary, but according to Hosea, the purpose of punishment is not to meet the demands of justice but rather to restore the ones who have done the wrong. This moral restoration is achieved by getting the wrongdoers themselves to recognize the error of their ways and then to repent in humility and turn from their evil paths. In other words, for Hosea, punishment is remedial rather than retributive, an expression of Yahweh's love for his people. Punishment should be used as a last resort to teach lessons that people have refused to learn in any other way. Israel will surely go into captivity, but it will not be a final or complete destruction of the nation. Rather, it will be an opportunity for Israelites to gain a clearer understanding of the character of Yahweh so that when they return to their land as free people, they will know how to worship Yahweh in an appropriate manner.

The responsibility for what has happened to the nation rests heavily on the priests, whose function was to guide the affairs of the nation, especially in regard to their religious duties. But this they have not done. They have been blind guides leading the people to believe that Yahweh demands nothing more than sacrifices, long prayers, solemn assemblies, and other forms of ritualistic observances. The truth of the matter, according to Hosea, is that Yahweh cares nothing at all for these services: "For I desire mercy, not sacrifice, and acknowledgement of God rather than burnt offerings." Yahweh's demands are moral. He desires the correct personal attitudes rather than external conformity to a given set of rules. If the people had a correct understanding of the character of Yahweh, they would not try to worship him after the manner in which the Canaanites worshiped their Baal gods. Because of this lack of understanding on their part, Hosea criticizes not only the priests but the people who have allowed themselves to be misled in this manner. The Israelites, and especially the priests, have had the chance to know better; their responsibilities include making the proper use of the opportunities given them: "My people are destroyed from lack of knowledge. Because you have rejected knowledge, I also reject you as my priests."

Failure to understand the nature of Yahweh has led to false ideas concerning the safety and security of the nation. Instead of putting their trust in righteousness, the Israelites have relied upon strength and military power. When it became evident that they could not match the strength of enemy nations who threatened to invade their land, there were those who advocated an alliance with some foreign power. One group urged an alliance with Egypt; another group insisted that the security of Israel depended on an alliance with Assyria. Hosea was convinced that both parties were wrong. He accused Israel's leaders of failing to understand the true cause of the nation's downfall. "Ephraim," says the prophet, "is like a flat cake not turned over." The people do not have any clear idea of what they are doing. Again, he says, "Ephraim is like a dove, easily deceived and senseless." The nation resembles a bird that is without brains. Its people have been following a stupid policy, trying to save their country by making it strong instead of making it morally right.

Commentary

Hosea was the last of the prophets of the northern kingdom. Fortunately, the book that bears his name has been preserved. When the Assyrians overran the land, someone escaped to the south and brought the manuscript to the city of Jerusalem. An important document, it represents in some respects the highest achievements in the development of the religious ideals of Israel. Here, we find for the first time the conception of Yahweh as a god of love. Earlier notions emphasized power and justice as the essential characteristics of the deity. Hosea does not eliminate these qualities, but he makes them subordinate to love and mercy. The way in which he arrives at this new conception is of particular interest: From the account given in the first three chapters of the book, we can infer that he came to his conclusions partly as a result of his own experiences. While in one sense Hosea's newfound wisdom was a revelation from Yahweh, we must bear in mind that even a divine revelation can be communicated to human beings only through the use of finite channels. True, a perfect understanding of the nature of deity is beyond any human capacity; nevertheless, it is possible to know something about the nature of deity provided similarities or resemblances exist between the human and the divine. On this assumption, we can reasonably suppose that the most adequate conception of deity will be derived from those experiences that are regarded as the noblest and best that human beings have ever observed in their own lives.

Such an observation is what seems to have happened in the case of Hosea. The attitude that he displayed toward Gomer in spite of her unfaithfulness to him and the efforts that he put forth to bring about her restoration were recognized at a later time as the noblest and best of all that he ever did. Fittingly, he thinks of Yahweh as one who possesses in an even greater measure those qualities of character that are similar to the best he experienced in his own life. From this reasoning, it follows that Yahweh's attitude toward the erring people of Israel is like that which Hosea displayed toward Gomer. Yahweh's main concern for his people would be to bring about their restoration rather than mete out to them the exact amount of punishment they deserve. In other words, Yahweh's justice is always subordinate to his mercy. Justice in human relationships is based on the idea of equality, which means giving to each person exactly that which is due. According to Hosea, divine justice is determined not so much by what people deserve as by what is necessary in order to bring about the desired reformation on their part.

This new element in the conception of deity had many important consequences for the future development of Israel's religion. For one thing, Yahweh's punishments could be interpreted as remedial rather than retributive. From this point of view, the entire history of the Hebrew people would appear in a new light. The hardships and tragedies that befell them from time to time were for the purpose of teaching them lessons that they refused to learn in any other way. Even the captivity of the nation by a foreign power would not mean that Yahweh had forsaken them. His love for the Israelites was so strong that he would never give them up. Israel was slow in learning the lessons these experiences were designed to teach, but now that an understanding was beginning to break through, at least some hope for the future remained. Eventually, the divine purpose with reference to Israel would be fully realized.

ISAIAH

Summary

The Book of Isaiah, as it now appears in our Old Testament, contains far more than can be attributed to the prophet. As a whole, the book is a rather large collection of writings that were produced by a number of different authors, some of whom were separated by relatively long periods of time. For example, Old Testament scholars have long recognized that Chapters 1-39 constitute a unit that is quite separate and distinct from Chapters 40-66.

Generally, Chapters 1-39 are attributed to the prophet Isaiah. These chapters deal primarily with Judah and Jerusalem at a time when the city was still standing and when the southern kingdom was threatened with invasion by the Assyrians. The group of chapters beginning with Chapter 40 appears to have been written from the point of view of conditions that prevailed more than a century later. In fact, the writer indicates very clearly that the Babylonian captivity has existed for a long time. He believes that the punishment is nearly complete; the time is close at hand when the captives will return to their homeland and rebuild the city of Jerusalem, which has long been in ruins.

A careful reading of each of these two groups of chapters reveals that the prophet Isaiah did not write all of the first thirty-nine chapters, nor did one person write all that is contained in Chapters 40-66. Ample evidence indicates the work of several different authors. The editors who assembled the entire collection of manuscripts placed them all under the name of Isaiah because they were quite certain of those materials that belonged to him, and putting them all together indicated their location in the sacred writings rather than precise authorship of each part.

Isaiah was a prophet of the southern kingdom. His call to a prophetic life took place in the year that King Uzziah died (740 B.C.), during a critical period in the history of the nation. Uzziah was one of Judah's greatest kings. He reigned for approximately half a century, and during this time, the kingdom enjoyed its greatest period of prosperity. Commercial relations were established with neighboring states, and the internal resources of the country were developed. However, this increase in wealth and the way in which it was distributed brought about some serious problems. The contrast between the rich and the poor reached an alarming state, which brought threats of a revolt from those who were deprived of their lands and other possessions. Then, too, there was an added threat from without, for the advance of the Assyrians against northern Israel was an indication that the time was not far distant when Judah might expect an invasion by the Assyrians. The situation was indeed ominous, but because Uzziah was a strong and able ruler, the people had confidence that he would know how to deal with these problems. Then came the startling news that the king had leprosy and would have to leave Jerusalem and live in a leper colony outside the city. Uzziah's son Jotham, heir to the throne, possessed none of the strong and admirable qualities characteristic of his father. Instead, he was a weak and vacillating person quite unable to inspire confidence on the part of his subjects. Uzziah lived for three years in the leper colony. The news of his death brought shock and consternation to the entire kingdom.

During this time and under these critical circumstances, Isaiah became a prophet. The vision that he interpreted as his call to service is recorded in Chapter 6 of the Book of Isaiah. The scene in which the vision occurred is the Temple in the city of Jerusalem. Here the religious life of the nation was centered, and to this place Isaiah, a young man probably in his early twenties, turned in an hour when the future of his country looked especially bleak. The vision is described in considerable detail. Its essential meaning is expressed in the prophet's deep conviction that despite Judah's dark hour, Yahweh still controls the nations. His glory and majesty fill the whole earth. The contrast between Yahweh's holiness and the sinful state into which the Judean kingdom has fallen is something that calls for immediate action. Someone must speak for Yahweh and communicate the divine message to the people. Knowing what a difficult task this would be, Isaiah pleads that he is quite unfit to perform it. Then an act takes place that symbolizes an inner cleansing of his heart and mind, after which he responds to the call with the words "Here am I. Send me!"

Isaiah's ministry lasted approximately half a century, continuing through the reigns of Jotham, Ahaz, and Hezekiah. Tradition tells us that he suffered a martyr's death during the reign of King Manasseh. His work brought him into direct contact with kings and priests, and he encountered strong opposition from both groups. At times, this opposition was so strong that he was forced to give up speaking in public and confine his ministry to a group of disciples with whom he met privately. With regard to the priests and the services that they performed, Isaiah expressed convictions that were similar to those spoken to the people of Israel by Amos and Hosea. For example, speaking for Yahweh, he says, "'The multitude of your sacrifices—what are they to me?' says the Lord." And again, "Your New Moon festivals and your appointed feasts my soul hates." He even insists that Yahweh will not listen to the multitude's prayers: "When you spread out your hands in prayer, I will hide my eyes from you; even if you offer many prayers, I will not listen. Your hands are full of blood."

In the same spirit, Isaiah criticizes the economic policies that were not only sanctioned but encouraged by the rulers of the land. In "The Song of the Vineyard," which was probably chanted by the prophet, we find these words: "Woe to you who add house to house and join field to field till no place is left and you live alone in the land." This chant protests the way in which the poor people were deprived of their property in order to satisfy the claims of their creditors, who had taken unfair advantages of these people's unfortunate circumstances in order to enrich themselves.

The prophet's criticism of kings was expressed on many occasions, but never was it more pronounced than when he protested against the foreign alliances that were being negotiated. Early in Isaiah's ministry, he warned King Ahaz against the dangers involved in an alliance with Assyria. The heads of two puppet kingdoms that were all that remained of northern Israel asked King Ahaz to join with them in a coalition against Assyria. When Ahaz refused, they threatened to make war against him. Ahaz was frightened and wanted to appeal to Assyria for help. Isaiah clearly saw the folly that would be involved in a move of this kind, and in a prophecy that has often been misinterpreted as a reference to a coming Messiah, he warned King Ahaz that within three or four years those two puppet kingdoms that he feared would be completely routed. On the other hand, if Ahaz wanted to protect Judah, he should give his attention to those conditions that needed moral reform. King Ahaz did not heed Isaiah's advice. He went ahead with his plans, and as a result, Judah was placed in a subservient relation to the Assyrian empire.

During the reign of King Hezekiah, on two different occasions an attempt was made to curb the rising power of the Assyrians by forming alliances that would resist any further Assyrian aggression. The first of these was promoted by the Egyptians, who invited the Judean king to join with them. The second one was initiated by Merodach-Baladan of Babylon, who visited King Hezekiah and tried to persuade him to have Judah join with the Babylonians and the Egyptians in a united front against Assyria. King Hezekiah, fearful that Judah would be unable to stand alone, was inclined to join the alliance, but Isaiah knew that it would be a grave mistake for the king to do so. In one of the strongest messages that he delivered to the king, the prophet declared, "Woe to those who go down to Egypt for help, who rely on horses, who trust in the multitude of their chariots. . . . But the Egyptians are men and not God; their horses are flesh and not spirit. When the

Lord stretches out his hand, he who helps will stumble, he who is helped will fall; both will perish together."

Despite the immediate dangers that the nation of Judah faced, Isaiah was confident of the ultimate triumph of the Hebrew people. Like Hosea, who had looked on the approaching captivity of northern Israel as merely a prelude to a reformed and triumphant Hebrew society, Isaiah was sure that any temporary disaster would not be the final end of the Judean kingdom. Yahweh's purpose in the world was to be realized through the Hebrew people, which meant that the city of Jerusalem and that for which it stood could never be overthrown completely. When the Assyrians did invade Judah, capturing many cities and demanding that Hezekiah surrender the city of Jerusalem, Isaiah advised the king not to yield to their demands. He insisted that Jerusalem was Zion's city and would never fall. Within a short time, the Assyrian army withdrew, and for a brief period, Isaiah was vindicated.

Closely related to Isaiah's teaching concerning the "surviving remnant" that would be the hope of Judah were his predictions with reference to the coming of a Messiah, or "anointed one," who will someday occupy the throne in Jerusalem and rule the nation with justice and righteousness. He will be a far better king than any of those who have preceded him. Under his leadership, the poor and the oppressed will find a champion, for he will judge their cases with a discerning mind and will not be unduly influenced by hearsay or mere outward appearances. His kingdom will be the fulfillment and realization of the divine purpose in the world.

Commentary

Israel's messianic hope, though implicit in the teachings of some of the earlier prophets, finds its first clear expression in the prophecies of Isaiah. The term *Messiah* means "anointed one," or one who has been chosen by Yahweh for the accomplishment of a specific purpose.

Hebrew kings and priests, as well as prophets, were usually anointed in a special ceremony that symbolized their dedication to the work for which they were called. When Saul was chosen as the first king of Israel, he was anointed by Samuel, and this ceremony symbolized people's hope that the nation, under Saul's leadership, would realize its chosen destiny. But Saul did not measure up to these expectations, and the same was true of all the kings that followed in the line of succession of King David. The man who succeeded King Uzziah was notoriously weak and incompetent, and it was during his reign that Isaiah centered his attention on the coming of a Messiah who would possess the good qualities that were so lacking in the kings. In one prophecy, the Messiah is portrayed as an ideal king; in another one, he is characterized as an ideal judge who will understand the problems of the poor and the oppressed. He will ensure that their rights are protected and that they are given their just dues. During the centuries that followed the career of Isaiah, the concept of a coming Messiah took on a number of different meanings and became one of the most important ideas of Judaism.

One of the best-known passages in the Book of Isaiah is recorded in Chapter 2 and deals with the subject of the coming of a warless world. Looking into the distant future, the writer envisions a time when the nations will "beat their swords into plowshares and their spears into pruning hooks. Nation will not take up swords against nation, nor will they train for war anymore." This prophecy, like the one recorded in Chapter 11, in which "The wolf will live with the lamb" and "They will neither harm nor destroy on all my holy mountain," seems to be an admirable supplement to the idea of a coming Messiah, who will be know as "Prince of Peace." Although these passages have often been attributed to Isaiah, the evidence indicates very strongly that these prophecies come from a later period. The same is true of several of the oracles concerning foreign nations, especially the ones having to do with the destruction of Babylon and the future regeneration of the Assyrian nation. That these oracles were finally included in the collection of Isaiah's own work indicates the high esteem with which they were regarded.

MICAH

Summary

The prophet Micah was a contemporary of Isaiah. He lived in a small village named Moresheth, not far from the city of Gath, which was destroyed by the Assyrians when they invaded Judah. Living in this village, Micah came into daily contact with the people who suffered most from the system of land tenure against which Isaiah protested. When Micah began his ministry, the northern kingdom still existed, and Micah's earliest messages were addressed to the people of Israel, as well as to those living in Judah. Micah lived among the poor people and sympathized with them because of their hard lot. In many respects, his work was similar to that of the prophet Amos, especially regarding what he said about social and economic conditions. Although little if anything is new in his criticism of the ruling classes, the manner in which he spoke caused his name to be remembered and honored among the prophets and teachers of later generations.

No writer in the entire Old Testament was ever more indignant than Micah over the ways in which the rich and powerful use every opportunity to exploit the poor and the weak. In deep earnestness he cries out, "Woe to those who plan iniquity [wickedness], to those who plot evil on their beds! At morning's light they carry it out because it is in their power to do it." He bitterly denounces the wealthy landowners because they "covet fields and seize them, and houses, and take them. They defraud a man of his house, a fellowman of his inheritance." He characterizes the way in which the poor and the unfortunate are treated as no better than that which is accorded to animals. Using the most forceful language, he denounces leaders who "tear the skin from my people . . . and break their bones in pieces; who chop them up like meat for the pan."

Because of these evil conditions, Micah tells his hearers that Yahweh will surely bring punishment on the land. The Assyrians' captivity of the northern kingdom is the punishment visited upon them due to their iniquities, and the prophet now sees a similar fate in store for Judah. Unlike Isaiah, who boldly proclaimed that Jerusalem was Zion's city and for that reason could never fall,

Micah sees no justice in having it spared. As the capital of the nation and the home of those persons most responsible for the corrupt practices that prevail throughout the land, it deserves punishment even more than the country villages, in which the victims of these unfair practices live. Micah proclaims in bold words, "Hear this, you leaders of the house of Jacob . . . who build Zion with bloodshed, and Jerusalem with wickedness. . . . Therefore because of you, Zion will be plowed like a field, Jerusalem will become a heap of rubble."

Micah's warnings were resented on the part of those who preferred to hear that all was well and that no evil would fall upon the land. Micah knew that his messages were not the kind that would gain popular approval, but true to his calling as a prophet, he declares, "But as for me, I am filled with power, with the Spirit of the Lord, and with justice and might, to declare to Jacob his transgression, to Israel his sin." We do not know if Micah believed that the judgments on Israel and Judah would be the final end of these nations—as Amos had taught—or that the judgments would be preparatory to a redeemed society—as Hosea had taught. Hope for the future is expressed in the messianic prophecy recorded in Chapter 5, but whether this prophecy is Micah's or an addition to the book made by a later writer is uncertain. What is unique about this prophecy is that it names Bethlehem as the place where the Messiah will be born. This prediction indicates that the coming Messiah will be a representative of the poorer classes of people; understanding their situation, the Messiah will champion their cause.

Commentary

Although there are seven chapters in the Book of Micah, only the first three can be attributed to the prophet Micah with certainty. Micah is usually classified with the minor prophets, but his work was evidently held in high esteem by later prophets and teachers. References to him were made on several occasions, and his writings are some of the choicest materials to be found in the entire Old Testament. For example, the prophecy concerning the coming of a warless world, found toward the beginning of Chapter 4, is quoted more frequently than any other portion of the book and is identical to one found in Chapter 2 of the Book of Isaiah. The original author is not known, but the editors of each of these two books valued the warless-world prophecy so highly that they included it in each collection of writings.

Another notable passage in the Book of Micah is found in 6:6-8. Here, we find a clear statement of prophetic religion at its best: "And what does the Lord require of you? To act justly and to love mercy and to walk humbly with your God." The writer of these words understands that Yahweh desires moral qualities on the part of his worshipers rather than sacrifices and burnt offerings. It is doubtful if one could find in the religious literature of any people a more exalted conception of the nature of true religion and the moral qualities that religion is designed to promote.

ZEPHANIAH, NAHUM, AND HABAKKUK

Summary

Not all of Israel's prophets were men of great vision. Some of them apparently made little or no impression on either their contemporaries or their successors, with the result that neither their names nor their writings have been recorded. The three who are included in this section were more fortunate: We know their names, and at least part of what they had to say has been preserved in the books that bear their names. But, as in the case of the other prophets, their messages are now combined with additions and editorial comments made by the people who brought the manuscripts into their present form.

Zephaniah. Zephaniah's ministry occurred during the reign of Josiah, king of Judah. Zephaniah was the grandson of Hezekiah, but we cannot be sure that this Hezekiah was the same Hezekiah who ruled Jerusalem during the time of Isaiah. Zephaniah was a prophet of doom in the true sense of the word: He saw no bright future for his people. He is remembered primarily for what he says concerning the coming of the Day of Yahweh: "'I will sweep away everything from the face of the earth,' declares the Lord. 'I will sweep away both men and animals.'" The immediate occasion that caused this prediction is generally assumed to be a threatened invasion of Judah by the Scythians, a barbarian horde that was invading neighboring countries with unparalleled devastation and destruction. We do know that an invasion by the Scythians occurred about this time, but whether the prophet had them in mind or the Assyrians, who had long been the oppressors of the Hebrew people, is uncertain. In either case, Zephaniah believed that events soon to take place should be interpreted as the judgment of Yahweh being visited upon Judah because of its sins. Specifically, he mentions the worship of foreign gods and the observance of ceremonies customary in connection with their worship.

Although Zephaniah was not the first prophet to predict the coming Day of Yahweh, he gave to this concept a specific meaning that was new to the people of his time. Amos proclaimed that the Day of Yahweh would come sometime in the future, but Zephaniah declares that it is already imminent: "The great day of the Lord is near—near and coming quickly. . . . That day will be a day of wrath, a day of distress and anguish." He sees its coming as a great climactic event in which the forces of evil will receive their just punishment. Whether he regarded this evil day as the termination of the Judean kingdom or as a necessary prelude to something better for his people, we do not know. Some parts of the Book of Zephaniah predict the coming of a better day, but it seems quite probable that these sections were added by editors who looked at the book as a whole from the perspective of later years.

Nahum. Nahum is usually classified with the minor prophets. Although we know practically nothing about Nahum as a person, we can judge from the contents of his book that he was not a prophet in the true sense of the word. He was a poet who possessed a remarkable style of writing and who described in unforgettable language the fall of Nineveh, the capital of the Assyrian empire, in 612 B.C. This event was an occasion for rejoicing on the part of the Jews, especially those in whom the spirit of nationalism was strong. Nahum's original poem is recorded in Chapters 2 and 3. The first chapter contains an acrostic poem—a poem in which the first letter of each line, taken together, forms a name or saying—that is used as an introduction to the book. Possibly the author of the main poem in the second and third chapters may have witnessed the battle that brought destruction to Nineveh, but of this we cannot be sure. The poem opens with a series of denunciations, is followed by a vivid account of the capture of the city, and concludes with a list of sarcastic remarks about a boastful power that is now laid low. For all of its remarkable qualities as an example of poetry, the poem is really a hymn of hate. For centuries, the Hebrew people suffered at the hands of the Assyrians; concerning those bitter experiences, we can see why this poem appealed to the editors who included it with the writings of the prophets.

Habakkuk. The Book of Habakkuk reveals a spirit that sharply contrasts Nahum's. The prophet for whom the book is named does not express hatred toward foreigners, nor does he pronounce doom upon the evildoers among his own people. Instead, he is deeply disturbed about certain events and earnestly prays for guidance that will help him understand the prevailing situation. His ministry occurred during the reign of Josiah (640-609 B.C.) and that of Josiah's son King Jehoiakim (609-598 B.C.). Josiah is usually regarded as one of the better kings of Judah. During his reign, a famous law book, which included the main text of what we now call the Book of Deuteronomy, was discovered in the Temple, and its provisions were made the law of the land. Despite his good deeds, Josiah was slain in a battle at Megiddo, where he had gone to stop the advance of the Egyptians across Judean territory. His son Jehoahaz was taken captive to Egypt, and another son, Jehoiakim, was allowed to occupy the Judean throne only because he pledged loyalty to the Egyptians. Later, when the Egyptians were defeated by the Babylonians at a battle at Carchemish, Jehoiakim pledged loyalty to the Babylonians. His attitude toward the people over whom he ruled was anything but honorable.

As Habakkuk observed these happenings, he could not understand why the evil forces in the world should prosper as well as they were. He believed that Yahweh was a just god who rewarded the righteous and punished the wicked, but the events that he observed seemed to indicate just the opposite. Josiah, a good king, was killed in battle; his son who was the rightful heir to the throne was in captivity; and Jehoiakim, who now ruled in Jerusalem, was a corrupt and incompetent king. The longer Jehoiakim's reign continued, the worse the situation became. The prophet cannot understand why Yahweh does not correct these grave injustices. In desperation, Habakkuk cries out: "How long, O Lord, must I call for help, but you do not listen? . . . Therefore the law is paralyzed, and justice never prevails. The wicked hem in the righteous, so that justice is perverted." He is told that the Babylonians are an instrument that Yahweh is using to punish the evildoers in Judah, but to Habakkuk, the Babylonians are no better than the ones who are punished. Habakkuk asks Yahweh, "Why then do you tolerate the treacherous? Why are you silent while the wicked swallow up those more righteous than themselves?" Although Habakkuk does not receive a direct answer to his question, he finds consolation in the assurance that ultimately the forces of righteousness will be triumphant. In the meantime, "the righteous will live by his faith."

Commentary

Zephaniah's references to the coming of the Day of Yahweh anticipate in some respects the development of the eschatological and apocalyptic ideas that play such important roles in the centuries preceding the beginning of the Christian era. Because the concept of a just god who is supreme over the nations of the earth implies the giving of rewards and punishments commensurate with the deeds of the people, the question of when and how this reckoning would take place received more and more attention on the part of prophets and teachers.

The Book of Nahum, which describes in exquisite language the fall of the city of Nineveh, contains no lofty religious sentiments. Its inclusion in the Old Testament has led to various interpretations of the imagery used in the poem. When these expressions are given a symbolic rather than a literal meaning, it is possible to read into the poem whatever one wishes to find. However, interpretations of this kind are legitimate only when the context indicates that the writer intended the work to be used that way. Nahum's poem does not indicate that he is talking about anything other than the destruction of the city responsible for so many of the woes inflicted on the Hebrew people.

The problem of injustice that troubled Habakkuk became even more acute during the centuries that followed his life. The earlier prophets' teaching that the calamities that befall a nation should be regarded as punishments for its sins was questioned more and more in light of observed experiences. The strong, powerful nations were not more righteous than the ones that were subservient to them. A righteous person often suffered the most unjust treatment, while the wicked person enjoyed comforts and prosperity. No final solution to the problem was ever found, but Habakkuk's statement that "the righteous will live by his faith" has inspired some of the most important movements in religious history.

JEREMIAH

Summary

With the single exception of the Book of Isaiah, which contains the works of more than one prophet, the Book of Jeremiah is the longest of the prophetic books of the Old Testament. Jeremiah contains a considerable amount of material of a biographical and historical nature in addition to the prophet's own words. This material is especially valuable because it reveals the personality of the prophet more clearly than any of the other prophetic books reveal their writers' personalities. Furthermore, the text provides information concerning the more important events in Jeremiah's career.

Jeremiah's life and teachings had a profound effect on the future development of both Judaism and Christianity. In the New Testament, many passages indicate that both Jesus and Paul not only accepted certain ideas from Jeremiah but gave them a central place in their own interpretations of the meaning of religion. For this reason, along with others, Jeremiah is often regarded as the greatest of the Hebrew prophets.

The period in which Jeremiah lived and worked was one of the most critical in Hebrew history. His public ministry began during the reign of King Josiah (640-609 B.C.) and lasted until sometime after the fall of Jerusalem and the beginning of the Babylonian captivity. He encountered strong opposition from King Jehoiakim (609-598 B.C.) and King Zedekiah (597-586 B.C.), and on more than one occasion, his life was threatened. After the fall of Jerusalem, the Babylonians permitted him to remain in his homeland; many of his fellow countrymen were taken into captivity. Later, he was taken to Egypt against his will by a group of exiles who found it necessary to flee Jerusalem for their own safety. In Egypt, Jeremiah died after a long and troublesome career.

The collection of writings that make up the Book of Jeremiah includes oracles, addresses, prayers, and exhortations, all of which were spoken by the prophet himself. Arranged without any reference to either topical or chronological order, the text is interspersed with materials that, though relevant to Jeremiah's work, were contributed by other persons. We shall attempt only a brief summary of the more important ideas set forth in Jeremiah's teachings.

The book begins with an account of Jeremiah's call to be a prophet. These passages are written from the perspective of Jeremiah's later years, when it seemed clear to him that even before Jeremiah was born, Yahweh had a plan or purpose for him to fulfill. Jeremiah's earliest prophecies, like those of Zephaniah, are believed to be concerned with the threatened invasion of Judah by the Scythians. He felt that his country would be completely devastated as proper punishment for the sins that its citizens committed. That his predictions in this respect were not fulfilled was seized upon by his critics as evidence that he was a false prophet.

One of the important events that took place a few years after Jeremiah began his prophetic work was the discovery of the law book in the Temple at Jerusalem. This book, the main part of what we now call the Book of Deuteronomy, was declared to be the word of Yahweh, and King Josiah made it a part of the law of the land. For a time, Jeremiah was enthusiastic about King Josiah's decision: The laws were intended not only to correct many of the social injustices that prevailed in the land but also to protect the worship of Yahweh from contamination by the evil influences of heathen forms of worship. It was hoped, and apparently with good reasons, that the enforcement of these laws would spark a great and sorely needed reformation. Jeremiah observed the situation both before and after the new laws were introduced. He became convinced that the conduct of the people was no better under these laws than it had been before, an observation that led to some very important consequences in Jeremiah's conception of religion and its purpose in the lives of the Hebrew people.

The reason for the failure of the Deuteronomic reformation was to be found not in the character of the laws but rather in the motives that were dominant in the lives of the people. The prophet's conception of human nature is well expressed in his statement "Can the Ethiopian change his skin or the leopard its spots? Neither can you do good who are accustomed to doing evil." Humans are so constituted that they follow their desires rather than their intellect; for this reason, they cannot change their evil ways until they experience a change of heart. Furthermore, Jeremiah contended that humans cannot change their nature by themselves. Such reform can occur only through cooperation with Yahweh, and Yahweh can act on human hearts only when humans recognize their need for it. Without this inner transformation in human nature, all reformative movements are destined to fail.

After leaving his hometown of Anathoth to live in the city of Jerusalem, Jeremiah experienced continual opposition from both political and religious leaders of Judah. The occasion that prompted some of this opposition was an address—or perhaps a series of addresses—concerning the Temple and the services that were being conducted in it. Because of the formal character of these services and their failure to change the spiritual lives of the people, Jeremiah saw that something very drastic would have to be done in order to bring people to their senses. People were putting their trust in the Temple, feeling certain that so long as it remained in their midst, no evil could befall them. For people to understand that the true meaning of religion consists in a change from within rather than conformity to external requirements, Jeremiah felt that it was necessary to undermine the trust that people placed in external objects. Therefore, the prophet declared that the day was coming when the Temple would be destroyed. The ark of the covenant would be taken away, and the nation that called itself the chosen of Yahweh would be taken into captivity. These statements aroused the anger of the priests and King Jehoiakim.

Jeremiah was charged with treason and would probably have been put to death had not some of his friends succeeded in hiding him until the wrath of his enemies subsided. When it was no longer considered safe for him to appear in public, Jeremiah dictated a series of oracles in which the policies of King Jehoiakim and his subordinates were severely criticized, and warnings were given concerning what would happen if these were not changed. The scroll on which these oracles were written was sent to the king by a messenger who saw to it that the document was read aloud in the king's presence. King Jehoiakim was displeased as he listened to the reading. Taking the scroll from the reader, he cut it into shreds and then threw the remnants into a fire. When news of what the king had done reached Jeremiah, he dictated the entire scroll over again, adding a specific warning to Jehoiakim, and sent the new copy back to be read again.

Nothing that Jeremiah taught during his career was more significant than his doctrine concerning the New Covenant. In Chapter 31 of his book, we read: "'The time is coming,' declares the Lord, 'when I will make a new covenant with the house of Israel and with the house of Judah.'" The Old Covenant, based on laws that were decreed as far back as the time of Moses, was a contract, or agreement, between Yahweh and the Israelites, in which the people agreed to obey all of the commandments given to them. But the Israelites did not live up to the terms of that agreement, and Jeremiah believed that he knew the principal reasons why they had not done so: the evil desires and wrong motives that were parts of their human nature. The only thing that could bring about a right relationship with Yahweh would be a change of heart—in other words, a new nature. Such change was unattainable except by means of the New Covenant, in which Yahweh promises to do for the Israelites that which they cannot do for themselves. Speaking for Yahweh, Jeremiah declares, "I will put my law in their minds and write it on their hearts. I will be their God, and they will be my people." Jeremiah concludes by saying that when this is done, specific rules no longer will be necessary in order for people to know how they ought to behave. With changed natures and the right desires present within them, people will know what is the morally correct thing to do in any situation.

Closely associated with this conception of the New Covenant is Jeremiah's teaching concerning individual responsibility. The prophets who preceded Jeremiah usually spoke in terms of a social solidarity, which meant that Yahweh's relationship to Israel concerned the nation as a whole. All citizens would be judged and either punished or rewarded. When the people of Judah responded to Jeremiah's warnings of impending disaster by saying that they were being punished not because of their own sins but because of the sins of their ancestors, Jeremiah challenged this ancient doctrine. He declared that each individual is accountable for his own conduct: "In those days people will no longer say,

'The fathers have eaten sour grapes, and the children's teeth are set on edge.'"

Commentary

The individual experience of religion, in contrast with mere external forms of worship, is the dominant theme in all of Jeremiah's teachings. For him, the relationship between a person and Yahweh is the most essential element in genuine religious experience. The external forms of worship, such as the offer of sacrifices, payment of vows, and participation in Temple services, are meaningless except insofar as they might contribute toward a changed nature in which Yahweh's spirit takes possession of a person's mind and heart.

Jeremiah believed that Yahweh used even the Babylonian captivity of Jerusalem as a means for bringing the Israelite people to a full realization of the fact that Yahweh could be worshiped in a strange land without any of the external factors associated with the Temple in Jerusalem. In a foreign land, they would learn that true religion is a matter of the heart and can be experienced by any individual who establishes a right relationship with the deity, a lofty conception of religion and one that was far beyond the understanding of the majority of people. Conformity to external requirements is always an easier course to follow, and during the centuries that followed Jeremiah's prophecies, the ritualistic element in religious practices received greater emphasis. Nevertheless, Jeremiah's conception of religion was never lost completely. Some people always adhered to it, and from time to time, new teachers emphasized Jeremiah's views.

Despite his pessimism with reference to the immediate future of the Judean kingdom, Jeremiah never abandoned the hope that eventually the divine purpose would be realized by his own people, in their own land. Throughout the Book of Jeremiah, predictions of impending disasters are usually followed by the words "Nevertheless, I will not make a full end." Jeremiah's hope is symbolized in his buying a piece of land even though he was well aware that his personal captivity was close at hand.

Jeremiah's own religious life is revealed to a considerable extent in his recorded prayers, which uniquely illustrate the intimate relationship that existed between the prophet and the deity whom he worshiped. These prayers are usually in the form of conversations and are characterized by a sincerity and frankness seldom found in prayer. Jeremiah opened his mind and heart to Yahweh and did not hesitate to state whatever he felt to be the truth. If he thought Yahweh had been unjust in dealing with him, he expressed his complaints in clear and unmistakable terms. But his prayers were never monologues in which he did all of the talking. After he spoke, he would listen for Yahweh's response, and the entire conversation would have a significance for him that went far beyond a more formal type of prayer. Jeremiah's personal honesty, as well as his courage and remarkable insights, inspired later generations to admire and esteem him.

EZEKIEL

Summary

The Book of Ezekiel has the most logical arrangement of any of the prophetic books. It contains three sections, each of which addresses a different subject matter. Chapters 1-24 concern the fall of Jerusalem. Chapters 25-39 contain a series of oracles addressed to foreign nations, concluding with a section in which the future of Israel is contrasted with that of the foreign nations. The third section, Chapters 40-48, presents a plan for rebuilding the Temple and reorganizing the restored state of Israel.

Ezekiel was one of the younger men taken to Babylon in the first captivity, which occurred in 597 B.C. He served as a kind of religious counselor to the Hebrew exiles who were allowed to live in a colony by themselves near the banks of the Kebar River. Scholars generally assume that most of what is contained in Ezekiel was written by the prophet himself. For some time, they believed that he wrote practically the entire book while living in the colony of exiles. However, more recent scholarship has pointed out several reasons for thinking that at least a portion of the chapters included in the first section contains speeches personally delivered by the prophet to the people who remained in Jerusalem until the city fell in 586 B.C.

The book opens with an account of the vision that summoned Ezekiel to his prophetic calling. Ezekiel describes his vision as an elaborate and complex image that symbolizes the majesty of Yahweh and proclaims Yahweh's sovereignty over all the nations of the earth. The prophet is so overcome by the vision that he falls on his face. A voice calls to him, saying "Son of man, I am sending you to the Israelites, to a rebellious nation that has rebelled against me. . . . And whether they listen or fail to listen—for they are a rebellious house—they will know that a prophet has been among them." Ezekiel is then handed a scroll, on which is written "words of lament and mourning and woe." Told to eat the scroll, when he does so he finds that it tastes as sweet as honey. Evidently, Ezekiel knows that the message he is to proclaim portends impending disaster, yet he thoroughly enjoys the task given to him.

The people who were left in Jerusalem after the first captivity consoled themselves with the idea that they were better off than their brethren who were taken to Babylon. They believed that Yahweh would protect them from any foreign power and that neither the city of Jerusalem nor the Judean kingdom would ever be overthrown. Ezekiel's task was to disillusion them with reference to this hope, to make clear to them that the city would be destroyed and also the reasons why it would be overthrown. To accomplish these tasks, the prophet performed a number of symbolic acts. For example, on a piece of tile, he drew a picture of Jerusalem under siege and placed the tile in a prominent place, where it could be seen plainly by all those who walked along the street. He lay on his left side for a period of time each day for three hundred and ninety days, and then he lay on his right side in a similar manner for forty days. Ezekiel explained that for each day he lay on his left side, northern Israel would be in captivity for one year, and for each day he lay on his right side, the southern kingdom—Judah—would spend a year in captivity. He cut off his hair, dividing it into three parts that symbolized northern Israel, the Judeans left in Jerusalem, and those in captivity in Babylon. He rationed his food, carried furniture out of his house, and did various other things to represent the disaster that would soon overtake the city of Jerusalem.

According to the prophet, the reason for the captivities that had already occurred, as well as for the one in store for the people left in Jerusalem, is the people's defiance of Yahweh's laws. Because Ezekiel believes that Yahweh rules supreme over all the nations of the earth, any violation of Yahweh's commands without appropriate punishment constitutes an infringement upon the deity's honor. Such violations are serious matters to Ezekiel, evidenced by the fact that his references to punishments are usually followed by the words "Then you will know that I am the Lord."

Jerusalem must be destroyed because of its sins. In his enumeration of these sins, Ezekiel includes both moral and ceremonial transgressions, but he noticeably places the greater emphasis on matters pertaining to the ceremonial. He condemns the worship of idols that represent foreign deities, and he severely censures people who eat forbidden meat or violate any of the other rules having to do with the conduct of worship. Coming into direct contact with that which is unclean contaminates Yahweh's sanctuary and profanes his holy name, which Yahweh will not tolerate.

Ezekiel, no less than Jeremiah, sees the significance of the individual in his relationship to Yahweh. Rejecting the ideas that fathers may be punished for the sins of their sons and the sons punished for the sins of their fathers, he boldly states that the soul that sins shall die. Furthermore, he carries this idea to the extreme position of maintaining that a person's entire life will be judged in terms of that individual's last act. Concerning the man who has lived wickedly all of his life but turns from his wickedness and does that which is lawful and right immediately before he dies, all of his wickedness will not be remembered: He will be judged as a righteous man. The reverse is true of the man who has lived righteously all of his life but turns to wickedness just before he dies: All of his righteousness will not be remembered.

The fall of the city of Jerusalem presented something of a problem, especially to those who believed that Yahweh's presence in the most holy place in the Temple was a sure guarantee that the place would never be overthrown. They remembered Isaiah's words uttered more than a century before, when he declared that Jerusalem was Zion's city and must stand forever. For Jeremiah, these words meant very little: Yahweh's dwelling place is in human hearts rather than in a specific place in the Temple. While this idea is not entirely absent in the Book of Ezekiel, the prophet nevertheless believes that Yahweh's presence is located in the Temple more than in any other place. How then could the Temple be destroyed so long as Yahweh's presence was in it? According to Ezekiel, Yahweh's presence went up out of the Temple and rested on a hill outside; then the Temple fell.

In the chapters dealing with foreign nations, Ezekiel has one predominant message: These nations are subject to Yahweh's laws, the same as the Hebrew people. That foreign powers have not recognized Yahweh's sovereignty does not alter their fate in the least. Ultimately, they will be destroyed, which will take place in order that "they will know that I am the Lord." Although Yahweh is, in Ezekiel's mind, a universal God, this universality does not mean that Yahweh stands in the same relationship to the foreign nations as he does to the people of Israel. In this respect, Ezekiel's views are decidedly nationalistic. Yahweh punishes the Israelites in order to teach them a lesson that they have refused to learn in any other way. But in the case of foreign nations, punishment is not meant to teach a lesson that will bring about their conversion. With them, the coming destruction is to be final and does not anticipate any reformation on their part. With reference to the Israelites, something quite different will happen: Yahweh will transform them by putting his own spirit into their hearts. This restoration will include both the people of the northern kingdom and the people of Judah. In the vision of the valley of dry bones, Ezekiel proclaims a complete restoration of the whole house of Israel. The Israelites will return to their own land and rebuild the kingdom that was overthrown, and Yahweh will dwell in their midst forever. The final destruction of all foreign nations is described as an event that will take place when the vast armies under the leadership of Gog and Magog attempt to capture the restored city of Jerusalem. At the crucial moment when victory appears near for the invaders, Yahweh will intervene and completely destroy all of their forces.

The last eight chapters of Ezekiel contain a description of the restored state as envisioned by the prophet. The Temple will be built outside the main part of Jerusalem, constructed in such a manner that will make it possible to keep out those persons and objects that might contaminate the holy place in which Yahweh will dwell. At this point in the text, Ezekiel introduces a distinction between priests and Levites in order that only qualified persons should enter the Temple, even for the purpose of keeping it clean.

The highest official no longer will be the king but rather the high priest, thus indicating that political affairs shall always be made subordinate to religious considerations.

Commentary

Ezekiel has often been called the father of Judaism. His influence on the future development of Israel's religion was, at least for several centuries, greater than that of any of the other prophets. His conception of holiness, which stands in sharp contrast to Isaiah's, became dominant in the period that followed his people's return from Babylonian exile. For Ezekiel, holiness was a quality present in both things and people. Holy objects would be profaned whenever anything common or unclean was brought into direct contact with them, a belief that led to a sharp distinction between the secular and the holy and gave new meanings to such items as the observance of dietary laws, payment of tithes, and observance of the Sabbath. Violation of any of these rules would constitute a profanation of that which was holy or sacred. This interpretation of rules and regulations pertaining only to the Israelite religion served to strengthen the spirit of nationalism and thus to increase the antagonism that already existed between Jews and non-Jews.

Ezekiel's conception of the final triumph of the Israelite people over all of their enemies and the complete destruction of foreign nations contributed much toward the development of the religious doctrines that played such prominent roles in the religion of post-exilic Judaism. The idea that the whole human race is divided into two classes, known as the righteous and the wicked, and that the righteous can be identified as the ones who live in strict conformity with all of Yahweh's laws, while the wicked are those who do not obey these laws, is derived from Ezekiel's teachings. Although this position was not accepted by all of the post-exilic Jews (some parts of the Old Testament were written for the specific purpose of refuting it), nevertheless this doctrine appealed to a large number of people and served to characterize in a general way the attitude of late Judaism.

Ezekiel's plans for rebuilding the Temple and reorganizing the state were carried out to a considerable extent when the exiles returned to their own land. The high priest, rather than a king, assumed the greatest responsibility in political and religious affairs. The use of servants and foreign slaves to do menial tasks in the Temple was discontinued; only those people who belonged to the tribe of Levi were permitted to enter the Temple for this purpose. In earlier times, the entire tribe was regarded as having been set apart for the priesthood, but now only a select group within this tribe was allowed to officiate in the Temple's services.

The spirit of Ezekiel's work determined to a very great extent the character of the religious life of the people during the centuries that followed his teachings. His influence is notable in the code of laws known as the Holiness Code, found in Leviticus, Chapters 17-26, and in the lengthy and detailed set of laws known as the Priests Code, now regarded as one of the four main narratives included in the Pentateuch—the first five books of the Old Testament.

DEUTERO-ISAIAH

Summary

Chapters 40-55 in the Book of Isaiah are believed to be the work of a prophet who lived with the Hebrew exiles during the Babylonian captivity. Because this prophet's real name is unknown and his work has been preserved in the collection of writings that include the prophecies of the earlier Isaiah, he is usually designated as Deutero-Isaiah—the second Isaiah. The chapters attributed to this prophet of the exile include some of the noblest religious ideals found in the entire Old Testament. The prophet was a pure monotheist. Rejecting the idea of Yahweh as a god who belonged only to the Hebrews, Deutero-Isaiah boldly proclaimed Yahweh as the only true God of the entire universe. He maintained that the so-called gods of foreign nations were but figments of the imagination. His conception of the people of Israel was also unique in that he regarded them as Yahweh's servants, whose primary function in the world is to carry religion to the ends of the earth. He made explicit an interpretation of history that, although it had been implied in the teachings of the earlier prophets, had never been stated as clearly by any of them. Finally, he introduced a new concept to account for the sufferings of people that could not, in all fairness, be explained as punishment for sins.

Deutero-Isaiah faced the task of giving new hope and encouragement to the exiles, who were on the verge of despair, feeling either that Yahweh had forsaken them entirely or that Yahweh's power had been broken by the superior gods of the Babylonians. To these disheartened people, Deutero-Isaiah calls out, "Here is your God!" He assures them that Yahweh has not forsaken the exiled people; neither has Yahweh been defeated by the Babylonians or any other foreign power. Yahweh is the supreme ruler of the universe, and all the nations of the earth are subject to him: "Surely the nations are like a drop in a bucket; they are regarded as dust on the scales." And again, "Before him all the nations are as nothing; they are regarded by him as worthless and less than nothing." Deutero-Isaiah ridicules people who bow down before man-made idols and who claim that these idols are representations of their gods. The only true God cannot be represented or symbolized by an image because there are no objects in nature to which he can be compared. Yahweh is the creator of the heavens and the earth. Whatever exists is dependent on him. He alone has the power to create and is the only presence whose purpose can be discerned in the course of history: "He sits enthroned above the circle of the earth, and its people are like grasshoppers. . . . He brings princes to nought and reduces the rulers of this world to nothing."

To those people who have grown weary of their captivity and who have despaired that the time will never come when they can return to their homeland, Deutero-Isaiah has a message of comfort and of hope: The time has arrived when warfare is over; their punishment is accomplished. Yahweh declares that already the captives have been punished too much, and he has called Cyrus, the Persian king, to take appropriate steps for their liberation. Yahweh is now ready to lead them himself. He will go before them, making the rough places smooth and gently carrying in his bosom the ones who are unable to travel by themselves.

Yahweh's sovereignty over the nations of the earth is illustrated in Deutero-Isaiah's conception of history. Humans may think they have complete control over the course of events, but they are mistaken. Yahweh orders events that make up the historical process. Although his order is moral rather than mechanical and allows for choice on the part of human beings, nevertheless it establishes a relationship between cause and effect that remains constant. Yahweh's constancy forms the basis for predictions. In this connection, Yahweh's power and foreknowledge cannot be matched by any of the foreign nations' gods. Speaking about this point, Deutero-Isaiah says for Yahweh, "Remember the former things, those of long ago; I am God, and there is no other; I am God, and there is none like me. I make known the end from the beginning, from ancient times, what is still to come. I say: My purpose will stand, and I will do all that I please."

In a series of poems called "Songs of the Suffering Servant," Deutero-Isaiah sets forth his greatest contribution to Israel's religious ideals. He points out the purpose and the opportunity that lie behind the unmerited suffering on the part of comparatively innocent persons. The problem that troubled Habakkuk—why the just suffer and the wicked prosper—had become one of the major issues for the exiles in Babylon. Granted, the exiles made many mistakes, but they were not as unjust or as wicked as the nations to which they were made captives. If suffering is to be interpreted as punishment for sins, it ought to be distributed on a different basis than what the exiles experienced and observed. Deutero-Isaiah does not deny that at times suffering may be a just punishment for sins, but he insists that not all suffering should be interpreted in this way. Having in mind the captivity of the Israelite people, he is able to see in their captivity something more than punishment for the mistakes they made. He views the captivity as an opportunity to do something generous and noble for the benefit of those who held them in bondage. Instead of the Israelites suffering for their own sins, he sees in the experience the possibility of a voluntary suffering because of the sins of others. Such suffering could be the means of winning over the Israelites' enemies to a new way of living that would be in harmony with the principles of justice and righteousness.

Deutero-Isaiah's thoughts on voluntary suffering were indeed new ways in which the captives might find at least a partial explanation—the realization of a divine purpose—for the hardships that they experienced. The prophet sees the Israelite people as Yahweh's servants and as his chosen people, but chosen for the task of suffering in order that true religion might be brought to those who could not be reached in any other way. What could not be accomplished by force or argument might be achieved through the power of love as manifested in the voluntary suffering of the innocent for the sake of the guilty. Speaking for Yahweh, Deutero-Isaiah says to the people of Israel and Judah, "It is too small a thing for you to be my servant to restore the tribes of Jacob and bring back those of Israel I have kept. I will also make you a light for the Gentiles, that you may bring my salvation to the ends of the earth."

Commentary

No prophet of the Old Testament ever reached loftier heights in his understanding of religion than did Deutero-Isaiah. In his conception of Yahweh as the creator of the heavens and the earth, he made a sharp distinction between Yahweh and the deities of foreign nations. Yahweh was the presence on which all existence depended; he could not be adequately conceived as like any of the objects in the created universe. Although Deutero-Isaiah speaks of Yahweh as a person—if the deity is to have any meaning for human beings, it must be conceived in terms that have been drawn from experience, and personality is the most appropriate symbol that can be found—Yahweh does not have a human personality in every respect, but only in some of them.

Deutero-Isaiah's interpretation of history recognizes that the course of events is something more than a chaotic sequence without meaning or order. A divine element, as well as a human element, exists in history; a purpose is achieved through the historical process, which is what Deutero-Isaiah means when he declares that Yahweh knows the end from the beginning. Deutero-Isaiah's predictions do not imply that all of the things that happen are known in advance, nor do they imply that human beings cannot alter the course of events by the choices they make.

Deutero-Isaiah's greatest achievement is his development of the idea of vicarious suffering. Although he was speaking primarily about the suffering of his own people, we must not think that he was attempting to give a historical account of the way only they were responding to their misfortunes. Rather, he was setting forth an ideal that, if followed, would throw new light on the question of unmerited suffering. People would realize that the situation in which they were placed provided an opportunity for them to exhibit to foreign nations the true spirit of their religion. Like the other prophets before him, Deutero-Isaiah never doubted that the divine purpose ultimately would be achieved, but the method by which it would be accomplished was something quite different from what was previously conceived. Vicarious suffering was an idea of great significance, and although it seems to have been too lofty an ideal for the majority of the people either to grasp or to follow, some individuals believed its truth. Through the centuries that followed, many occasions exemplified this ideal. Christians have long recognized that the life and death of Jesus of Nazareth are supreme examples of what Deutero-Isaiah proclaimed to his contemporary exiles in Babylon.

THE POST-EXILIC PROPHETS

Summary

Prophecy in the Old Testament reached its greatest heights preceding and during the Babylonian exile. Jeremiah, Ezekiel, and the two Isaiahs made the most profound impressions on the religious development of the Israelite people. The period following the exile is characterized by the work of many prophets, some of whom produced writings that are preserved in the Old Testament. In general, these prophets were men of limited vision, but there were some exceptions, and the literature that belongs to this period contains some of the best insights found in any of the prophetic writings, although in most instances the authors of these passages are unknown. In this section, only those prophets for whom books in the Old Testament are named are discussed.

Haggai. When the exiles returned from Babylon, they experienced many bitter disappointments. Both Ezekiel and Deutero-Isaiah promised so much that the people expected an era of great happiness and material prosperity. However, despite the help and encouragement given the exiles by Cyrus, the Persian ruler, when they returned to their own land, they experienced miserable conditions. The land was neglected, the buildings were dilapidated, and the people who had remained behind had become careless and indifferent toward their religious obligations. To make matters worse, the neighboring states assumed a hostile attitude toward the Hebrews; in attempting to rebuild the walls of their city, the Hebrews found it necessary to have their swords close at hand while working with bricks and mortar. Under these conditions, Haggai appeared as a spokesman for Yahweh.

Haggai's message is essentially one of reproof because the people have neglected to rebuild the Temple so that Yahweh might dwell in their midst. The people responded to Haggai's message and set to work with a newfound will. Handicapped by a lack of means and materials, they did the best they could under the circumstances. When they had finished, Haggai told them that even though the building they erected was poor in comparison with the earlier Temple, Yahweh would be with them; in due time, the promises Yahweh made would be fully realized.

Zechariah. Joining with Haggai in bringing a message of hope and encouragement to those who returned from the exile was Zechariah, whose analysis of the situation was more profound than that of his contemporary. Zechariah realized that something more than a rebuilding of the Temple was necessary before Israel's hopes could be realized. A moral transformation must take place within the people themselves, who must be cleansed of their evil nature. Furthermore, the foreign nations whom the people consider their enemies must be subdued, but not by the Israelites' taking up arms against them: Yahweh will quash the aggressors when the time is right for him to act.

Zechariah's messages are expressed in a series of eight visions, each of which symbolizes some aspect of the situation having to do with the future of his people. In one of these visions, the prophet sees an angelic surveyor measuring the area on which Jerusalem is to be built and marking the line of a wall. Another angel explains that the city will have no need of a wall because Yahweh's protection is all that is necessary. In another vision, the high priest Joshua, dressed in soiled clothes, stands before an angel. At Joshua's right stands Satan, the accuser, who brings charges against Joshua and the people to whom he ministers. The angel does not accept these accusations. Joshua is then clothed in a white robe, which symbolizes forgiveness of the sins of the people. Other visions symbolize the destruction of the forces of evil. One of the most significant statements found in the book is Yahweh's message to Zerubbabel, including the saying "Not by might nor by power, but by my Spirit, says the Lord Almighty."

Malachi. A prophet whose name we do not know spoke to the returned exiles and offered them an explanation of the situation that they faced. He is known as Malachi not because this was his name but because the word means "messenger," and in his predictions concerning the future, he says that a messenger will precede the coming of the Day of Yahweh and will prepare the people for it. Later editors supposed erroneously that the prophet was referring to himself, and hence this name was attached to the writings. He was not a great prophet, but he did have some words of encouragement, as well as words of rebuke, for the people to whom he addressed his messages. Insisting that Yahweh still loves the Israelites in spite of all the misfortunes that have befallen them, Malachi calls attention to the fact that the Edomites were severely punished, which was good news to the Israelites because they despised the Edomites as traitors to those whom they should have befriended. The prophet quotes Yahweh as saying "Yet I have loved Jacob, but Esau I have hated, and I have turned his mountains into a wasteland and left his inheritance to the desert jackals."

According to Malachi, one of the reasons why Yahweh withheld his blessings from the Israelites for so long a time was their frequent use of sick and inferior animals for sacrificial offerings. Yahweh demands the best and will be satisfied with nothing less. Another reason why Yahweh did not bless them was their failure in the matters of tithes and offerings; here the prophet accuses his people of robbing God. Also, some men divorced their wives in order to marry women of foreign ancestry, which is contrary to the will of Yahweh. So careless and indifferent have many of the people become that the prophet says that even among the Gentiles, Yahweh's name is honored and feared more than it is among the Israelites. When the Israelites repent and correct all of these mistakes, Yahweh will open the windows of heaven and pour out a blessing so great that the people will not be able to receive all of it. This blessing will include such material benefits as bountiful crops, increase of their flocks, and freedom from sickness.

Obadiah. Obadiah's work is preserved in a book that contains a single chapter. Usually works of this length were placed in larger collections of manuscripts and included under the name of a different author. Presumably in this case, editors or compilers believed that the work would attract more attention if placed by itself. The book is the least significant of all the prophetic writings both from a literary and a religious point of view. Decidedly nationalistic in tone, the first part of the chapter rejoices in the fall of the Edomites. The remaining portion predicts the triumph of the Hebrew people at a time when all of their enemies will be destroyed.

Joel. Nothing is known concerning the life of this prophet. A lack of agreement exists concerning the time when he lived, but this is not a matter of great importance. The book opens with the description of an unusually severe plague of locusts and is followed by Joel's instructing the priests to proclaim a fast and to call a solemn assembly, the purpose of which is to arouse the people to repent and reform. After the people "rend [their] heart and not [their] garments," Yahweh will pour out his spirit on all flesh, causing sons and daughters to prophesy, young men to see visions, and old men to dream.

Commentary

The prophets of the post-exilic period are of particular interest because they indicate the various trends of thought that were taking shape during the centuries that immediately followed the return of the exiles from Babylon. The Temple in Jerusalem and the many ceremonies and activities associated with it came to occupy a most important place in the religious lives of the people, and especially in the case of Haggai, who believed that Yahweh's presence, as well as his blessings, was dependent upon a proper place in which he might dwell in their midst. The distinction between the secular and the sacred, emphasized by Malachi and implied in the works of other prophets, came to occupy more and more attention on the part of the priests. The spirit of nationalism, which in some cases reached the point of hatred toward Israel's enemies, can be seen in Obadiah and, to a lesser extent, in Joel.

It would, however, be a mistake to suppose that these tendencies were present in all of the prophetic writers. Voices were heard from time to time in which the spirits of Jeremiah and

Deutero-Isaiah found magnificent expression. We do not know the persons who possessed these voices, but many of their messages have been preserved in the later chapters of the Book of Isaiah. The introduction of the figure of Satan in the prophecies of Zechariah, as well as the eschatological implications of Zechariah's visions, marks an important trend in the development of post-exilic Judaism.

THE HISTORICAL WRITINGS

Approximately one-third of the Old Testament consists of historical documents, including the Pentateuch, or what has often been called the five books of Moses, and the books of Joshua, Judges, Samuel, Kings, Chronicles, Ezra, and Nehemiah. Taken together, these writings may be regarded as covering the high points in the history of the Hebrew people from the time of the Exodus from Egypt to the post-exilic period. In addition, they are presumed to cover important events pertaining to the same people from the creation of the world to the time of the Egyptian bondage. The Hebrew prophets were especially concerned with history because they believed that the course of events revealed Yahweh's nature and will. In this connection, the law codes were presented in a historical setting. Thus we find that the prophetic literature of the Old Testament includes the historical narratives, as well as the writings attributed to the prophets for whom books were named.

THE PENTATEUCH

Summary

The first five books of the Old Testament were, according to both Jewish and Christian traditions, attributed to Moses until comparatively recent times. To be sure, there were some exceptions, but generally the Mosaic authorship of these books was not questioned until the era of the movement known as "higher criticism." Biblical scholars today almost universally agree that the Pentateuch is composed of at least four separate and distinct narratives written by different persons who were widely separated historically. Evidence overwhelmingly suggests that within each of these four documents, the work of more than one author is present. Nothing in the first four of these books asserts, or even suggests, that Moses was the author. Deuteronomy, the fifth book, is presented as though it were an address delivered by Moses, but the contents of the book indicate quite clearly that it was written a long time after Moses' death. Hebrew authors commonly wrote as though the words they used had been spoken a long time before.

Early Judean History . The earliest of these four main narratives is known as the Early Judean History. The unknown author is designated by the letter *J* because supposedly he was a prophet of the southern kingdom of Judah. The narrative begins with the story of Creation as it is recorded in the second chapter of the Book of Genesis and concludes with an account of the establishment of the monarchy in the land of Canaan. There are several distinctive characteristics of this history. Yahweh is the name used for the deity and stands for a god who is conceived in terms that are crudely anthropomorphic, or humanlike. He possesses a physical body, walks in the Garden of Eden during the cool of the day, talks directly with Adam, and is a dinner guest in the tent of Abraham. In many respects, he behaves in a manner that resembles the typical chief of a primitive tribe. The place names that are used belong to the southern kingdom. The implied ethical standards are somewhat lower than those of later narratives. The various parts of the history are organized in a manner that sets forth the author's conception of the divine purpose to be realized on earth and the reasons why its fulfillment has been delayed.

This history appears to have been written about 850 B.C. The source materials used for its composition include not only the written documents available at that time but a number of traditions that were passed on orally from older generations. In the Creation story, man is formed out of the dust of the earth, and Eve, the first woman, is created from Adam's rib. The story of the Fall, which has to do with the eating of forbidden fruit, is followed by an account of the brothers Cain and Abel. Because sin has become so widespread over the face of the earth, Yahweh causes the Great Flood to appear but spares Noah and everything that is with him in the ark. After the flood, Noah pronounces a curse on Canaan and gives blessings to Shem and Japheth.

Abraham's calling to perform Yahweh's work is followed by an account of his journey to Egypt. After Abraham's return home, a promise is made to him concerning the birth of a son and the inheritance of the land of Canaan by his descendants. Although Abraham and his wife have reached an advanced age, Isaac is born in fulfillment of the promise. Isaac's two sons, Jacob and Esau, struggled in their mother's womb before they are born, thus indicating the strife that will continue for centuries between the Israelites and the Edomites. Jacob deceives his father and tricks his brother, Esau, out of his birthright. He then goes to a distant land, where he marries the two daughters of Laban and enters into an agreement whereby he obtains a large share of his uncle's property. On his return home with the members of his family, he meets his brother, and the two are reconciled.

Jacob's favorite son, Joseph, is sold by his brothers into slavery but eventually comes to hold a powerful place in the government of Egypt. Jacob and his sons and their families move to Egypt because of a famine in the land of Canaan. Their descendants increase in number, which causes an Egyptian pharaoh to become alarmed lest the Israelite colony become too powerful. Accordingly, the pharaoh begins a policy of oppression that places burdens on the Hebrews that are greater than they can bear. Moses is summoned by Yahweh to deliver his people from this oppression. After a series of plagues is visited upon the Egyptians, the Hebrews leave the land where they were enslaved and begin their march through the wilderness toward the land of Canaan. After a description of the difficulties that they encounter during this march, the author concludes his history with an account of their entrance into the land and the conquering of a portion of it.

Ephraimite History. The second of the four Pentateuch narratives is known as the Ephraimite History. The author is designated by the letter *E* for two reasons. *E* is the first letter in the word *Ephraimite,* which is used interchangeably with the northern kingdom. Because the place names in this history belong to the northern kingdom, it is assumed that the author was a native of this place. The second reason that *E* is designated for this material is that *E* is the first letter in the word *Elohim,* which is the name for the deity in that part of the history that precedes the story of Moses and the burning bush. In our bibles today, the *J* and *E* histories have been interwoven to present a single narrative. However, careful analysis reveals with a fair degree of accuracy the materials that belong to each of the original histories. The *E* narrative has several distinctive characteristics, including the use of the term *Elohim,* place names that belong to the north, a more advanced conception of the deity, higher ethical standards implied in the stories concerning the patriarchs, strong opposition to idol worship, and an unfavorable attitude toward the establishment of a monarchy.

This history is believed to have been written about 750 B.C., a century later than the *J* narrative. Although these two histories are in many respects parallel versions of the same events, the *E* version begins with the story of Abraham and makes no references to what may have happened prior to that time. The stories pertaining to the patriarchs Abraham, Isaac, Jacob, and Joseph are told in a more favorable light than in the *J* narrative, indicating something of an advance in ethical ideals, for these heroes of the Israelite people are not regarded as guilty of acts of deception as they are in the *J* account of the same events. The story of the sacrifice of Isaac occurs only in the *E* narrative. Here, the purpose of the story is twofold: The author wants to illustrate perfect obedience to the will of God on the part of Abraham, and he also wants to make it clear that the deity no longer requires human sacrifices. Animals may be substituted in their place.

The great masterpiece of the *E* narrative is the Joseph story, which is related in greater detail than in *J*. The underlying motive of the story is that a divine purpose is being realized through the course of human events even though the individuals who are involved in it may not be entirely conscious of it. Moses, according to *E*, introduced the name of Yahweh to the Hebrew people. Although Yahweh may be regarded as the same god who appeared to the early patriarchs, he was not known by this name until the time of Moses. Not until after Moses returns from a lengthy sojourn in the land of Midian does Yahweh appear to him in a burning bush and call upon him to deliver his own people from the oppression of the Egyptian pharaoh. When Moses protests that he is slow of speech and unable to present his demands before the Egyptian ruler, Aaron, his brother, becomes his spokesman.

The experiences during the march through the wilderness are described at considerable length. When the people are encamped near Mount Sinai, Moses goes up onto the mount and receives the law tablets from Yahweh. The story of Aaron and the golden calf idols is told in a manner that is intended to make idol worship appear ridiculous. Because Moses is not permitted to enter into the land of Canaan, Joshua is chosen to be the leader in Moses' place. An account is given of an important meeting at Shechem, where representatives of the different tribes meet and form themselves into a confederacy. This action introduces the period of the judges, designed as a form of government in which Yahweh rules by communicating his will directly to those who have been appointed to receive it. This type of organization continued until the people clamored for a king to rule over them.

Deuteronomy. The third narrative, designated by the letter *D*, is found in our present Book of Deuteronomy. Like the other narratives, it appears to be written by several authors. Its distinctive characteristic is the body of laws that forms the book's main core. These laws are recorded in Chapters 12-26. Chapters 5-11 consist of an introduction to the laws. The remaining chapters are believed to be later additions to the original book, added in order that the entire book might be regarded as an integral part of a complete history that reaches from the time of Creation to the post-exilic period.

Although the introductory statements indicate that the words included in this part of the history were spoken by Moses, the contents of Deuteronomy tell a different story. Many, if not most, of the specific laws that are set forth are not appropriate to the time of Moses but rather are designed to deal with situations that did not arise until long after the era of Moses. For example, the story of the finding of a law book in the Temple, which is recorded in 2 Kings 22, is believed to be a reference to the Deuteronomic code of laws. If this story is correct, then the laws were formulated by disciples of the eighth-century B.C. prophets and were designed to correct those conditions that Amos, Hosea, and Isaiah had protested so vigorously. Especially prominent in this code is the law of the Central Sanctuary, which forbade the offering of sacrifices at any place other than the particular one designated for that purpose. Obviously, the authors had the Temple in Jerusalem in mind, but the naming of that place would have been inappropriate in a document attributed to Moses. Not until after the law book was discovered in the Temple during the reign of Josiah was this particular law either recognized or enforced.

Another important law is known as the Year of Release, which provided that at the end of each six-year period, all property that had been forfeited to satisfy debts should be returned to its original owners. This law was intended not only to prevent an undue accumulation of wealth on the part of a few but also to provide new opportunities for those who had been deprived of their possessions through unfortunate circumstances over which they had no control. Other laws were designed to protect people who had been falsely accused. By fleeing to one of the cities of refuge, the accused person would be safe until the charge had been thoroughly investigated.

Not all of the laws in Deuteronomy are of an ethical nature. Ritualistic requirements, such as the prohibition of eating certain kinds of meat, sowing mixed seed in the same field, purification rites, and numerous ceremonies, are included along with the other laws. The nationalistic character of this legislation is illustrated in the fact that Hebrews and non-Hebrews are not subject to the same requirements. For example, animals that died a natural death could not be sold to the Hebrews for food but could be sold to foreigners. The treatment of slaves was another instance in which Israelites were entitled to privileges denied to foreigners.

The introduction to the law codes is presented as an address given by Moses. The motive that should prompt obedience to these laws is gratitude for the way in which Yahweh delivered his people from bondage in Egypt. The Sabbath, for example, should be observed as a memorial to the people's deliverance and should constantly remind them of their obligation to treat with kindness the laborers in their employ. Later additions supplement the earlier portions of Deuteronomy by placing all the laws under the same historical setting. Blessings are pronounced on people who obey all the statutes and ordinances of the book; those who refuse to obey are cursed.

Late Priestly History. The fourth and last of the Pentateuch narratives is called the Late Priestly History and is designated by the letter *P.* Called a priestly history because it represents the point of view generally held by the priests, who were inclined to greatly emphasize ritualistic requirements, the date of its composition is usually placed somewhere near 450 B.C. Although written in the form of a history, it contains a number of law codes, one of which is known as the Holiness Code, as recorded in Leviticus 17-26. The *P* narrative includes many other regulations pertaining chiefly to the place, manner, and forms of worship. One of the priests' chief duties during the post-exilic period was to enforce these regulations.

The history begins with the Creation story as it is reported in the first chapter of the Book of Genesis. Although this narrative is now interwoven with the *J* and *E* histories, its unique characteristics make it somewhat easier to distinguish the materials that belong to it. Its style of writing is formal and legalistic, with a concern for exact and precise statements. For example, in the creation story, stating that the heavens and the earth were created by a divine act was insufficient; stating exactly what was accomplished on each of the six days of the creation week was necessary. Also, the age of each of the early patriarchs is recorded in an exact number of years, and the dates when Noah entered the ark and again when he left it are also recorded. The author's interpretation of history has much to do with such recording of particular events. For example, because a person's life span was supposedly proportionate to the amount of sin that that person had committed, the lives of the earliest inhabitants were said to have been much longer—eight or nine hundred years—than at the time when the history was written. As sin increased in the world, life spans became shorter and shorter.

Because it was important in the post-exilic period to give a new emphasis to the religious institutions that had been neglected, an attempt was made to show the very ancient origin of each of them. For example, the story of Creation culminates in the institution of the Sabbath. The Deuteronomic narrative indicates that the Sabbath is to be observed as a memorial to the Israelites' deliverance from Egypt, but in the *P* narrative, the reason for observing the Sabbath dates to the time of Adam and the creation of the world. The story of Noah and the Flood provides a setting for the laws that prohibit murder and the eating of blood. Circumcision, of a deep religious significance for the Hebrews, is now said to have been introduced by Abraham, and the Feast of Passover was established by Moses. Each of these religious institutions or practices was not only of ancient origin but was introduced by one of the great characters of the past.

The history of the periods covered in the *J* and *E* narratives is passed over quickly except for those particular points that needed special emphasis. The story of the march through the wilderness includes a great deal of material not found in the older narratives. This new material largely details instructions concerning the offering of sacrifices and other ritualistic performances. The reason for these in-depth instructions was the obvious desire on the part of the authors to show that the priestly requirements of the post-exilic age were really in force from the time when the Hebrews left Egypt. Although the law of the Central Sanctuary, which deals with the Temple in Jerusalem, is actually a later development, the *P* historians explain the ancient character of the law in their account of a moving sanctuary made according to instructions given to Moses and carried by the Hebrews as they journeyed through the wilderness. This moving sanctuary was no more than a tent, but it contained rooms and equipment that corresponded to the Temple of later years. Of the many ceremonies that are described in detail, the most important are those pertaining to the services to be performed on the Day of Atonement.

Commentary

The Pentateuch, or what came to be known as the Torah or the Book of the Law, is regarded as the most authoritative and highly inspired of all the Old Testament writings, in large part because these books contain the laws given to the Israelites by Yahweh. These laws, like the source from which they are derived, were eternal and would forever remain the standard by which people's conduct would be judged. Because Moses has long been recognized as the great lawgiver who transmitted the words of Yahweh to the people of Israel, it seemed appropriate to attribute the writing of all the law books to him. Actually, we know from the contents of the Old Testament itself that the concept of divine law and its application to the problems and situations that occurred in Hebrew history was a developmental process that took place over a long period of time. Attributing all of these laws to Moses was not meant to deceive the people but rather was a device used to indicate the eternal character of the laws and a continuation of the spirit and purpose of Moses' work. Then, too, the laws constitute the basis upon which the covenant relationship between Yahweh and the Hebrew people was established. The significance of the covenant idea in the Old Testament can scarcely be overestimated. The prophets constantly make reference to it by insisting that the fate of Israel will always be determined by the extent to which its people are faithful or unfaithful to the obligations placed upon them by the covenant.

JOSHUA, JUDGES, AND 1 AND 2 SAMUEL

Summary

Joshua. Consisting of twenty-four chapters, approximately the first half of the Book of Joshua is an extension of the history recorded in Deuteronomy; the remainder appears to have been added by authors of the Late Priestly History. The story of the conquest of Canaan is told briefly and in a manner that indicates that it was accomplished easily and within a relatively short period of time. The crossing of the Jordan River is attended by Yahweh's miraculous intervention, reminiscent of the crossing of the Red Sea that followed the Exodus from Egypt. In commemoration of the Jordan River crossing, twelve stones are taken from the river bed and erected as a monument. The first city to be attacked is Jericho, where the walls tumble down at the moment when trumpet blasts are heard. Because Achan steals a wedge of gold and a fine Babylonian garment, the Hebrews fail to capture the city of Ai. Not until punishment is meted out for Achan's sin does the city fall into the Hebrews' hands.

Joshua, in accordance with the instruction that he receives, gathers representatives of all the people in one place and delivers to them the statutes and ordinances given by Moses. In a battle with the Gibeonites, Joshua commands the sun and moon to stand still, with the result that the day is lengthened, thus enabling Joshua's forces to achieve a remarkable victory over their enemies. The latter chapters of the book describe the division of the land among the various tribes. The authors of this book were evidently interested in personalities. They had a very high regard for Joshua, ranking him as second only to Moses. The farewell address that this hero delivers before all Israel praises Yahweh for the victories that he has given and counsels the people to remain faithful to the god who has already done so much in their behalf.

Judges. Really a continuation of the history in Joshua, the Book of Judges' central theme is the settlement in the land of Canaan, a period that preceded the establishment of the monarchy. Although the leaders of the people were known as judges, their chief function was not that of deciding cases of law but rather providing political and military leadership in times of crises. These crises occurred one after another in rapid succession, indicating quite clearly that after the death of Joshua, the situation that the Israelites faced was chaotic. Whenever conditions became intolerable, a leader would arise and deliver his people from the hands of the enemy. But the victory would never bring about anything more than temporary relief. Within a short time, a new crisis would develop and the cycle of events would be repeated.

The first judge, or deliverer, was Othniel, who brought victory to the Israelites after they suffered eight years of oppression by the king of Mesopotamia. Then came Ehud, who delivered his people from the Moabites. Deborah, both a judge and a prophet, sent out a call to the various tribes to unite in a battle against the Canaanites. Responding to her call, the Israelites defeated the armies of Sisera at a battle at Megiddo. Gideon was another judge who delivered the people of Israel, this time from the Midianites. The story of Gideon is related at considerable length, for he is regarded as one of the better judges. As a result of his activities, the land is said to have had rest for a period of forty years. Jephthah was the judge who made a vow to Yahweh: If Yahweh would grant him victory in his war with the Ammonites, Jephthah would offer as a sacrifice whatever first came out of his house on his return home. The victory was achieved, and on his way home, he was met first by his own daughter. With great emotion, he told her of his vow and shortly thereafter carried it out.

Samson, one of the more prominent judges, tricked the Philistines on several occasions. At one time, he slew thousands of them with the jawbone of an ass. His affair with Delilah, who betrayed him to the Philistines, cost him his eyesight, but ultimately he was restored to Yahweh's favor and was able to pull down the temple that housed the Philistine god Dagon. Many other judges are mentioned, and some interesting stories are related concerning a few of them. The historian of this period was convinced that Israel should have had a different type of leadership and expresses this attitude in these words: "In those days Israel had no king; everyone did as he saw fit."

1 and 2 Samuel. The two books of Samuel record an important transition in political organization. The period of the judges came to an end with Samuel, who is also referred to as a seer and a prophet, and who anointed Saul to be the first king of Israel. The history of the monarchy contained in these books is believed to have been compiled during the reign of King Josiah of Judah. Because of the reformation that he inaugurated, Josiah was regarded as a great king. Under his leadership, the aspirations for Israel's future hopefully would soon be realized, for it seemed reasonable enough to suppose that Israel's troubles during the early period of the settlement in Canaan were due to the fact that the people had no king to rule over them, at least according to certain parts of Samuel. However, the story as we have it now is a bit confusing because the compiler of Samuel used some source materials that express an opposite idea. We are told that the establishment of the monarchy was a great achievement, but we also read that it was Israel's greatest mistake. According to the latter view, Samuel warned his people of the dangers involved in having a king, and only after their persistent demands did Yahweh relent and allow them to have their own way.

Because the career of Samuel marks an important transition point in the history of the Hebrew people, many stories concerning him are preserved. In 1 Samuel, we read that even before Samuel was born, he was dedicated to Yahweh. His birth was a miraculous event, for his mother, Hannah, had been childless. While only a small boy, Samuel was taken to the home of Eli, a priest, so that he might be reared under influences that would prepare him for his future work. One night, Yahweh called to Samuel and spoke a message of reproof that Samuel was to deliver to Eli. On another occasion, when the elders of Israel gathered for a consultation concerning their political future, they called upon Samuel to select someone to be anointed as king, but here we have two conflicting accounts: According to one account, Samuel protested vigorously against a movement of this kind; in the other account, Saul arrived at Samuel's house after a prolonged search for his father's lost animals, but Samuel was warned in advance of Saul's coming, and knowing that Yahweh's chosen leader was before him, Samuel made arrangements for him to be anointed as king. The brief account of Saul's reign also appears to be based on conflicting source materials. The most probable explanation for this conflict is that these sources were written by both supporters and detractors of the idea of a monarchy for Israel.

Saul's disobedience in sparing the life of the Amalekite king, along with animals that were offered as sacrifices, was bitterly denounced by Samuel. This failure on the part of Saul is used as an introduction to the story of David. Samuel, in response to instruction that he received from Yahweh, went to the home of a certain Jesse who had several sons, one of whom was to be selected as king in place of Saul. David, although the youngest of Jesse's sons, was chosen. Eventually Saul became jealous of David, and his antagonism is illustrated in a number of different stories. 1 Samuel closes with an account of the war with the Philistines and Saul's tragic death on Mount Gilboa.

2 Samuel is concerned almost entirely with the career of David. An excerpt from the Book of Yashur the Upright reports a eulogy spoken by David in commemoration of Saul and Jonathan. An account is given of the way in which David was made king first over Judah and later over all of Israel. The story of Abner, Saul's trusted general, is followed by a short poem, in which David expresses lamentation over the way in which Abner met his death. We are told how David captured the city of Jerusalem and made it the headquarters of his kingdom, how the ark was brought to Jerusalem, and how David achieved many victories. David's sin against Uriah is reported, as is the way in which he was reproved by Nathan the prophet. Absalom's rebellion is narrated at considerable length, and the book ends with the story of David's sin in numbering the people of Israel.

Commentary

The history that is recorded in these historical writings represents the points of view of post-exilic writers. In their accounts of the events that followed the entrance of the Hebrews into the land of Canaan, the writers were influenced by the religious ideals and practices current at the time when they lived. The primary purpose of the history is not to preserve an accurate record of what happened in the past but rather to emphasize the religious lessons that are illustrated in the course of events. The Deuteronomic law of the Central Sanctuary, the regulations embodied in the Holiness Code, and the detailed instructions of the Priests Code were considered extremely important for the preservation of the Hebrew religion. By projecting these ideals and institutions back to the early history of the Hebrew people, the writers intended to show that such codes and laws were not innovations invented by contemporary priests but rather were continuations of principles recognized as far back as the time of Moses. Further support for these institutions was provided by showing that the course of Hebrew history was determined primarily by the attitude of these people with regard to the requirements specified in these codes.

In writing their history, these Old Testament authors made use of older source materials, including the Book of the Wars of Yahweh, the Book of Yashur the Upright, "The Song of Deborah," and other fragments of the early literature available to them. The primitive character of some of these sources is understandable given that they were produced in an earlier age, going back as far as the period of the united kingdom and in some instances even earlier than that, which helps explain in part the strange and barbaric stories that are incorporated into the history. Actions that would not have been condoned at all in later times are related without any apparent censure or blame. In their original form, these sources represent a period of Hebrew history that preceded the teachings of the great prophets and the corresponding development of ethical ideals.

Because these sources were produced by men who held opposing views about such institutions as the establishment of the monarchy, we can see why conflicting accounts of the same event are found side by side in the Old Testament history. In some instances, two different accounts are presented without any attempt to reconcile the disagreements. At other times, explanatory passages inserted by editors and copyists in an attempt to harmonize the accounts with one another are detectable. Despite these conflicts, throughout this history the underlying conception of a moral order characterizes the historical process. This moral order in the historic process illustrates what the Hebrew writers believed to be the divine element in history. Obedience to Yahweh's commands was certain to cause consequences quite different from the ones that were sure to follow disobedience of these same commands. To the prophetic historians, either obeying or disobeying Yahweh's directives meant choosing between life and death, respectively.

1 AND 2 KINGS, 1 AND 2 CHRONICLES, EZRA, AND NEHEMIAH

Summary

1 and 2 Kings. Often called the Deuteronomic History of the Kings of Israel and Judah because of the prominence attached to the Deuteronomic law of the Central Sanctuary, Kings discusses the attitudes of Israel's kings toward the observance of the law of the Central Sanctuary as the most important factor in their various reigns. In this respect, the kings' conduct determined more than anything else whether they did that which was evil or that which was good in the sight of Yahweh. Although some of the kings ruled for a comparatively long time and others occupied the throne for only a brief period, all were judged by the same standards. Any king who failed to destroy the high places of worship or permitted the people to offer sacrifices at any place other than the Temple in Jerusalem was said to have performed evil in the sight of Yahweh and was responsible for the disasters that fell upon the nation.

Kings begins with the history of the kingdom at the point where the history ends in Samuel and continues the account until the time of King Josiah of Judah. The work is divided into three parts: The first part deals with the united kingdom under David and Solomon; the second division discusses the parallel history of the divided kingdom until the fall of Samaria; and part three focuses only on the southern kingdom of Judah. The writer used a number of sources, including the Book of the Acts of Solomon, the "Temple Annals," stories about Elisha, and other documents that report particular events. Taking from these sources only the materials that were suited to his purpose, the Kings author shaped the materials to emphasize the lessons that he wanted to teach.

1 Kings begins with an account of how Solomon was chosen as the successor of King David. The author of this history was evidently an admirer of Solomon, for he credits him with great wisdom in administering the affairs of the kingdom. He tells of the prayer that Solomon offered at the dedication of the Temple and of his wise decisions in dealing with difficult problems. He does mention that Solomon did not destroy the high places of worship and that Solomon brought many foreign wives to the court in Jerusalem, conduct that the writer strongly suggests is the main reason for the rebellion and division of the monarchy that occurred after Solomon's death.

The second part of the history follows a very definite pattern in describing the activities of the kings of both the northern and the southern kingdoms. The writer begins by telling when it was that a king began his reign and for how long his reign lasted. Next, he states whether the king was good or evil. In some instances, the record of events that occurred during the reign of a particular king is fairly long, while in others it is comparatively short, but the standard of judgment is always the same: the attitude of a king toward the law of the Central Sanctuary. The writer regards a king's permitting worship at any of the local shrines, or so-called high places, as a more serious offense than any other form of social injustice. Because the only legitimate sanctuary was located in Jerusalem, which was now the capital of the southern kingdom, the kings of the north did not have access to it; consequently, any worship that they authorized had to take place at some local site, which is why the writer of Kings opens his account of each one of the northern kings by saying "He did evil in the eyes of the Lord." Of course, the southern kings did not always destroy the high places either, but the writer is more charitable in dealing with them: He usually finds some excuse for their failure in this respect.

An interesting feature in this second part of the history is the system of chronology that the writer uses. Dates are recorded in terms of the number of years that the corresponding ruler of the other kingdom has reigned. For example, one northern king is said to have begun his reign during the fifth year of the corresponding king of the southern kingdom.

The history's third part focuses only on Judah. The northern kingdom is held in captivity because of the transgressions of its inhabitants; now, only in the southern kingdom are the hopes of the Hebrew people to be realized. King Hezekiah's reign is described at greater length than those of most of the other kings because the writer regards him as a great reformer. The invasion of the Judean kingdom by the Assyrian ruler Sennacherib is reported, as is the visit to Jerusalem by Merodach-Baladan of Babylon. The reign of Manasseh, Hezekiah's son, lasted for over fifty years but is passed over lightly, as is the reign of his son and successor, Amon, who was assassinated. With the coming to the throne of King Josiah, Amon's son, the writer expresses great optimism, for it was during Josiah's reign that the law book was discovered in the Temple and the great reformation inaugurated. Probably at this point, the Kings writer ended his history, for scholars assume that Josiah was still king when the author wrote. Later writers extended the Deuteronomic history, but their work is recorded in Judges, Samuel, and other portions of the Old Testament.

1 and 2 Chronicles. If the Deuteronomic law is the standard of judgment in 1 and 2 Kings, then the Priests Code is the standard in 1 and 2 Chronicles. Chronicles' history appears to have been written later than Kings'; the date usually given is approximately 300 B.C. The authors of the two books have the advantage of using the Deuteronomic history, as well as the many other documents that appeared prior to 300 B.C., as source material. Apparently, they accepted the older histories' idea that personal suffering and national disasters are punishments for wrongdoing, while long life and material prosperity are rewards for righteous conduct.

This conception of punishments and rewards adequately explains some historical events, but other events contradict this view. For example, King Uzziah, whose reign preceded Isaiah's becoming a prophet, was regarded as one of the ablest and best kings of Judah, yet he was smitten with leprosy and died in a leper colony; King Manasseh, judged by all the accepted standards of both priests and prophets, was a wicked man but reigned for more than half a century and died a natural death; and Josiah, the good king who started the Deuteronomic reformation and followed as closely as he could the teachings of the great prophets, was slain on the field of battle, and his son was taken to Egypt as a prisoner. The chronicler felt it necessary to explain these events. Believing as he did that Yahweh orders the course of events, he interpreted the entire course of Hebrew history from the point of view of the laws and regulations embodied in the Priests Code.

The introduction to Chronicles consists of a brief sketch of the period from Adam to David, whom the chronicler idealizes—in contrast to the record preserved in 1 and 2 Samuel. The law of the Central Sanctuary is projected back into this early period by identifying it with the tabernacle that the Israelites carried with them in their march through the wilderness. The Priests Code, too, is presumed to have been in force during the early periods of Hebrew history. No mention is made of the kings of northern Israel: The assumption is that the people in that kingdom were no better than heathens and, as a consequence of their behavior, were no longer to be counted among the true people of Israel.

Ezra. This book, which along with the Book of Nehemiah is also part of the history produced by the writers of Chronicles, contains ten chapters, six of which are concerned almost entirely with recounting events that led to the return of the Jews to Jerusalem. Ezra had in his possession a royal decree authorizing him to make the return along with all the Jews who wished to return with him. As soon as they entered Jerusalem, they built an altar and later rebuilt the Temple, having overcome Samaritan opposition. Ezra protests against the intermarriage of Jews with foreigners and insists that such guilty Jews should obtain divorces from their spouses.

Nehemiah. In the first part of this book, Nehemiah is presented as the cup bearer to Artaxerxes, the Persian king who granted Nehemiah permission to visit the city of Jerusalem. During this visit, Nehemiah takes an active part in helping to rebuild the walls that were demolished. The book's second part centers on Ezra rather than on Nehemiah. Ezra gathers the people into one great assembly and reads to them from the law book. Part three contains a number of miscellaneous items, including lists of those who returned from exile. The Book of Nehemiah closes with an account of Nehemiah's second visit to Jerusalem after an interval of twelve years.

Commentary

With the Book of Ezra and the Book of Nehemiah, the historical survey from Adam to the rebuilding of the Temple in the postexilic period is nearly complete and includes the words of many different authors who lived at different times and, in some cases, represented conflicting points of view. The work as a whole began with the Judean and the Ephraimite histories, which form part of the Pentateuch, and was continued at various intervals by Deuteronomic and priestly historians. These later writers not only used as source materials the older narratives that were available to them, but they supplemented and revised the accounts according to the ideals and institutions that were dominant when they did their work. The rewriting of the *J* and *E* histories did not, however, replace the earlier accounts, whose value and prestige were too well established for them to be put aside. Hence, the newer histories have been preserved in the Old Testament along with the older ones.

1 and 2 Kings relate the historical story as seen by an enthusiastic supporter of the Deuteronomic code of laws. Although this code includes both moral and ritualistic requirements, the later historian emphasizes ritual. Perhaps one reason for this emphasis is that ritualistic observances can be enforced in a manner that is not possible in the case of moral requirements, which involve motives, as well as overt acts. The work of supplementing and revising the older histories continued over a long period of time, with an increasing emphasis on details concerning the place, form, time, and manner of worship. Although such emphasis is expected of priestly historians, they did not ignore moral matters. They wanted, no less than the prophets, to bring the people into harmony with the will of Yahweh. But the priests' business was to conduct the various forms of worship, and it seemed obvious to them that obedience to divine commands was a prerequisite to any satisfactory relationship with Yahweh, a point of view expressed so clearly in 1 and 2 Chronicles, Ezra, and Nehemiah.

THE WISDOM LITERATURE

The Book of Jeremiah makes reference to three distinct groups of people: priests, prophets, and sages. Of these three, the prophets are responsible for the largest portion of Old Testament writings. They produced not only the books that bear their names but the historical writings that include a record of the specific laws and requirements that pertained to the priests' work. Three books in the Old Testament represent the work of Israel's teachers, the sages or so-called wise men: Job, Ecclesiastes, and Proverbs. In contrast with the prophetic writings, the writers of these three books do not preface their remarks with a "thus says the Lord" but instead appeal to reason and common sense to support what they say. Their writings are characterized by a broad and universal appeal that avoids the nationalistic spirit so prevalent in many of the prophetic writings. Because the sages address themselves to the problems that arise in everyday living, their counsel and advice are applicable to non-Jews just as much as to the people of Israel. They speak to individuals rather than to the nation, and they consider problems that have nothing to do with race or nationality. If the religion of the Old Testament can be said to have reached its greatest heights in the teachings of the prophets, then in the sages' work it reached its greatest breadth.

JOB

Summary

The Book of Job is often referred to as one of the great classics of world literature. Its subject matter is the all-important question, "Why, in a world over which Yahweh has jurisdiction, should innocent persons have to suffer when at the same time the wicked escape suffering and are permitted to have comfort and security?" All people—not just Jews—sooner or later confront this universal problem. Some of the Hebrew prophets attempted to deal with this question insofar as it affected the nation as a whole, but the writer of the Book of Job deals with it on an individual basis. The book, in its present form, loosely divides into five parts: the prologue, the symposium, the speeches of Elihu, the nature poems, and the epilogue. As a whole, the book appears to have been written as a direct challenge to the time-honored doctrine that people are rewarded or punished according to their merits.

The prologue, which consists of the book's first two chapters, is believed to have been based on an older folktale in which a wager is made between Yahweh and Satan. Satan contends that no one serves Yahweh except for selfish reasons, but Yahweh disagrees and presents Job, a righteous man who "fears God and shuns evil," as an example to counter Satan's claim. In order to prove to Satan that Job's loyalty is not based on material reward, Yahweh permits Satan to take from Job all of the material benefits Job has received and to afflict him with the most severe and excruciating pain. Through all of this suffering, Job never complains. His only response is "The Lord gave and the Lord has taken away; may the name of the Lord be praised." However, Job's wife urges him to "curse God and die" in order to gain relief from his suffering. Three friends—Eliphaz the Temanite, Bildad the Shuhite, and Zophar the Naamathite—come from afar and express their sympathy by remaining silent and by clothing themselves in sackcloth and sitting in ashes.

The symposium, consisting of speeches by Job and by each of his three friends, tells a very different story. In the first speech, Job curses the day that he was born, insisting that life under the conditions that he must bear is not worthwhile. Because he is conscious of no wrongdoing, he sees no justice in the way he must suffer. To this speech, Eliphaz replies that righteous people do not suffer; only the wicked are tormented in this fashion. For Job to declare himself innocent is to charge Yahweh with injustice; that a man should be more just than God is unreasonable. Eliphaz argues that in God's sight, no human being is righteous. All humans have sinned, and any suffering they must endure is a just punishment for their transgressions. Bildad adds his support to what Eliphaz says by insisting that God does not pervert justice; neither does he ever act unrighteously. Zophar goes even further in his accusations against Job: Job is not being punished as much as he deserves, for Yahweh is both a just *and* a merciful God, and mercy always means treating a person better than that person deserves.

To each of these speeches, Job makes an effective reply. He challenges his accusers to point out any evil deed that he has committed. If he has failed simply because he is mortal, it is not his fault, for he was created that way. His conduct has been as good as that of his accusers. After the first round of speeches, the cycle is repeated, with Job again making a reply after each friend speaks. In the third cycle of speeches, only Eliphaz and Bildad speak. In Job's final reply, he makes a masterful defense of his own position, at the conclusion of which we are told, "The words of Job are ended."

The speeches of Elihu represent a further attempt to find justification for Job's affliction. Elihu admits that the arguments of the three friends have been adequately refuted by Job, but he believes he can present other ones that will show how Job has been in the wrong. He suggests that Job's suffering may be a warning so that he won't sin, and then he repeats the same arguments that the three friends made.

The nature poems are presented as speeches by Yahweh that are addressed to Job. They picture in the most exquisite language the wonders and the grandeur of the created universe. However, as beautiful as the poems are, they do not deal with Job's problem. True, they contrast the power and wisdom of the deity with the inferior lot of human beings, but they still leave unanswered the question of why innocent people have to suffer in the manner that Job experiences.

In the epilogue, which is found in the last chapter of the book, Job acknowledges the justice of Yahweh and repents for all that he said in his own defense. After this admission, Yahweh recompenses Job by returning to him all the material wealth that was taken away from him and even doubling the amount of property Job originally possessed.

Commentary

The Book of Job does not present concrete solutions about why innocent people suffer. As far as the symposium is concerned, the author's purpose seems to be none other than to challenge the view presented by both prophets and historians to the effect that suffering is in itself evidence of wrongdoing. For centuries, it was accepted as true that because Yahweh is a just ruler of the universe, the distribution of rewards and punishments must be in strict accordance with what people actually deserve. The author of the symposium is convinced that this line of reasoning is not true. In order to make his position clear, he constructs the story of a righteous man named Job. As an introduction to his theme, the author makes use of a popular folktale in which a good man suffers in order to prove to Satan that he does not serve Yahweh for selfish reasons. That the author of the symposium did not accept this solution to the problem is shown very clearly in the arguments between Job and the three friends. Job's final speech in his own defense is probably where the book originally ended.

The skeptical character of the symposium, with its challenge to time-honored views, most likely would have kept the Book of Job out of the canon of Old Testament writings had some additions not been made to the original book. The speeches of Elihu appear to be added for the purpose of giving to the book an interpretation more in accord with the older views of the prophets. Quite possibly the same is true of the nature poems, which are presented as words spoken by Yahweh. Although neither the speeches of Elihu nor the nature poems gives any direct answer to the question of why innocent persons suffer, their presence in the book as a whole suggests that there may be a reason for such suffering that human beings are unable to grasp. The epilogue is, of course, a kind of anticlimax in that it tends to support the charges made by Satan in the prologue. However, it also presents an ending to the book quite in keeping with the older and more orthodox position concerning suffering.

ECCLESIASTES

Summary

The Book of Ecclesiastes is an essay on the topic "Is life worthwhile?" Ironically, the writer answers this question in the negative. He considers the various ends or goals for which people live and finds that each of these reasons brings only vanity and frustration: "Yet when I surveyed all that my hands had done and what I had toiled to achieve, everything was meaningless, a chasing after the wind; nothing was gained under the sun." Referring to himself as an elderly person of considerable means and as a man who personally has tested the ways by which people pursue a meaning-ful life, the writer finds that life, ultimately, is self-defeating. He has tried riches and found that they do not satisfy. He has sought fame and found that it, too, is an empty feeling. He has even pur-sued wisdom, but it, likewise, fails to satisfy the human spirit. The more he learns, the more dissatisfied he becomes with that which he has already attained.

Some people follow the course of justice, believing that they will be rewarded, but the author of Ecclesiastes is convinced that there are no rewards. His observations tell him that a righteous person fares no better than a wicked person; at times, the righteous person doesn't even fare as well. Regardless of how an individual lives, we will all be forgotten after we die, for death comes to the righteous and the wicked alike. The writer appears to be familiar with some people's belief that rewards and punishments will be meted out to individuals in a future life that is beyond the grave, but he takes no stock in this notion. He tells us that the death of a human is comparable to that of a beast, and he asks ironically, "Who knows if the spirit of man rises upward and if the spirit of the animal goes down into the earth?" He says emphatically, "All have the same breath; man has no advantage over the animal. Everything is meaningless." He does not believe in progress but is committed to a theory of cyclical history: "What has been will be again, what has been done will be done again; there is nothing new under the sun." True, each generation thinks it develops something new, but the achievements of former generations are forgotten, just as those of the present generation will not be remembered. Furthermore, the writer sees no point in trying to make the world better: "What is twisted cannot be straightened; what is lacking cannot be counted." People's desires cannot be satisfied, for the more people see, the more they want to see; the more things people acquire, the less satisfied they become with what they have obtained.

The Ecclesiastes writer is indeed a cynic, but he is a gentle cynic who has not become embittered toward the world, for he re-solves to make the best of what he can. Unlike the author of Job, who is emotionally troubled that innocent people suffer, the Ecclesiastes writer accepts his situation as it is and refuses to be-come upset about it. Throughout the book, again and again he says, "A man can do nothing better than to eat and drink and find satisfaction in his work." Although he accepts a kind of fatalism according to which there is a definite time and place for everything, his book is filled with advice about how a person should live in order to get the greatest enjoyment out of life. Above all else, he counsels moderation: "Do not be overrighteous, neither be overwise—why destroy yourself?" A person should find a happy medium. One of the tragedies of life, the author tells us, is for a person to spend so much time and energy preparing for old age that when it arrives, the person is unable to enjoy it. We should enjoy life while we are young, for old age is characterized by weakness and infirmities that are but a prelude to the time when "the dust returns to the ground it came from, and the spirit returns to God who gave it."

Commentary

The Book of Ecclesiastes is unique in many respects. One wonders how it happened that a book so skeptical in tone and so unorthodox in its contents would ever have been placed in the canon of sacred writings. Presumably, several factors secured its inclusion among the books of the Old Testament. Ecclesiastes strongly appeals to many individuals because of the honesty with which the author expresses his own convictions. He knows that what he says is not in accord with generally accepted ideas, but he has the courage to say what he believes to be true. Because the name of King Solomon had long been associated with the work of the sages, it became attached to this particular piece of writing and gave an added prestige to it. But even with these two factors in support of the book's inclusion in the Old Testament, Ecclesiastes probably would have been excluded from the canon of Scriptures had it not been for an addition that appears to have been made to the last chapter. Here, we find the words "Fear God and keep his commandments, for this is the whole duty of man. For God will bring every deed into judgment, including every hidden thing, whether it is good or evil."

PROVERBS

Summary

The Book of Proverbs is exactly what the name implies, a collection of short sayings gathered from different places and produced over long periods of time. In general, these sayings represent wisdom derived from practical experience. Although they contain no profound contributions to theological ideas, they constitute wholesome advice about the way a person should live in order to attain a happy and satisfactory life. Late tradition attributed the entire Book of Proverbs to King Solomon, but we may be sure that this is historically incorrect. Many of the proverbs, especially those that extol the virtues of monogamy, would have been most inappropriate coming from King Solomon, who is reported to have had many wives. Solomon may have been the author of some of the proverbs included in the book, but most of them originated from other sources. Within the book itself, there are different collections of proverbs, some of which are attributed to men who were not Hebrews, which gives added emphasis to the universal character of this work of the sages. Overall, the wisdom contained in the Book of Proverbs can be said to have been drawn from a wide range of experiences, including those of both Jews and non-Jews.

In its present form, the book is made up of different collections of proverbs. The first collection, found in Chapters 1-9, consists of a series of instructions given by a father to his son. The purpose of the instruction is that of guiding youth in doing what is "right and just and fair; for giving prudence to the simple, knowledge and discretion to the young." The proverbs in the second group, found in Chapters 10-22 and titled "Proverbs of Solomon," are usually written in couplet form and are quite different from the ones included in the first section. Because this collection probably constituted the original core of the book, the first nine chapters serve as an introduction to the entire collection and the remaining sections as appendices. The short sections found in Chapters 22-24 bear the titles "Sayings of the Wise" and "Further Sayings of the Wise." Chapters 25-29 begin, "These are more proverbs of Solomon, copied by the men of Hezekiah king of Judah." The last two chapters of the book contain two groups of sayings called "Sayings of Agur" and "Sayings of King Lemuel." Because both Agur and Lemuel have Arabic rather than Jewish names, the inclusion of their proverbs in the final collection indicates a recognition on the part of the editors that genuine wisdom can be obtained through non-Hebraic sources. The Book of Proverbs closes with a significant poem written in praise of a worthy wife.

Throughout the entire Book of Proverbs, wisdom receives the highest praise. The following statements are typical: "Get wisdom, get understanding; . . . Wisdom is supreme; therefore get wisdom. Though it cost all you have, get understanding."

In one sense, the wisdom to which reference is made is a human achievement, but wisdom is also of divine origin. It has its source in the deity even though it must be received and understood by human minds. The Book of Proverbs assumes that divine revelation is communicated to individuals through careful and correct thinking, as well as through prophetic inspiration. This conception leads to the view that the wise man lives in harmony with the divine will; the fool brings disaster upon himself. This concept of wisdom is so closely related to that of the deity that in some instances it is personified and said to be the divine agent involved in the creation of the world. However, this emphasis on wisdom is not intended to encourage original thinking; it is the wisdom received by the men of old that should be passed on from one generation to another.

The practical character of the Book of Proverbs can be seen in the instruction concerning the type of conduct that should be observed in the affairs of daily living. A wise man is described as one who looks to the future but makes plans for the present. He does not squander his time or his money on momentary pleasures; he is a hard worker who does not try to gain his livelihood by infringing on the rights of other people; he is diligent in his business and courteous to friends and neighbors, and he governs well the affairs of his own household; he is generous in his giving, but he does not lavish gifts on those who fail to put forth efforts to supply their own needs; finally, he is temperate in his habits, respectful of the rights of others, and obedient to the laws of the land.

Commentary

The Book of Proverbs has sometimes been regarded as a text-book in the field of ethics. Although it avoids any theoretical discussion concerning the basis for determining what is right or wrong, it advocates a very high standard of personal conduct. The man of wisdom will abstain from idle gossip; he will not seek the company of idle men, nor will he testify falsely before the judges of the land. He will avoid loose women as he would the plague; he will not waste his time in idleness, but he will use his leisure hours to reflect on the meaning of life and the paths of conduct that he should follow. The compiler of Proverbs is well aware of life's hardships, but unlike the writers of Job and Ecclesiastes, he believes that happiness and material prosperity are distributed according to merit. The lazy man or the fool comes to want, and the distress and suffering that he experiences are exactly what he deserves. On the other hand, Yahweh rewards the wise and the prudent with the good things in life.

The proverbs express the conviction that loyalty to Yahweh is extremely important. In this respect, they fully agree with the teachings of the Hebrew prophets. They differ, however, in that they define this loyalty in terms of personal conduct rather than national policy. Although the Book of Proverbs places a great deal of emphasis on selfish motives as means of promoting good conduct, such motives, although not the highest, are better than no motives at all.

MISCELLANEOUS WRITINGS

In addition to the writings of the prophets and the sages, several other books are included in the canon of the Old Testament. These books can scarcely be classified according to any one basic characteristic; they represent different styles of writing and deal with a variety of subjects. Regarded as inspired writings but not on as high a level as the prophets, some of the books are of relatively late origin; not until after the beginning of the Christian era was agreement reached concerning their inclusion among the sacred writings. The books included in this group are Jonah, Ruth, Esther, and Daniel, a collection of psalms, Lamentations, and a love poem called Song of Songs.

JONAH, RUTH, AND ESTHER

Summary

Jonah. Although often classified with the prophets, the Book of Jonah is not a prophetic book. The story, about a prophet named Jonah, was written to criticize and rebuke the narrow spirit of nationalism that Jonah observed among so many of the Jewish people. To accomplish this purpose, he constructed a story that would illustrate the spirit he wished to counteract. In the story, Jonah acts in a manner that is similar to the way the Jewish people behaved in their attitude toward foreign nations. Anyone reading the story cannot help but see how foolish Jonah's actions are. The author hoped that the Jewish nationalists would see themselves in the role that Jonah played.

Jonah is told to go to Nineveh, the Assyrian capital, and deliver a message that Yahweh entrusts to him. Refusing to go to Nineveh, Jonah instead flees to Joppa, where he boards a boat that is bound for Tarshish. The ship on which he is riding encounters a storm, and the sailors in charge, in order to save themselves, throw Jonah overboard. Jonah is swallowed by a whale. However, he not only lives inside the whale but is carried to shore and thrown out onto the land.

When the call to go to Nineveh comes to Jonah a second time, he very reluctantly obeys. The only message that he proclaims is one of destruction that will be visited on the Ninevites because of their sins. When the people of Nineveh hear what Jonah has to say, they repent of their sins, expressing their remorse by sitting in sackcloth and ashes. Their repentance makes the threatened punishment unnecessary, which greatly disappoints Jonah, for it means that he has not judged them correctly. He starts to feel sorry for himself and complains to Yahweh of his bitter lot. At this point, Yahweh rebukes him in no uncertain terms, explaining that the fate of one hundred and twenty thousand people is a matter of more importance than the comfort and vanity of a single individual.

Ruth. Like the Book of Jonah, the Book of Ruth, a master-piece of storytelling, has a moral lesson, but this lesson may not be the chief reason why the book was written. It is a story about a Hebrew woman named Naomi who lives during the period of the judges, prior to the establishment of the monarchy. After the death of her husband, Naomi accompanies her two sons to a land occupied by the Moabites. Here the two sons marry Moabite women. Later, after both of her sons have died, Naomi decides to return to the land of the Hebrews so that she might dwell among her own people. She urges her two daughters-in-law to stay with the Moabites. One of the daughters-in-law, Orpah, yields to Naomi's request and bids farewell to her mother-in-law. The other one, Ruth, refuses to let her mother-in-law return home alone. Her affection and loyalty are expressed in the words "Where you go I will go, and where you stay I will stay. Your people will be my people and your God my God."

As Naomi and Ruth journey back to the land of the Hebrews, they come near Bethlehem at the time of a grain harvest. Naomi's kinsman, a wealthy Hebrew named Boaz, owns a large field of grain. Ruth asks that she be allowed to work with the gleaners, who gather the grain that the reapers have missed. Boaz grants Ruth's request, giving instructions to his servants to see to it that plenty of grain is left for Ruth and her mother-in-law. Because Naomi is a relative of Boaz, she and Ruth are treated generously. In time, Ruth becomes Boaz' wife; their son Obed will be the grandfather of King David.

Esther. The story of Esther is unique in several respects. It does not set forth any important moral or religious ideals. No mention is made of Yahweh, nor is anything said about rewards for righteous living or punishment for evil deeds. In the story, a Jewish maiden named Esther is made queen in the court of the Persian king Xerxes; she is instrumental in defeating a plot intended to bring about the complete slaughter of the Jewish people. In the end, the people who plotted against the Jews suffer defeat, while at the same time the Jews achieve a remarkable victory over their enemies. In many respects, the story resembles the typical historical novel, for while there may be some basis in history for the events that are related, the details of the account cannot be regarded as historical fact. The author has constructed the kind of story suited to the purpose he had in mind.

The setting of Esther's story is in the court of a Persian king. The narrative opens with an account of a royal feast that lasts for seven days. On the last day of the feast, the king asks his queen, Vashti, to display her royal beauty before the guests. She refuses, and the king becomes so angry that he issues a decree that a new queen shall reign in her place. To this end, he orders that beautiful maidens shall be brought to his court from various parts of his realm; from these women, one shall be selected as the new queen. A Jew named Mordecai has a beautiful niece named Esther, whom he presents before the king, taking special care not to reveal that she is a Jew. After Esther is made queen, her uncle, who is now employed as one of the king's gatekeepers, learns of a plot made against the king's life. He reports it to Esther, who makes it known to the king, and the plotters are put to death.

Meanwhile, a man named Haman has been promoted to a very high place in the government, and orders have been given that whenever he passes by, people must bow to him. Mordecai, because of his Jewish scruples, refuses to do so, which makes Haman angry and determined to destroy him. Haman persuades the king to pass a decree that on a certain day all Jews are to be slaughtered. Realizing the terrible plight in which his people have been placed by this decree, Mordecai pleads with Esther to go before the king and intercede on the Jews' behalf. Although such a mission is dangerous for Esther to undertake because she is a Jew, she willingly risks her life in order to carry it out. Haman is delighted that the king has issued this decree, and in anticipation of the slaughter being carried out, he constructs a gallows, on which Mordecai is to be hanged.

One night, the king, unable to sleep, gives orders to his servants to read to him from the official records. They read the account of the plot against the king's life that was revealed by Mordecai, thus saving the life of the king. When the king realizes that nothing has been done to reward the man who saved him, he begins to wonder what would constitute an appropriate reward for one who has rendered such a great service. Seeing Haman outside, the king calls him into his chambers and asks what should be done for one whom the king "delights to honor." Haman, supposing that he is the one to be honored, suggests many elaborate things. When Haman has finished, the king orders that all these shall be done to honor Mordecai. Ultimately, Haman is hanged on the very gallows that he prepared for Mordecai, and on the day originally appointed for the slaughter of the Jews, the decree is reversed and the Jews are permitted and encouraged to slaughter their enemies.

Commentary

Although the prophetic period in Israel's history came to a close and it was no longer possible to make a direct declaration concerning the word of Yahweh, the ideals that were proclaimed by the earlier prophets still persisted. However, finding new literary forms for their expression was necessary. These new forms included the short story, in which an author's message could be concretely illustrated. Many advantages were gained from this type of writing. Because it was not necessary to report accurate historical events in every detail of the story, the author was free to construct the characters and events in a way that would illustrate precisely the lesson he wanted to teach. For example, in the Book of Jonah, the author selected a person who reportedly lived during the times of the prophet Amos. The story concerning this man was designed to show the attitude that the Jewish people had taken toward foreign nations. Jonah behaves so badly in the story that the average reader becomes quite disgusted with him. By making it obvious that Jonah's behavior toward the Ninevites typifies the Jewish nation as a whole, the writer hoped that his story would counteract the narrow nationalism of the Israelite people.

Jonah's call to go to the people of Nineveh was analogous to what the author believed Yahweh wanted the people of Israel to do. Like Deutero-Isaiah, he held that it was Israel's function to proclaim religion throughout the world. But Israel tried to run away from its responsibility. In the end, it was swallowed by Babylon, but just as Jonah survives his experience in the whale, so the Israelites returned to their own land. Still, Israel felt reluctant to carry out its mission to the other nations. When it did come into contact with foreign nations, its only message was a warning of coming destruction. The author of the Jonah story did not believe that the foreign nations were inferior to the Hebrews or that

Yahweh was prejudiced against them. If they were given the opportunity to learn of Yahweh's ways, they would respond as well as the Hebrews had done. It was absurd to think that Hebrew pride was more important than the welfare of vast numbers of people.

The Book of Ruth is another short story written in the interests of internationalism. The main purpose of the story is to protest the enforcement of the law forbidding intermarriages between Hebrews and foreigners. This law was being used under the leadership of Ezra and Nehemiah to help restore loyalty on the part of those who had grown careless with reference to the observance of Hebrew rites and ceremonies. Ezra and Nehemiah went so far as to demand that a person who had married a foreigner must either get a divorce or leave the community. In many instances, such actions involved real hardships on account of the breaking up of family relationships. The story of Ruth attempted to show that in ancient times, Yahweh did not disapprove of foreign marriages. Although the setting of the story is placed during the period of the judges, the story itself is of post-exilic origin, clearly indicated by the fact that one of the customs referred to was observed in ancient times. Throughout the story, no indication is given of any divine displeasure over foreign marriages. The two Moabite women, Ruth and Orpah, are described as persons of excellent character. They are loyal and devoted to their husbands and in every respect are the equal of wives chosen from among the Hebrews. The marriage of Ruth and Boaz is blessed with children, one of whom will be the grandfather of King David. Because it was from the line of David that the Messiah was to be born, that Yahweh would forbid foreign marriages is inconceivable.

The story of Esther, unlike the stories of Jonah and Ruth, illustrates the spirit of Jewish nationalism. Because it is a patriotic rather than a religious story, some people question its inclusion with the other books in the Old Testament. Its admission to the canon of the sacred Scriptures is due primarily to the fact that it contains an account of the origin of the Feast of Purim, which celebrates Esther's saving the Persian Jews. The story is set during the days of the Persian king Xerxes, and the author evidently drew upon his imagination for the details of the story since no evidence exists among Persian records of a Jewish maiden becoming a queen in a Persian court. However, historical accuracy was not the purpose of the story, which illustrates the antagonism between foreign nations and the Jews. This antagonism is exemplified in the stories concerning Mordecai and Haman, and especially in the plot that Haman forms in order to have the Jews massacred. Esther's decision to risk her own life to save her people is the noblest point of the story.

DANIEL

Summary

The Book of Daniel is the chief example of apocalyptic writing in the Old Testament, a form of writing that came into use largely in response to the disappointments that were experienced by the Hebrews. For centuries, they had looked forward to a reign of justice and righteousness on earth. Instead of these hopes being realized, the lot of the Hebrew people was becoming more difficult with each generation, while at the same time the forces of evil were constantly becoming stronger. These circumstances led to a conviction that only a supernatural intervention by Yahweh could bring about the desired goal. Prior to this time, the forces of evil would continue to grow stronger, and persecutions of the righteous would become even more severe. At the appointed time, a great catastrophic event would engulf the world. The wicked would be destroyed, and the messianic kingdom would be established for all time to come. The purpose of the apocalyptic literature was to offer encouragement to the righteous to remain true and faithful to the principles of their religion. Apocalyptic literature gave them the assurance that the time was not far distant when their deliverance would be at hand.

One of the chief characteristics of apocalyptic writing is an account of a dream or vision given to someone who lived a long time before the date of the actual writing. In such a vision, a series of predictions is made concerning events that will occur prior to the establishment of the messianic kingdom. These predictions will come to pass exactly as outlined in the vision, with the exception of the last ones before the coming of the catastrophic event. The recital of these apocalyptic fulfillments inspired confidence that the remaining ones would take place in the near future. Apparently, the apocalyptic writers assumed that Yahweh knew the future as well as the past and could reveal these secrets to individuals who were chosen to receive them. These predictions concerned specific events and definite time periods, thus indicating the exact time when particular events would occur. The occasion for writing an apocalypse was always a period of crisis during which righteous people were persecuted and threatened with death at the hands of their enemies.

The persecution of the Jews under Antiochus Epiphanes led to the writing of the Book of Daniel. During this period of crisis, the Jews were threatened with death if they refused to worship images, continued to offer prayers to Yahweh, observed their dietary laws, and worshiped on the Sabbath day. Many Jews yielded to the demands of Antiochus and his Syrian officers in order to save their lives, but others remained faithful to their customs and beliefs despite certain punishment. To encourage these persons whose faith was being put to so severe a test, the Book of Daniel was written.

The book consists of two parts, one of which is a series of stories about Hebrews who lived at the time of the Babylonian captivity and who experienced hardships similar to those faced by the Jews under Antiochus. The other part, which is more directly apocalyptic in form, consists of a series of visions that predict future events.

Among the stories related in the first part of the book is one concerning four young Hebrews who refuse to follow the king's dietary laws even though they are ordered to do so and are threatened with death if they disobey. The young men remain faithful to the principles of their religion, and as a reward for their loyalty, they are not only spared any punishment for their disobedience but are given high honors and declared to be superior.

In another story, three young Hebrews, commanded by the king of Babylon to bow down and worship a statue erected in his honor, refuse to obey this command and, as a result of their decision, are thrown into a fiery furnace heated to seven times its normal temperature. But Yahweh works a miracle on their behalf, and they emerge from the furnace unharmed and without even the smell of smoke on their clothing. In still another story, a plot is formed to destroy Daniel, who, though a Hebrew, holds an important position in the government of King Darius. The king is urged to sign a decree making it a capital offense for anyone, during a certain period of time, to offer prayers to any god except those approved by the king. When Daniel ignores this decree and continues to pray to Yahweh with his windows open toward Jerusalem, he is thrown into a den of lions. Again Yahweh rescues his faithful servant and delivers him from the lions.

In the apocalyptic portions of the book, certain dreams and visions are interpreted as predictions concerning the rise and fall of nations from the time of the Babylonian captivity to the establishment of the messianic kingdom. In one chapter, we are told about King Nebuchadnezzar's dream in which he sees a great image with a head of gold, breast and arms of silver, a belly of brass, legs of iron, and feet of iron mixed with clay. In another vision, Daniel sees four beasts emerging out of the sea. One of these beasts is a lion with eagle's wings; another is a bear with three ribs in its mouth; the third beast is a leopard with four heads and four wings; and the fourth beast is described as great and terrible: It has seven heads and ten horns, among which is another horn with humanlike eyes and a mouth that speaks terrible things. Other visions include one of a ram and a he-goat. Prophetic periods of 2300 days, 70 weeks, 1235 days, and other specific periods of time are described and interpreted. Toward the end of the book, we find one of the first definite references in the Old Testament to a resurrection of the dead.

Commentary

The Book of Daniel has sometimes been classified with the prophetic books of the Old Testament, a mistake owing largely to a failure to distinguish between the predominant characteristics of prophetic and apocalyptic writings. Daniel belongs to the latter group, a type of writing that in many respects sharply contrasts prophetic literature. For example, predictions of coming events in the apocalyptic writings are definite and specific, thus indicating the precise time when certain events will occur; predictions made in the prophetic writings are of a general nature and are always conditioned by the decisions of people with reference to moral issues. In other words, the prophets' statements concerning the future are always consistent with the free choice of human beings, which is not true of the apocalypses. So far as the apocalypses are concerned, what was predicted would necessarily come to pass; nothing that anyone could do would alter the situation. The impression that predictions made in the distant past were fulfilled accurately is due to the fact that the apocalypses were written after these events had already taken place, but their predictions are presented as though they were made prior to their predicted events.

Evidence in the Book of Daniel supports the idea that the book was written during the period of the Maccabean wars, but many of the book's predictions are presented as though they were revealed to one of the Hebrews involved in the Babylonian captivity. Nebuchadnezzar's dream is interpreted to mean a prediction concerning the rise and fall of four great world empires: the kingdom of Babylon; the kingdoms of the Medes and Persians; the kingdom of Greece; and the monstrous power under which the Jews suffered persecution at the hands of Antiochus. The stone that is cut out of the mountain and that strikes the image on its feet, grinding the stone to pieces, symbolizes the destruction of this evil power and the establishment of the messianic kingdom. The same set of predictions is made again in Daniel's vision of the four beasts emerging out of the sea. In this vision, a more specific characterization is given of Antiochus and the power that he represents. He is designated by the little horn among the ten horns, rooting up three of them in order to make room for itself. This horn, with eyes like a human's and a mouth, speaks words of blasphemy, persecutes the saints, and endeavors to change laws. A further account of this same evil power is given in the vision of the ram and the he-goat. The specific time periods cited in the book all have reference to the time when this evil power will be destroyed through supernatural intervention and when the new kingdom of righteousness will be created. The reference to a resurrection of the dead indicates that the idea of resurrection was beginning to find acceptance among the Hebrews.

PSALMS

Summary

The Book of Psalms, which is generally believed to be the most widely read and the most highly treasured of all the books in the Old Testament, is a collection of poems, hymns, and prayers that express the religious feelings of Jews throughout the various periods of their national history. The intrinsic beauty of the poems and the sentiments that they convey have contributed toward their appreciation. Especially adapted for use in worship services, the psalms have been used in Christian churches, as well as in Jewish temples and synagogues. The Book of Psalms has a special significance for understanding the religious life of ancient Israel. The prophets and the sages provide some insight concerning what the Hebrews thought, but the psalms give the clearest indication of what the Hebrews felt. Here, we find a revelation of the hopes, the joys, the sorrows, the loyalties, the doubts, and the aspirations of the human heart.

The psalms are difficult to classify because of the wide variety of experiences and sentiments reflected in them. A further difficulty is trying to reconstruct the background or historical situation from which the different ones were produced. In the case of the prophets, this reconstruction can usually be done with a fair degree of accuracy, but not so of the psalms. They represent the inner life of individuals who lived under differing circumstances and who reacted in various ways to the critical situations that developed throughout the entire course of Israel's history. These individuals did not think alike, nor did they feel the same way about the rites and ceremonies that they observed. It would be helpful if we could know the exact circumstances that are reflected in the different psalms, but the best we can do in this respect is to find the particular occasions for which the individual psalms seem to be most appropriate. As a whole, the Book of Psalms may be regarded as a kind of epitome of the entire range of the Hebrews' religious life. It has been said that if all the rest of the Old Testament were lost, the essential faith of the Israelite people could be recovered from this single book.

The authorship of most of the psalms is anonymous, although tradition has long attributed the entire collection to King David. It is possible, but not probable, that David may have written some of them. Recent excavations and discoveries indicate quite clearly that parallels to certain of the psalms were in existence as early as the period of the monarchy, and the fact that David has been referred to as the "sweet singer of Israel" lends some support to the tradition. However, most of the psalms reflect ideas and conditions that came into existence long after the time of King David. For example, one psalm in particular discusses an event that occurred during the life of Isaiah. Others describe experiences pertaining to the Babylonian captivity, and still others appear to have originated during the period of the Maccabean wars. The earliest collection of psalms was probably titled "Psalms of David," and to this group several others were added at various times, including what was known as the "Korah Psalter," the "Asaph Psalter," the "Hallelujah Psalter," the "Pilgrim Psalter," and others. In its present form, the book is divided into five sections: Psalms 1-41; Psalms 42-72; Psalms 73-89; Psalms 90-106; and Psalms 107-150.

The psalms were used in connection with worship services conducted in the Temple at Jerusalem. Some of them were sung by the pilgrims on their journeys to the Central Sanctuary, for all of the faithful were required to attend services at this place at least once a year if it was at all possible for them to do so. Some of the hymns would be sung when the pilgrims first came in sight of the city of Jerusalem and others as they stood before the entrance to the Temple. Some of the hymns were antiphonal numbers, and their use constituted an essential part of the worship service. Hymns and prayers of adoration were used on appropriate occasions, such as the beginning of the new year, particular feast days, the enthronement of Yahweh, and celebrations of important events in Hebrew history. There were songs of praise to Yahweh for the mighty works that he had performed, and there were songs of thanksgiving for the way in which the Hebrews had been delivered from the hands of their enemies. Other songs were written in praise of the Law.

Many different themes are treated in the Book of Psalms. For example, one psalm praises Yahweh for coming to the defense of his people when the Assyrian armies invaded Judah. The sudden withdrawal of the army, leaving the city of Jerusalem standing, was indeed an occasion for great rejoicing. Yahweh's love for the poor and the oppressed is the theme of Psalm 146. Sorrow and discouragement because of the fate that befell the nation when the people were taken into captivity by a foreign power are expressed in the prayers that are recorded in Psalms 42 and 43. The same attitude can be found in Psalm 22, in which the author cries out from the depths of his soul, "My God, my God, why have you forsaken me?" The Babylonian captivity is the setting for Psalm 137, which reports, "By the rivers of Babylon we sat and wept when we remembered Zion." Psalm 119, the longest one in the entire book, is an alphabetical poem written in praise of the Law.

The psalms' teachings are difficult to summarize because their main purpose is not instruction but expressions of the heart made in the spirit of worship. Nevertheless, certain ideas are set forth in the psalms that are essential to the purposes for which they were written, including the reality and significance of Yahweh in relation to the experiences of individuals and the nation as a whole. True, the conception of Yahweh is not always the same in the different psalms, but this difference is due to the fact that each author must find for himself the conception that seems most adequate to him. Sometimes Yahweh is portrayed as a god of loving kindness and mercy, but at other times he is a god of wrath who brings destruction on those who disobey his commands. Always Yahweh is presented as an everlasting God, one who is omnipotent and omniscient, and whose power and goodness endure throughout all generations.

Commentary

The Book of Psalms in the canon of the sacred Scriptures gives to the modern reader an insight into the religious life of the Hebrews that cannot be obtained from any of the other Old Testament writings. Although Jeremiah and some of the other prophets emphasized the inwardness of religion, they did so primarily to counteract the formalism that had become conspicuous in the Temple services and other practices that they observed. In Psalms, the longings, the hopes, the sorrows, and the disappointments of individual worshipers find their clearest expression. Here, we find what the various authors felt even in those situations that they were not able to understand. Although some of the psalms are probably as old as the time of King David, not until a relatively late period was the entire collection gathered and organized in the form in which it has been preserved.

Like other portions of Old Testament literature, the original psalms were edited and supplemented from time to time. Frequently we find evidence of a tendency to add something to a psalm as it first appeared in order to give to it an interpretation that would be more in accord with generally accepted ideas. For example, in Psalm 51, the first seventeen verses are written in the spirit of the great prophets, who insisted that the true worship of Yahweh consists not in sacrifices made on an altar nor in the observance of ritualistic requirements but in the inner attitudes of the human heart. The next two verses of the psalm present a very different idea, for an editor who was evidently under the influence of the post-exilic emphasis on the importance of ritual and ceremony added a statement that was intended to show that the attitude of the human heart was but a prelude to the sacrificing of bulls on the altar. It is not uncommon, even at the present time, to find hymn books that continue to use ancient conceptions, even though these have long been replaced with ideas that are more in harmony with the spirit of the times.

LAMENTATIONS AND SONG OF SONGS

Summary

Lamentations. The fall of Jerusalem and the fate of the captives who were led into exile form the subject matter of the Book of Lamentations. Five poems are included in the book, each of which may have been written by as many different individuals. All of the poems deal with the destruction of the city and the events closely related to that event, a terrifying experience that severely tested the faith of those who put their trust in Yahweh. The poems portray some of these horrors. Jerusalem was placed under siege, and famine drove the people to despair. When King Zedekiah and a band of his soldiers tried to escape during the night, they were overtaken by the Babylonians and brought before Nebuchadnezzar for punishment. Zedekiah was forced to witness the execution of his own sons. He was then blinded and taken to a Babylonian dungeon to spend the rest of his life. The suffering caused by the famine and the bitter anxiety brought on by the terrible fate of Judah's last king were clearly in the mind of the poet who wrote one of the poems included in Lamentations. His poem closes with a prediction that Edom, who in the hour of Judah's agony gave its support to the Babylonians, would meet its doom in the very near future.

In another poem, an attempt is made to understand the reason for this terrible tragedy that has befallen the Hebrew people. The author bemoans the ruin that Yahweh wrought in his anger, and then he addresses the people of Zion, blaming the prophets for the miserable plight that evoked only scorn from the enemies of Israel and calling upon the people to weep and cry to Yahweh for mercy. A third poem, which is an acrostic in structure and style, meaning that certain letters, taken together, form a name or saying, is placed in the center of the book, and the others are arranged with reference to it. The last poem of the book contains a prayer in which someone who has survived the catastrophe implores Yahweh for mercy and help.

Song of Songs. Not a religious book but rather a collection of secular love poems and wedding songs, Song of Songs portrays the scenes of a typical Oriental wedding feast. The bridegroom is a king, the bride is a queen, and the feast lasts for a period of seven days. The songs celebrate the physical beauty of the royal pair, especially the bride. Nothing in any of these songs concerns the sanctity of marriage or any of the moral and spiritual aspects associated with it. They are about human love, with all of its passion and deep emotion. One of the songs discusses the springtime of love and is full of erotic suggestions that would have offended Occidental readers. It should be remembered, however, that physical love was not regarded as base or obscene to the Oriental mind but rather as an important factor in human life and a proper theme to be celebrated in poetry. It is extremely unlikely that these poems would ever have been included in the Old Testament had it not been for the allegorical interpretation that was placed on them.

Commentary

The authorship of the Book of Lamentations is unknown. The earliest collection of the poems included in the book was called "Lamentations" without assigning any name to them. Later, they were called "The Lamentations of Jeremiah," which is the title given to them in various editions of the Old Testament. The Greek translation states in the preface to the book, "And it came to pass, after Israel was led into captivity and Jerusalem laid waste, that Jeremiah sat weeping, and lamented with this lamentation over Jerusalem." Nothing in the Book of Jeremiah indicates that Jeremiah is the author of these poems, and we may be quite certain that they were produced by other persons. Because later generations regarded Jeremiah as an inspired author, attributing these poems to him gave to them an added prestige, which is probably the reason why it was done.

Song of Songs was attributed to King Solomon probably because his name is mentioned several times in the songs, or poems. Because the songs describe the wedding feast of a king and his bride, it was assumed that the chief participants in the wedding were King Solomon and a Shulamite maiden. Interpreted literally, these songs would scarcely have been included in the Old Testament. But it was possible to interpret them allegorically and find their meaning in the relationship between Yahweh and his people. As the Hebrew people understood the songs, Yahweh was the bridegroom and Israel was the bride. In later generations, Christians interpreted the same songs as representing the union between Jesus Christ and his church. We have no reason for thinking that King Solomon or any single poet is the author of these songs. They are a group of folk songs, some of which may have been in existence for a long time before they were edited and arranged in their present form, which was probably sometime during the third century B.C.

THE APOCRYPHA AND THE PSEUDEPIGRAPHA

When the author of Ecclesiastes wrote, "Of making many books there is no end, and much study is a weariness of the flesh," he apparently thought that everything worth knowing had already been written; nothing could be gained by writing more books. But writing did not cease with the completion of the Ecclesiastes manuscript. So far as the Hebrew people were concerned, each succeeding generation continued to write books, many of which were regarded as worthy of inclusion along with the other writings that ultimately became part of the Old Testament. Eventually, which writings to accept as the authoritative word of Yahweh and which ones to exclude from the list of inspired or sacred Scriptures became necessary. The decision was not reached all at once. Some of the writings were accepted without question, others were regarded as somewhat doubtful, and still others were not accepted at all.

Several centuries were required before there was any general agreement among the Jewish rabbis concerning all of the books that are now included in the Old Testament. Apparently, the majority of the Jewish people accepted the idea of degrees of inspiration. For example, the so-called books of Moses, known as the Torah or the Book of the Law, were regarded as the most highly inspired and therefore the most authoritative of all the writings. Next to the Law came the group of prophetic books, which included both the historical writings and the ones named for the prophets. These texts were considered to be inspired and authoritative but on a somewhat lower level than the Book of the Law. A third group, known as the Hagiographa, or miscellaneous writings, while still inspired and authoritative, was believed to be on a level that was somewhat lower than that of the prophets. In addition to these books, two more groups of writings were recognized as valuable and appropriate for use in religious service but not as authoritative sources for the establishment of doctrine: the Apocrypha and the Pseudepigrapha, both of which are relevant to the study of the Old Testament.

THE APOCRYPHA

The Apocrypha is the name given to a group of writings found in some versions of the Old Testament but not in others. These texts are usually included in Catholic bibles but not in Protestant ones. They were, however, included in Protestant versions until the second quarter of the nineteenth century. When, in the year

382 A.D., Jerome was commissioned by the pope to make a new translation of the Scriptures, he went to Palestine rather than to Alexandria, Egypt, to obtain original copies. By doing so, he discovered fourteen books included in the Alexandrian, or Greek, version of the Old Testament that were missing in the Palestinian version. The question then arose concerning the status of these newly discovered books. The name Apocrypha, which means "hidden things," was given to these books because of the belief that the men who wrote them were not addressing their contemporaries but were writing for the benefit of future generations; the meaning of these books would be hidden until their interpretation would be disclosed at some future date by persons qualified to do so.

The books in the Apocrypha include histories, short stories, wisdom literature, and additions to canonical books. Among the historical writings are 1 and 2 Maccabees and 1 and 2 Esdras. The two books of Maccabees contain accounts of the Maccabean wars written from different points of view. 1 Maccabees tells the story from what came to be known as the position of the Sadducees, and 2 Maccabees reflects the position of the Pharisee sect. The two books of Esdras are apocalyptic in character, but they portray certain aspects of Jewish history presented as fulfillments of predictions made in the distant past. The wisdom literature includes Ecclesiasticus, or what has sometimes been called "The Wisdom of Jesus ben Sirach." Ecclesiasticus, which resembles the Book of Proverbs but covers many more topics, concludes with a famous discourse introduced by the words "Let us now praise famous men." The author includes himself in the list of Israel's most famous men. Another text, "The Wisdom of Solomon," appears to have been written as a reply to the argument given in the Book of Ecclesiastes. In it, the author affirms his belief in Yahweh, whose activities influence the course of Hebrew history. Interestingly, the author believes in a life after death.

Tobit and Judith are short stories included in the Apocrypha. Tobit, called Tobias in some versions, discusses Jews who have been faithful to the ritualistic requirements of their religion and have been abundantly rewarded for their good works. Judith, which in many ways is similar to the Book of Esther, tells of a Jewish woman living in the city of Jerusalem at a time when the city is besieged by the Assyrians and her people are in a desperate situation. She is not only a faithful Jew but a courageous person who invades the camp of the enemy and succeeds in a plot that enables the Jews to achieve a remarkable victory.

Several additions to the Book of Daniel are included in the Apocrypha. One of these, "The Prayer of Azariah," is said to be a record of the prayer that was offered by a Hebrew who was thrown into a fiery furnace by King Nebuchadnezzar. Another addition, "The Song of the Three Children," claims to be the song of praise that was sung by Hebrews as an expression of gratitude for the marvelous way in which they were delivered from Nebuchadnezzar's furnace. "The History of Susanna" tells of a woman who has been accused unjustly of the sin of adultery. The wickedness of her accusers and the innocence of the woman are established by the prophet Daniel. The story "Bel and the Dragon" relates how Daniel was delivered from the hands of his enemies, who were trying to put him to death. An addition to the Book of Esther reports a dream given to Mordecai in which forthcoming events are revealed to him. The Book of Baruch is an addition to the Book of Jeremiah. In some versions, it contains a section called "An Epistle of Jeremiah." The "Prayer of Manasseh" supplements a story recorded in the Book of Chronicles, telling how Manasseh, who had done so many wicked things during his life, repented of his sins before he died.

THE PSEUDEPIGRAPHA

The Pseudepigrapha is a group of writings, each one of which is attributed to someone other than its real author. Many writings of this kind appeared during the centuries immediately preceding and immediately following the beginning of the Christian era. Most are apocalyptic in character. In several instances, they reflect the legalistic attitude that was especially strong among the majority of Jews during those periods when the Jews were subject to the domination of the Roman government. This type of literature was used during New Testament times; there are references to books in both the Apocrypha and the Pseudepigrapha in the books of the New Testament.

The most important of the apocalyptic writings is the Book of Enoch, a relatively late book but one attributed to Enoch, who received visions revealing all sorts of mysteries pertaining to both heaven and earth. One section of the book contains "The Apocalypse of Weeks," which tells of a vision in which the whole course of history, from creation to the setting up of the messianic kingdom, is revealed to Enoch. "The Testament of the Twelve Patriarchs," which purports to have come from the twelve sons of Jacob, contains a series of predictions concerning the future of each of the twelve tribes of Israel. "The Sibylline Oracles" is a collection of so-called revelations made to ancient prophetesses but which have been edited and rewritten in light of contemporary events.

"The Assumption of Moses" is another apocalypse, written as if it were an address delivered by Moses to his successor. In the vision that was given to Moses shortly before his death, the whole course of Hebrew history was revealed in advance. The final triumph of the people of Israel will be brought about through supernatural intervention. "The Secrets of Enoch" concerns a dream-vision in which Enoch is transported through a series of heavens to the presence of the deity. Here, many mysteries about the created universe are explained to him, including the length of time that will elapse before the setting up of the messianic kingdom. Other examples of apocalyptic writing are 2 and 3 Baruch and 4 Ezra, which discusses such questions as the origin of evil and the way in which evil will finally be banished from the universe.

Not all of the writings in the Pseudepigrapha are of an apocalyptic nature. "The Psalms of Solomon" is a collection of eighteen psalms that extol the Pharisaic conception of righteousness. The standard that is set forth is complete obedience to the perfect Law of God. The Fourth Book of Maccabees, concerning the field of ethics, is a discourse on the power of reason to control passions; illustrations are drawn from the experiences of such men as Jacob, Joseph, Moses, and David. "The Story of Ahikar" belongs to the folktales of the ancient Hebrews. The hero of the story is an official in the court of an Assyrian king. An evil plot against him is formed by men who wish to kill him. The plot fails, and Ahikar is able to take full revenge on his enemies. The Book of Jubilees praises the Law revealed to Moses. The Law is declared to be everlasting, and the importance of obedience to its demands is illustrated throughout the entire course of history. A somewhat different attitude toward the Law is presented in the Book of Zodak, which was written in support of a reform movement designed to counteract the formalism and irregularities of the priesthood. Among the sacred legends, one finds the Epistle of Aristeas, in which the circumstances that led to the making of the Septuagint version of the Hebrew writings are described. The Books of Adam and Eve record popular beliefs concerning the events that occurred immediately after Adam and Eve were driven out of the Garden of Eden. Finally, "The Martyrdom of Isaiah" describes the way in which the prophet Isaiah met his death at the hands of wicked King Manasseh.

THE NEW
TESTAMENT

INTRODUCTION TO THE NEW TESTAMENT

The New Testament is a collection of writings in which different people set forth their convictions concerning the meaning and significance of the earthly life of Jesus of Nazareth. No one of these writings appeared until some years after Jesus' physical death. He left no written records concerning himself, and any information about him must be gleaned from what other people have written. By the end of the first century of the Christian era or thereabouts, several biographies of Jesus had been written, four of which are now part of the New Testament. Before any of these biographies were written, Christian communities — what was later known as churches — had been established, and letters instructing the members about the Christian way of life and telling them how to deal with local problems were sent to them. Some of these letters were written by a man named Paul, who, although raised in the strict traditions of the Jewish religion, had converted to Christianity, and who spent the remainder of his life as a missionary, founding new churches and nurturing members in their newly acquired faith. After Paul's death, other leaders of the movement continued to write letters to churches; in this way, they hoped to strengthen the organization and prepare its followers for any emergencies.

As the number of Christians increased and their influence was felt in various parts of the then-known world, opposition to the movement arose from different quarters. Jews deeply resented the fact that many of their own people were forsaking Judaism and becoming Christians, but the most severe opposition came from the Roman government, which tried in various ways to suppress, if not to annihilate, the whole Christian movement on the grounds that it constituted a danger and a threat to the security of the empire.

When persecution of the Christians became extreme, messages were sent to them by church leaders. These messages, usually in the form of letters or public addresses, encouraged the sufferers and advised them concerning the ways in which they should respond to the demands that were being made upon them. Some of these messages are now part of the New Testament. Other letters, several of which have been preserved, were written to counteract false doctrines that arose within the churches. However, these writings were not intended by their respective authors to be regarded as sacred literature comparable to that of the prophets of the Old Testament. Eventually, Christians did come to think of these writings in this way, but the transition from a collection of writings originally designed to meet certain local problems to the status of sacred Scriptures either replacing or else being added to the Old Testament required a comparatively long period of time.

The twenty-seven writings in the New Testament of today were selected from a larger list of writings, and not until the fourth century of our era was any general agreement reached among the Christian churches as to the exact number and selection of writings that should be included. The Gospels and Paul's letters generally were accepted prior to that time, but other writings' inclusion was a matter of serious controversy.

In view of these facts, an adequate understanding of the books in the New Testament cannot be had without some knowledge of the historical background from which they were written, but just how this knowledge can be obtained presents something of a problem. Our chief source of information is the New Testament itself, but there are some references to Jesus and the Christian movement in Roman history and in Jewish literature pertaining to the period in which he lived. However, these non-Christian sources are very meager, and we have good reasons for believing that they are somewhat biased. Christian sources are no doubt biased too, but in the case of both Christian and non-Christian sources, we know the direction in which each of them is biased, and we can make proper allowances. Because only in the Christian sources do we have any detailed account of the life and teachings of Jesus and the general character of the early Christian movement, we need to center our attention on them.

The New Testament biographies of Jesus, usually referred to as the Gospels, contain the most extensive records of what Jesus did and of what he taught. But it is also in connection with these same biographies that readers of the New Testament encounter difficult problems. How are these records to be evaluated? To what extent do they reveal what *actually* happened, and to what extent do they merely indicate what the author *believed* to have happened? Answering these questions by asserting that these are all inspired writings and are therefore infallible in every respect will not do. Divine inspiration is always and necessarily a two-fold process involving both a giving and a receiving. The giving may well be regarded as the divine part, but the receiving or the understanding of whatever it is that has been revealed is the human part, and that which is human is never infallible. Anyone who is at all sympathetic with the meaning and message of the New Testament will not be hesitant about regarding it as a divinely inspired book, but the intellectually honest person will also recognize that a human element is involved in the receiving and the interpreting of that revelation. And the human element must be understood first, for it is the medium through which the divine element is communicated.

The human element present in the Gospels is necessarily conditioned by the circumstances under which the Gospels were written. Because these texts were not written until after the death of Jesus, they must be viewed from the perspective of the conditions that prevailed at the time of their writing. In this connection, it is important to remember that the Christian community was in existence for a considerable period of time and that it came into existence because a group of people believed that the man Jesus who had been crucified was the long-awaited Messiah. The Christian community was convinced that his life had met with divine approval and that his death was not the result of any wrongdoing on his part. He died for a righteous cause and in so doing achieved victory over the forces of evil, for he did not yield to any temptations in order to save himself. He was, in the Christians' judgment, the Messiah about whom the Old Testament prophets had spoken. By the time the Gospels were written, stories preserved orally by those who associated with Jesus were viewed in light of more recent events and interpreted in accordance with the beliefs that had become firmly established in the biographers' minds. Reconstructing the original stories as they existed prior to later interpretations of them has been one of the main tasks of what is known as "form criticism." Although the methods used for this purpose have their limitations, these methods are of value as a means toward understanding the New Testament.

The letters written by the apostle Paul constitute nearly one third of the New Testament. They were written long before any of the Gospels that we now have were in existence. Paul evidently knew something about the life of Jesus, although he never saw him in the flesh. Paul's information, so far as we can determine, must have been obtained from the oral traditions that were passed on to him by those who associated with Jesus. Paul reports very little concerning the teachings of Jesus, but his interpretation of the life, death, and resurrection of Jesus has had a profound influence on Christian history.

The remaining portions of the New Testament, although concerned primarily with specific problems and situations, nevertheless reflect the generally accepted beliefs concerning Jesus that were current among Christians at that time. Written accounts of what Jesus did during the course of his life were not considered necessary by the earliest Christians, who believed that Jesus would return to earth in the very near future and establish the messianic kingdom. Until that time, the memories of his disciples and friends would be sufficient to preserve his deeds and his teachings. Not until after many of those who associated with him had died was the need for written records recognized. And not until some time after the New Testament texts were written were the manuscripts assembled in their present form and used along with the Old Testament Scriptures in the worship services of Christian churches. Their status as inspired writings that were authoritative for the establishment of doctrines came about in response to a whole series of situations that developed within the Christian movement.

The study of the New Testament may be pursued several different ways, and although benefits may be derived from any one of these ways, no one method is better than the others. For example, reading the books of the New Testament in the order in which they are now assembled means starting with the Gospel of Matthew. However, the Gospel of Matthew was not the first gospel to be written; because Matthew was regarded as the most important of the Gospels, it was placed first in the New Testament. Understanding the contents of this gospel is difficult if not impossible until one relates it to the other Gospels and to the historical situation from which it was produced. One needs to know the sources from which the author obtained his materials and the scheme that he followed in the materials' selection and organization. It is also essential to know the purpose that the author had in mind and the way in which his materials were used for the accomplishment of that purpose. Elements in the Gospels that appear to be in conflict with one another can scarcely be understood until one becomes familiar with the background from which each of them was derived. These difficulties, along with many others, are necessarily involved in the use of this method.

Another way of studying the New Testament consists of putting together all of the material found on a given subject in any of the writings. If this method could be done successfully, one might speak about the New Testament teachings on such subjects as money, divorce, Sabbath observance, spiritual gifts, and many other topics. Aside from the fact that an inquiry of this kind would be practically endless because of the number of topics that are mentioned, a more serious difficulty is fitting together the statements made by different persons under different circumstances and from different points of view. Nor can it be assumed without supporting evidence that different writers thought alike about any given subject.

Studying the books in the chronological order in which they were written does have some advantages in that it enables us to trace more directly the development of Christian thought through the period during which the New Testament was being written. The chief objection to this method lies in the fact that Christianity was an ongoing concern before any portion of the New Testament was written. The literature that the New Testament contains was the product of the Christian movement, not the cause of it. For this reason, an understanding of what was written presupposes a certain familiarity with what had taken place before the writing began. For example, when Paul wrote his letters to the Christian churches of his day, he was writing to people who already knew something about the life of Jesus and the significance of what Jesus had done, which the people must have obtained from oral traditions because the sources from which we derive our information about Jesus had not yet been written. Hence, we must consult the later literature of the New Testament in order to understand what was known earlier. In the case of the Gospels and other portions of the literature, it is quite impossible to comprehend what the respective authors were saying apart from the beliefs that they were trying to establish.

In view of these considerations, it seems wise to begin the study of the New Testament with a survey of the historical background that is implicit in the literature itself. This survey will necessarily include some of the more important elements in the religious life of the Jewish people prior to the beginning of the Christian era, as well as an account of the religious hopes and ideals that were current among the Gentile or non-Jewish parts of the population. Some familiarity with both of these backgrounds is a prerequisite for the study of the New Testament, for while Christianity had its earliest beginnings among the Jews, it was not long until Christianity began to spread among the Gentiles. For each of these groups, Christianity's meaning had to be formulated in terms of the ideas and concepts to which they were accustomed. Knowing something about the religious beliefs and practices of these two groups, together with the more pertinent facts in connection with the life of Jesus as it was understood by the early Christians, prepares one for a more intelligent reading of the literature included in the New Testament.

THE HISTORICAL BACKGROUND OF THE NEW TESTAMENT

The Christian churches of the first century drew their membership from both Jews and Gentiles. The first Christians were Jews, and their first missionary activities were directed toward winning members from this group. However, not long thereafter, their activities were extended to include Gentiles, and many of those who had been non-Jews were welcomed into the newly formed Christian communities. The common element shared by both those who had been Jews and those who were Gentiles was loyalty to the person known as Jesus of Nazareth. Both groups recognized Jesus as a man of God and looked forward to a time when the message that he proclaimed would be spread throughout the world, bringing salvation to all those who would receive it.

Although both groups were loyal to Jesus, they did not, as a rule, interpret his life and ministry in the same way, nor could it reasonably be expected that they would. Each group interpreted his teachings in terms of the religious concepts with which they had long been familiar. For those who had been reared in the Jewish faith, he was the Messiah, the anointed one, the chosen of God, about whom the Old Testament prophets had written. He was the one under whose guidance and leadership the kingdom of God would be established, thus bringing about the full realization of the divine purpose in history. But while the Messiahship of Jesus meant a great deal to those whose training had been in Judaism, it meant very little to the non-Jews, or Gentiles, who were accustomed to thinking of religion in terms of the ideas and concepts associated with the mystery religions. To them, Jesus was comparable to the heroic redeemer of the mystery cults, which were numerous in the Greco-Roman world of New Testament times. Members of these cults were concerned primarily with the idea of salvation from physical death, to be followed by participation in the life of another world free of all the trials and hardships so characteristic of earthly life. The chief function of the heroic redeemer was to bring about this salvation. He would be a heavenly being who would descend to earth; after a life of service and self-sacrifice, he would rise from the dead. By achieving a mystical union with him, his followers would gain the power to triumph over death. For many of the Christians who had been Gentiles, it seemed perfectly natural to think of Jesus as one who fulfilled the role of the heroic redeemer; on this basis, they accepted him. The different conceptions of Jesus that are found in the various writings of the New Testament can be understood only in relation to the different backgrounds from which they were developed.

THE JEWISH BACKGROUND

Christianity began with the belief that Jesus of Nazareth was the Messiah. As far back as the eighth century B.C., the prophets of the Old Testament expressed their conviction that some day a leader would arise in their midst, and under his guidance a kingdom of justice and righteousness would be established on earth. During the centuries that followed, this belief was modified in various ways but was never completely abandoned. Three different stages can be noted in the development of the messianic idea: prophetic messianism, apocalyptic messianism, and revolutionary messianism. All three concern the earthly establishment of the kingdom of God, the ultimate goal of history or the final realization of the divine purpose in regard to the destiny of the human race. The three types of messianism differ from one another in respect to the time and manner of their accomplishments.

Prophetic messianism taught that the earthly kingdom of God would be reached with the coming of the Messiah, or anointed one. He would be an actual king who would reign over the Israelite nation and direct its affairs in such a way that the evils in society would be overcome and peace and happiness would be the lot of all.

When Saul was chosen as the first king of Israel, supposedly he was anointed with oil by the prophet Samuel in the presence of a multitude of people. This important ceremony symbolized the hope that this anointed one would be the Messiah under whose leadership the divine purpose would be realized. Saul's reign was a disappointment, and when things were going rather badly, David was chosen to be king in place of Saul. In many respects, David's reign was more successful. Later generations looked back upon it as a kind of golden age in the history of the Israelite people. The hope for the coming of the Messiah was emphasized more and more in the teachings of the prophets. Because so many of Israel's kings had been disappointing in what they did, the prophets talked about the coming of an ideal king who would appear in the future and do for his people that which other kings had been unable to do. This king, they said, would be like King David. Later, they maintained that he would be a descendant from the line of David, an idea expressed in the writings of the prophet Isaiah.

The course of Hebrew history over the centuries did not fulfill the prophets' hopes. Instead, one disaster after another overtook the nation. After the death of King Solomon, Israel was divided into a northern and a southern kingdom, and each kingdom went through a series of tragic experiences. In 722 B.C., the northern kingdom was taken captive by the Assyrians. A century and a half later, the southern kingdom suffered a similar fate at the hands of the Babylonians. Eventually, a Hebrew state was restored for a time, but conditions were far from ideal. Internal strife was present, and the nation was under a constant threat of destruction from foreign enemies. Under these conditions, prophetic messianism began to wane, and apocalyptic messianism appeared in its place.

The dominant characteristic of apocalyptic messianism was a conviction that the kingdom of God would not come about by a gradual transformation of society under the leadership of a great and good king. Rather, it would be brought about by a sudden supernatural intervention. When the right time arrived, God would act, bringing punishment to all the forces of evil and establishing his kingdom as a dwelling place for the righteous for all time to come. This event, referred to as the coming of the Day of the Lord, what in the Old Testament is referred to as the Day of Yahweh, was described as a great catastrophic event, an end of the world and the ushering in of a new age. Although there are variations in the different apocalyptic texts, some of these writings convey the idea that the Messiah will be a heavenly being who will descend to earth and inaugurate the new era. His appearance will bring destruction to the wicked and deliverance to the righteous. A resurrection of the dead and a judgment of all the people who have lived on the earth will occur. After the wicked have been completely destroyed, a new heaven and a new earth in which only justice and righteousness prevail will exist.

Apocalyptic messianism was especially meaningful in times of crises, which for the Jews meant most of the time. The Book of Daniel in the Old Testament was written primarily for those who were suffering persecution from the Syrians under Antiochus Epiphanes during the period that preceded the Maccabean wars. In New Testament times, the Roman government persecuted the Christians, and the Book of Revelation did for the Christians of that day what the Book of Daniel did for the Jews of an earlier date: assure those who were suffering for their faith that although the evil forces in the world were then in the ascendancy, the time was not far distant when God would intervene and bring an end to the reign of evil by establishing a kingdom of righteousness in which those who had proved faithful through all of their trials and afflictions would dwell forever in peace.

Not all Jews were satisfied with the notion that they should endure suffering and persecution while waiting for God to intervene on their behalf. The revolutionary messianists argued that God would come to their aid only after they had done all that they could for themselves. Accordingly, they believed that the Day of the Lord would be hastened if they took up arms against their enemies and fought for their own freedom and independence. In other words, God would use his own people as the instruments through which he would bring punishment upon unrighteous nations. The belief that God would aid in this task was strengthened by what the people had experienced during the period of the Maccabean wars. When Mattathias and his small band of renegade fighters took up arms against the Syrians, they achieved one remarkable victory after another. Despite being greatly outnumbered by Syrian soldiers, they were able to win back the territory that had been taken from them, including regaining possession of the city of Jerusalem and restoring the worship services of the Temple. All of these successes were interpreted to mean that God would protect them in battle and give them victory over their enemies. What he had done for them in times past he would do again if they would only follow a similar course.

After the Romans conquered the Jewish territory and made the Jews subjects of their dominion, revolutionary messianists continued their efforts by calling upon Jews to launch a revolt against the government of Rome. Not long before the birth of Jesus of Nazareth, a certain Judas of Galilee, claiming the messianic role for himself, organized a revolt that the Romans put down with unmistakable cruelty. This fear of rebellion made the Romans suspicious whenever it was rumored that a Jewish Messiah had appeared among his people.

Another important characteristic of Judaism can be seen in its conception of the Law and its relation to the conduct of people. According to its tradition, the Law was from God. It was revealed to Moses and through him was communicated to the entire Israelite nation. Because God was the author of the Law, the precepts contained in it were binding for all time to come. The Law, as unchangeable as God himself, included not only the Ten Commandments but all the statutes and ordinances found in the Book of the Law, or what is now recognized as the first five books of the Old Testament—the Pentateuch. Many of these laws were no doubt added to the original codes long after the death of Moses. Nevertheless, tradition attributed all of them to Moses. Taken as a whole, they constituted for the orthodox Jew the standard of righteousness according to which not only the people who were living then but all succeeding generations would be judged.

Obedience with reference to the laws that God commanded was the measure of goodness. This being true, knowing exactly what the requirements of the laws were and how they were to be applied to particular cases were matters of great importance. These concerns were not always easy to determine; instances occurred in which different laws appeared to be in conflict. One of the main tasks of the Scribes was to determine matters of this kind. Their job was to state precisely the conditions under which a given law would be applicable. Frequently, it was necessary for them to state when exceptions should be made to certain laws. Additionally, occasions arose when the Scribes had to make exceptions to these exceptions, a very complicated and confusing process but an important one, for if a person was to be judged solely on the basis of whether he had obeyed the laws, there must be some authoritative way of knowing exactly what the laws required under a given set of circumstances. Remember that throughout the Gospels of the New Testament, the chief accusation brought by the Jews against Jesus is that he is a law-breaker.

Although Judaism is often referred to as a single type of religious belief and practice, complete agreement among all the Jews concerning either doctrine or manner of living did not occur. We can distinguish several sects or parties within Judaism itself. The largest and most influential of these sects was known as the Pharisees, who took their religion most seriously, especially with reference to their attitude toward the Law. The Pharisees believed that Jews were God's chosen people, distinguished from all others because God revealed his standard of goodness to them, and they alone lived in conformity to it. Their zeal for the Law made them appear exclusive and self-righteous to those who did not belong to their group. To avoid contamination with the evil ways of the world, they avoided contact with foreigners and foreign customs so far as it was possible for them to do so, and they were especially antagonistic toward the influences derived from the cultures of the Greeks and the Romans. They believed in a life after death in which the righteous would be rewarded and the sinners punished for the deeds that they had committed. In many parts of the New Testament, the Pharisees are severely criticized, but we must bear in mind that these accounts were written by people who did not belong to their group. Without doubt, the accounts given are accurate with reference to some of the Pharisees, but it would be a mistake to think that they were all alike. Many of them were men of the finest character, representing in some instances Judaism at its very best.

The Sadducees was another sect, smaller in number than the Pharisees but very influential in determining the policies that affected the lives of the people as a whole. In some respects, they were a conservative group that held a strict and literal interpretation of the Law as recorded in the first five books of the Old Testament. They rejected the so-called oral law, which consisted of the comments and interpretations of prominent rabbis made over long periods of time. Neither did they take seriously many of the ideas presented in the later books of the Old Testament—for example, the resurrection of the dead as set forth in the Book of Daniel. But in their attitude toward Hellenic culture and Roman law, they were far more liberal than the Pharisees. The Sadducees believed that although some important truths had been revealed to the Jews, other nations had important contributions to make as well. They advocated an intermingling of the various cultures of their day, thus giving to each group the opportunity to enrich their own lives through contact with others. Because the priesthood was controlled by the Sadducees and appointments had to be confirmed by officials of the civil government, this sect was able to exercise political power. However, sometimes this power was used more to promote selfish interests than to benefit people as a whole.

A third sect was known as the Essenes, the group that produced the famous Dead Sea Scrolls. From these scrolls, much has been learned concerning the history of the period that preceded the writings that constitute the New Testament. The Essenes were a group of Jews who were seriously disturbed by the way things were going in and around the city of Jerusalem. To them, the religion proclaimed by priests and prophets of old ceased to have any meaningful relation to the lives of the people. They saw so much wickedness in the society around them that they felt impelled to live in a secluded colony where they would be sheltered from such evil. In this respect, their attitude was similar to that of the medieval monks of later generations who withdrew from a worldly society in order to live a holier type of life. Initially, the Essenes, like the later monks, advocated celibacy, hoping to maintain their numbers by adding new converts to their order. Later, marriages were permitted, but both sexes were required to conform to a very rigid set of disciplinary rules. They were a communal society, sharing their goods with one another and making spiritual preparations for the end of the world and the establishment of the messianic kingdom that they expected in the near future. Much of their time was spent in study and in copying the manuscripts of the Old Testament writings. In addition to these copied works, the Essenes produced a considerable amount of literature of their own, some of which describes their manner of living and the rites and ceremonies that they observed.

In addition to the Pharisees, Sadducees, and Essenes, other smaller and less influential groups existed. One of these was known as the Zealots, revolutionary messianists who believed in the use of violent methods in order to gain freedom from their oppressors. They were feared by the Romans because of their tendency to stir up rebellion against the recognized government. We read in the New Testament that one of the twelve disciples whom Jesus chose was Simon the Zealot. Another sect was the Zadokites, reformed priests who resented the way in which the Sadducees made political offices out of the priesthood. The Zadokites believed in the religious ideals advocated by the great prophets of the Old Testament, and they tried as best they could to make these ideals effective. They produced some of the apocalyptic literature to which Paul makes reference in one of his letters to the Thessalonians. The comparatively large number of people who belonged to the poorer classes were known as the Am'ha'aretz, or people of the land, manual laborers who performed menial tasks. They were, to some extent, held in contempt by the Pharisees and Sadducees, who considered themselves morally superior to these persons whose hard lot they believed was precisely what they deserved because of their laxity in the observance of ritualistic requirements of the Law. From this class of discouraged and oppressed persons, Jesus drew many of his followers. They are referred to in the Gospels as "the common people [who] heard him gladly."

THE NON-JEWISH BACKGROUND

Because early Christianity made its appeal to Gentiles as well as to those who had been Jews, the New Testament reflects something of the Gentiles' background, along with that of the Israelite people. Of course, to mention more than a few of the more important influences that have a direct bearing on the literature produced by the early Christians is impossible. However, three major influences on the Gentile version of Christianity are mystery cults, emperor worship, and Greek philosophy.

Mystery cults were secret organizations whose membership was restricted to people who made application for admittance and then passed through a probationary period during which their conduct was carefully observed by qualified officials. Unless they performed the necessary rites and met all of the specified tests, they were not allowed to become members. Many mystery cults existed throughout the Greco-Roman world during New Testament times, including the Eleusinian Mysteries, the Orphic Mysteries, the Attis-Adonis Mysteries, and the Isis-Osiris Mysteries.

The actual ceremonies that took place within any of these cults were supposed to be kept secret. However, certain general characteristics of the mystery religions are fairly well known. All of them were concerned primarily with the means of obtaining salvation. Life in this present world was so infected with evil that no permanent good could be achieved in it. Consequently, salvation meant leaving this world and entering into a new type of existence in a life that comes after physical death.

Each of the mystery cults had its own peculiar mythology describing in some detail the activities of the gods that were involved. Many of the myths appear to have originated in order to explain the change of seasons, which causes the death of vegetation in the fall of the year and its rebirth in the spring. As the mythology developed, the death and resurrection that occur in the vegetable kingdom came to be regarded as appropriate symbols for the lives of human beings. Because vegetation overcomes death through the power of the gods, humankind, through the aid of a supernatural power, might also triumph over death.

The agent through whom this power to overcome death would be made available was known as the heroic redeemer.

Unlike the Jewish concept of the Messiah, whose function was that of establishing a kingdom of justice and righteousness on this earth, the heroic redeemer of the mystery cults was a savior able to conquer death not only for himself but for all of his faithful followers. He was a heavenly being who would come to earth in human form and use his miraculous power to perform deeds of mercy and kindness toward human beings. His work would encounter opposition from the forces of evil, and his earthly career would be brought to an end by a sacrificial death. By virtue of his power as a divine being, he would rise from the dead and ascend back to the heaven from whence he came.

The power that was manifest in the experiences of the heroic redeemer could be imparted to the members of the cult who were prepared to receive it. In order to prepare for this experience, the applicants for membership were required to go through certain initiatory rites, which usually included a sprinkling ceremony in which either water or blood was used, thus signifying a purifying process that cleansed the individual of evil. After the applicant became a member, other ceremonies were designed to bring about a mystical union between the believer and the redeemer. In one of these ceremonies, the initiates would sit in front of a stage, where they would witness a dramatic performance that portrayed the life, death, and resurrection of the redeemer. As they saw this drama enacted, they would feel a sense of kinship with the hero. Being united in spirit with him, they, too, would possess the power to overcome the evils of mortal existence, including even death itself.

In another type of ceremony, union with the redeemer was accomplished through participation in a common meal. The members of the cult gathered around a table and partook in a symbol of the body and blood of the redeemer, believing that in this way the life present in the redeemer was imparted to them. Membership in the cult and participation in its many rites and ceremonies were regarded as essential means for transforming the quality of one's living on this earth in preparation for the true salvation achieved in a life to come after death.

Emperor worship was another factor that had an important bearing on the religious life of the Gentile world. Its chief significance lies in the concept of a human being who, over the course of time, is elevated in the minds of his followers to the status of deity.

In other words, a person becomes a god. This way of thinking contrasts that of the Jews. Judaism always made a sharp distinction between the human and the divine. Yahweh, the god of the Jewish religion, was regarded as the creator and, in a sense, the father of all humankind. But he was not a father in any physical or biological sense of the term. Human beings were born of two human parents, not of one human parent and one divine parent. However, among some non-Jews of the world, the concept of an individual who has one human parent and one divine parent was fairly common. To be sure, only the exceptional individual's earthly career could be explained in this way, the most frequent example of which was found in the ruler of a country. One way of accounting for the extraordinary achievements of a head of government was to credit him with supernatural ancestry on the grounds that no ordinary human being born in the usual way could have accomplished so much. Having a divine parent was interpreted to mean that the individual belonged to the race of the gods and was therefore not comparable to ordinary mortals.

The so-called deification of a ruler did not always take place during the ruler's lifetime. After his death, later generations might idealize both his reign and his person, thus giving rise to the belief that he was something more than a mere mortal. For example, this process happened in the case of the Greek ruler who came to be known as Alexander the Great. One of the most revered of the Roman emperors was Augustus Caesar, who, after his death, was declared by the Roman Senate to have been a god. Worship of his image was encouraged in various parts of the empire, and not only was he deified in the minds of his admirers of later generations, but legends indicating his supernatural character evolved and were given wide publicity. A heavenly messenger supposedly had foretold his birth, strange phenomena had been observed in the heavens at the time of his birth, miraculous power had been manifested in many of his earthly activities, and he had even triumphed over death. We have the testimony of one Roman historian who claims that eyewitnesses told of Augustus Caesar's resurrection from the dead and his ascension to heaven.

The deification of earthly rulers by their subjects was not confined to the Greeks and the Romans. For centuries, it was a common practice among Egyptians, Babylonians, and other peoples of the ancient world. Nor were the rulers the only ones deified by their followers. Some of the most noted of the Greek philosophers were said to have descended from the gods since their remarkable wisdom could be accounted for in no other way. Among the Gentiles of New Testament times, explanations of this kind were commonly given to account for the activities of a person who accomplished extraordinary things.

By the end of the first century of the Christian era, emperor worship led to a serious conflict between officials of the Roman government and members of Christian communities. Certain Roman emperors, in order to strengthen their prestige and establish further unity among their subjects, decided that their deification should not be postponed until after their deaths. Accordingly, they not only proclaimed their own deity but gave orders that statues in their honor should be erected in the provinces and that worship should be accorded them at specified times and places. Christians were thus placed in a precarious position: To refuse to conform to an emperor's orders would brand them as enemies of the civil government, but obeying these same orders would be an act of disloyalty to the one and only god whom they recognized. Portions of the New Testament are addressed to Christians who faced this dilemma and who needed both advice and encouragement with reference to the course that they should follow.

The influence of Greek philosophy was widespread throughout the Greco-Roman world. The Greek language was used by educated people, Greek-inspired schools of philosophy were established in leading cities of the Roman Empire, and the writings of the Old Testament were translated into Greek by the seventy scholars whose work was known as the Septuagint version of the Hebrew Scriptures. The influence of Greek ideas can be seen in many instances of New Testament writing, especially in those parts of the literature that attempt to interpret the Christian religion of people whose prior experience was in a Gentile rather than a Jewish environment. Such attempts are true to a considerable extent in the Pauline letters and also in the Gospel of John. In both of these instances, the writings were addressed to communities composed of Gentile and Jewish Christians. Therefore, these authors necessarily had to use language with which the people to whom they were writing were familiar and could readily understand.

Greek influences can be noted, too, in other parts of the New Testament, although they are not as conspicuous there as they are in the writings of Paul and John.

To say just how much of the New Testament was influenced either directly or indirectly by Greek conceptions is difficult, but such influences are recognized readily in the doctrine of the Logos, which may be translated as Word or Reason; in ethical conceptions having to do with the conflict between flesh and spirit; and in the belief in immortality.

When the author of the Fourth Gospel, commonly known as the Gospel of John, begins his account of Christianity by saying "In the beginning was the Word, and the Word was with God, and the Word was God," he uses a concept that had long been familiar to students of Greek philosophy. The Word, or Logos, which was the term used by the Greeks, has a long and interesting history. One finds it in the writings of Heracleitus, one of the Pre-Socratics whose work appears to have had considerable influence on the philosophies of Plato and Aristotle. For Heracleitus, the Logos was a kind of cosmic order, or divine justice, that presides over the destinies of a changing world. Whenever either of two opposite forces operating in the world oversteps its bounds, the Logos ensures that a proper balance is restored. Light and darkness, heat and cold, wet and dry, male and female, like all other pairs of opposites, are thus kept in proper relation to one another. Nor is the work of the Logos confined to the physical aspect of nature, for it affects the moral order as well. Whenever the requirements of justice are violated, either by individuals or by nations, the Logos acts in a compensatory manner and punishes the evildoers and thus restores the proper balance of things. Plato regarded the Logos, or Reason, as the divine element that is present in human beings. Its demand for harmony among the elements, including those in human nature, provides the key to the real meaning of the good life.

In Stoicism more than in any other branch of Greek philosophy, the doctrine of the Logos was emphasized. The Stoic philosophers identified Reason with God. They did not conceive of it as having an existence apart from the world; they believed that it permeates every part of the world. By virtue of the Logos, or Reason, the world is a cosmos rather than a chaos. Reason is present in the minds of humans, and knowledge is possible because the rational element in human nature is akin to the Reason that exists in nature, the only difference being that in the former case, Reason becomes conscious of itself. So far as humanity is concerned, Reason functions to give guidance and direction to the activities of life. Because all humans are rational beings, a common bond exists between them, and this bond was recognized by the Stoics as the basis for their belief in the universal brotherhood of humanity. Reason operating in the lives of human beings made possible the realization of what constituted for them the real meaning of the good life.

The Stoic ideal is expressed in the words "life according to nature," which means a life directed by the rational element that is present in both nature and humanity. This ideal can be achieved by bringing one's feelings and desires under the control of Reason, which the Stoics believed was a real possibility for any normal human being. Epictetus, a well-known Stoic writer, describes this way of life in his essay "Things within our Power and Things not within our Power." The individual has power over his own inner attitudes. He can govern his own spirit, control his temper, and follow the path of duty rather than yield to his feelings or be led by his emotions. On the other hand, circumstances arise over which there is no control. Some things that happen are inevitable, and the wise person will accept them without fear or complaint. The apostle Paul reflects this ideal when he writes in one of his letters, "I have learned, in whatsoever state I am, there to be content."

Closely related to the concept of the Logos, or Reason, is the notion of conflict between flesh and spirit, an idea that pervades the whole structure of Greek philosophy and is illustrated in the teachings of Plato, who held that the world of ideas, or the realm of the spirit, constitutes reality. This realm is eternal and unchanging. In contrast, the world that is experienced through the senses is a changing and unstable one. We could not have any knowledge concerning such a world except for the unchanging ideas that participate in it. The presence of these ideas, which are copied or imitated in particular things, gives to them the appearance of reality. But when ideas are embodied or imitated in material things, the result is always somewhat inferior to the original. In other words, matter is the source of corruption and deterioration.

Ideas conceived in this way are something more than a basis for the existence of particular things: They are also ideals or standards of perfection, thus making it possible for particular things to be evaluated in terms of their approximation to the ideal. To call an object good means that it is a close approximation to the ideal, one that is as nearly like the ideal as it is possible for a physical object to be. In a similar way of thinking, a person is morally good who conforms to the pattern of the ideal as much as it is possible for a human being to do. Centuries after Plato, Christians illustrated this point when they said of Jesus of Nazareth, "The Word became flesh and made his dwelling among us." Jesus is regarded as an embodiment of the ideal. He is the ideal man, the standard according to which the goodness of any other human being is to be judged.

For the Greeks, the source of goodness is spirit, and evil has its roots in matter. Because a human being is composed of both matter and spirit, a struggle is constantly going on within one's own nature. The conflict between good and evil that takes place in the life of an individual is a conflict between the desires of the flesh and the demands of the reason, which is the ruling part of one's spiritual nature. The Greek idea of a good mind and an evil body was never accepted by Jews, who teach that man is created in the image of God. Body, soul, and spirit constitute a unit that is good. Evil entered the world with the Fall of man and infected all of the elements in his nature, including his mind and his body. The apostle Paul was brought up in the Jewish tradition, and nothing indicates that he ever abandoned the notion of original sin. Nevertheless, in writing to Gentile Christians, he frequently uses the language of Greek philosophy. For example, in the Epistle to the Galatians, he writes, "So I say, live by the Spirit, and you will not gratify the desires of the sinful nature. For the sinful nature desires what is contrary to the Spirit, and the Spirit what is contrary to the sinful nature. They are in conflict with each other. . . . But the fruit of the Spirit is love, joy, peace, patience, kindness, goodness, faithfulness, gentleness, and self-control."

The Greek conception of a good mind but an evil body is illustrated also in the teaching concerning the immortality of the soul. Unlike the Hebrews, who never accepted the idea of a soul existing apart from the body, Plato and many of his followers believed that souls have neither a beginning nor an end. They belong to the eternal realm of the spirit but are capable of entering human bodies and remaining there until the body dies. During this time, they can be influenced by their contact with that which is physical. As a result, they may be dragged down toward the level of matter or may so direct the physical body that its activities will be in the direction of spiritual attainments. In one of Plato's well-known dialogues, the soul is described as being something like that of a charioteer who is driving two steeds, one of which is wild and unruly, the other of which behaves in an orderly manner. The charioteer determines which one of these steeds will be subdued by the other. The two steeds represent the flesh and the spirit, and the charioteer is the soul. The soul, throughout the course of its embodied existence, is engaged in a conflict between flesh and spirit, which is also a conflict between evil and good. Souls that yield to the demands of the flesh are deserving of a different fate than those that follow the prompting of the spirit. This belief is one of the main reasons why Plato believed in the immortality of the soul. Souls that do not receive the happiness that they deserve in one life can be given a just compensation in another one. This argument provides a solution for the problem concerning the suffering of comparatively innocent persons: They may be receiving just punishment for deeds done in a former existence, or they may be given an appropriate reward in a future one.

Another reason for believing in the immortality of the soul lies in the fact that ideas present in the soul have neither beginning nor end. They are eternal; therefore, the soul in which they have their existence must also be eternal. On no other basis does Plato think it possible to account for the ideas that one can think of but that are never experienced through the senses. One can think of a perfect circle or a perfectly straight line, although neither has ever been seen. Plato's explanation is that the ideas have always been present in the soul. One's awareness of such perfect ideas is a recollection of what happened in some former existence. They are latent in the soul of a human being and are raised to the level of consciousness as a result of the stimuli provided by sensations.

When Plato writes his account of the death of Socrates, he makes a clear distinction between what happens to the physical body and what happens to the soul. When Socrates' friends visit Socrates in prison during his last hours, Socrates explains that his imminent death is not an occasion for sadness because the time is close at hand when his soul will be released from the body in which it has been imprisoned for so many years. Only the physical body dies. The soul journeys to another world unencumbered with the difficulties that have attended its existence in a mortal body. In this future existence, the soul will receive a just reward for whatever goodness it has achieved; because Socrates believes that he has lived well, he looks to the future with joyful anticipation.

This conception of the soul and its relation to a life beyond physical death was widely accepted by the Gentiles of the Greco-Roman world during New Testament times. Although neither the Jews nor the early Jewish Christians thought of this issue in this way, many, if not most, of them believed in some kind of survival after physical death. We know that the early Christian movement was greatly based on a firm belief in the resurrection of Jesus. Because the story of this resurrection was told in various places, it was not always interpreted in the same way. People whose orientation was in the Greek tradition were bound to see in it something quite different from people who were brought up in a Jewish environment.

A BRIEF OUTLINE OF THE LIFE OF JESUS

Our information concerning events in the life of Jesus is obtained almost entirely from the Gospels of the New Testament. Before any of the Gospels were written, the Christian community had already existed for some time. Community members had formulated a number of specific beliefs concerning Jesus and the significance of his life, death, and resurrection. When the Gospels were written, the materials contained in them necessarily reflected to a considerable extent those beliefs that were generally accepted by Christians at that time. Not only Christians' specific beliefs but also their interpretation and significance for coming generations were bound to become part of the written biographies. There is nothing strange or unusual about this practice, for it is the kind of thing that is always involved in historical writing. Historians make use of source materials and record actual happenings with as much accuracy as possible. Even so, their selection of facts is recorded, and their interpretations of these materials govern the way in which histories are put together, which is true of the New Testament writings no less than it is of other historical writings.

The authors of the Gospels, inspired as they undoubtedly were, could not help but be influenced by their beliefs about Jesus. For them to fill in the gaps that occurred in their accounts by telling what they believed must have happened or even to insert at various points what seemed appropriate given their knowledge of subsequent events after Jesus' physical death would have been most natural. Determining just how much of the record as it exists at the present time is due to the interpretations of the authors is not always an easy task, nor can this determination be done with complete accuracy. So far as the main outline of events is concerned, no reason exists for doubting the biographies' historical accuracy, but like any other historical writing, appropriate allowances must be made for the limitations under which the different authors carried on their work.

The oldest of the biographies of Jesus, which according to most New Testament scholars is the Gospel of Mark, tells us nothing of the time or place of Jesus' birth, nor does it record anything of his life prior to the time when he was baptized by John in the Jordan River. Perhaps information concerning the early part of Jesus' life was not available or was not regarded as important. Other Gospels report that he was born in Bethlehem of Judea and grew up in the town of Nazareth in Galilee. His public ministry did not begin until after his baptism, which was apparently a turning point in his career. John the Baptist was conducting a vigorous campaign in preparation for the great day when God would establish his kingdom here on earth, which John believed to be near at hand. John called upon people to repent of their sins and in witness thereof to be baptized. That Jesus responded to this call and was baptized indicates that he was in full accord with the work John was doing. Shortly thereafter, Jesus began to proclaim the coming of the heavenly kingdom on earth and called upon his fellow men to make preparation for it. The work of John the Baptist was brought to a close when he was imprisoned and later beheaded by Herod Antipas. His death may have been one of the reasons why Jesus continued, at least in part, the type of work that John was doing, although there are good reasons for believing that

Jesus would have carried out a program of his own quite independent of what happened to the Baptist.

Before beginning his own public ministry, Jesus, like many of
Israel's prophets, retired to the solitude of the wilderness for a period of fasting and meditation. At the end of this period, we are
told that he was tempted by Satan, the archenemy of God and the
personification of the forces of evil. Although the details of the
temptation stories are somewhat varied, there can be little doubt
that they report an actual event, and the meaning of the experience
is essentially the same in all of them. They tell us that Jesus was
tempted to do evil in the manner that is typical of the temptations
that come to all human beings. That Jesus was able—with divine
help—to resist these temptations brings assurances that any person
may overcome evil by cooperating with divine aid, the same as
Jesus did.

According to the Gospel of Mark, Jesus began his public
ministry in the towns and villages of Galilee by proclaiming that
the kingdom of God was at hand. He spoke in synagogues, in pri-
vate homes, on lakeshores, and wherever people would gather to
see and to hear him. Two elements in his ministry—teaching and
healing—were so closely linked together that neither one can be
understood apart from the other. Both of them concerned overcoming the forces of evil in preparation for the coming of God's
kingdom. The purpose of the preaching, or teaching mission, was
to make people aware of their need for repentance and to give
them a clearer understanding of the way they should live in order
to be ready for a place in God's kingdom. One of the chief devices
used by Satan to lead people astray is the development of people's
sense of complete satisfaction with themselves, which is often designated as the sin of pride, a feeling on the part of individuals that
they are already good enough, that there is no need for any reform
on their part. Jesus wanted to counteract this aspect of Satan's
work, and preaching was one of the means he used to accomplish
this end.

Jesus' healing mission was another means employed for the
same purpose. The Jewish people generally accepted that physical
suffering was predominantly the main punishment for sin. This
point is well illustrated in the story concerning the healing of a
man who was born blind. The first question put to Jesus by those

who were standing nearby was, "Who sinned, this man or his parents, that he was born blind?" But if suffering is a punishment for sin, then an assurance that one's sins have been forgiven would be followed by a removal of the punishment. The Gospels indicate that in Jesus' ministry, the healing of the sick and the forgiveness of sins were linked so closely together that they were but different ways of reporting the same event. Overcoming sickness, as well as erroneous beliefs, counteracts the work of Satan and thus prepares for the coming of the kingdom.

According to the account in the Gospel of Mark, Jesus' early ministry in Galilee was quite successful. Large crowds gathered to hear him, and many sick individuals were brought to him in order that they might be healed. To assist him in the work he was doing, as well as to instruct the listeners further concerning life in the kingdom, Jesus chose a group of disciples. The disciples came from different walks of life and were so deeply impressed by the character of Jesus' mission that they wanted to be closely associated with it. This willingness does not mean that they fully understood it. Apparently, they all believed that the kingdom was soon to be established, but they were not in complete agreement concerning the manner in which it would be brought about, and there was some doubt in their minds with reference to the precise role of Jesus in connection with it. For a long time, the Jews believed that the coming of the Messiah would precede the establishment of the kingdom, but there was some question in the minds of the disciples concerning whether Jesus was the one who long had been expected. In the Gospel of Mark, Jesus' Messiahship was a secret known only by Jesus himself and the demons whom he encountered. His Messiahship was not revealed even to the disciples until he discussed it with them at Caesarea Philippi shortly before the journey to Jerusalem, and then he warned them that they should say nothing about it.

We have no definite information concerning the length of Jesus' public ministry. So far as the events related in the Gospel of Mark are used as the basis for calculating its length, we can say that it would have been possible for all of the events to have occurred within a single year. Other Gospels indicate a longer period of time. Whatever length of time it may have been, evidently the only purpose of the ministry was that of preparing the people for life in God's kingdom. None of Jesus' mighty works was done in order to attract attention to Jesus himself. The miracles were manifestations of God's power, which is always available to those who are prepared to make use of it. Some people saw in these miracles nothing more than a type of magic or an exhibition of some spectacular power, but they were the ones who failed to grasp the true meaning or significance of Jesus' work.

At some point in his Galilean ministry, Jesus had a disappointing experience in his hometown of Nazareth. Jesus could do no more mighty works in Nazareth because of the citizens' lack of belief, but his enthusiasm for carrying forward the mission he had set out to perform was not dampened; he intensified his efforts. He sent his disciples into the outlying territory with instructions to do the same type of work that he was doing. The disciples' efforts appear to have been successful, for when they brought back their report, Jesus said with reference to it, "I saw Satan fall like lightning from heaven." Later, Jesus and the disciples carried their mission into the region northeast of Galilee, including such places as Tyre, Sidon, and Caesarea Philippi.

After a brief return to Galilee, during which he visited the city of Capernaum, Jesus decided to go to Jerusalem. The growing opposition to his work on the part of those who were engaged in the activities that he criticized seems to have been one of the reasons that prompted this decision. But more important, the success of his entire mission was at stake, for it was crucial that the cause that he represented be placed squarely before the leaders of the Jewish people in their headquarters at Jerusalem. Jesus realized the danger that was involved in an attempt of this kind, for he was familiar with what had happened to Israel's ancient prophets whenever they challenged government officials' policies. Nevertheless, despite the dangers to him personally, "he set his face steadfastly toward Jerusalem" no matter what it might cost him to do so. As he talked with his disciples about what might happen to him in Jerusalem, they were shocked, for they did not believe anything of that kind would happen to the promised Messiah. When Jesus tried to explain to them the true nature of the work of the Messiah, they did not understand.

The journey to Jerusalem was relatively uneventful, but after Jesus' entrance into the city, opposition to his program soon became so strong that it resulted in his death. Jesus' coming into the city is described by the gospel writers as a triumphal entry, for evidently many people welcomed him, believing that the time was at hand when the promised Messiah would take part in the establishment of God's kingdom. Their hopes were soon frustrated by the turn of events. The chief priests and rulers of the people were infuriated by Jesus' attacks on the use that was being made of the Temple. When Jesus drove out the buyers and sellers and denounced the commercialism involved in priests' and rulers' activities, he aroused the antagonism of the Jewish leaders, which led to their decision to denounce him.

Because it was the season for the celebration of the Jewish Passover, multitudes were entering the city to participate in the services. Jesus observed the Passover meal with his disciples, but in the meantime, his enemies plotted against him by charging that he was not only disloyal to the Jewish faith but an enemy of the Roman government. After the Passover meal, Jesus was betrayed by Judas, one of his own disciples, and arrested by soldiers. In the course of his trial before the Roman governor, he was examined by Pilate, who declared that he found no fault in Jesus. Pilate wanted Jesus released, but a mob that had gathered to press charges against him demanded that he be crucified, and in the end, Pilate yielded to their demand. From the point of view of Jesus' followers, everything for which they had hoped was lost. Even the disciples forsook Jesus and fled in order to save their own lives. Jesus died on the cross and was buried in Joseph's new tomb.

Later, a remarkable change took place in the experience of these same disciples. They became convinced that Jesus' cause was not lost. The man who died on the cross was one whose life met with divine approval. He died not because of his own sins but, like the suffering servant of the prophet Isaiah, for the sake of others. The disciples were now sure that he was the true Messiah, the nature of whose mission they did not understand before his crucifixion. His death on the cross did not mean the end of the cause for which he stood. In fact, that cause was now more alive than it had ever been before. God's kingdom would yet be established. Jesus' return to earth to complete the program already begun would be accomplished in the near future. With these convictions in the minds of the disciples, the Christian movement was inaugurated, a movement that produced the writings in the New Testament.

CRITICAL COMMENTARIES

THE PAULINE LETTERS

Approximately one third of the New Testament consists of letters, or epistles, written by the apostle Paul and addressed to the Christian churches of his day. Because these letters are older than any of the gospel accounts of the life of Jesus, they constitute the most reliable source that we have today for information concerning the early history of the Christian movement. With few exceptions, these letters were written in response to conditions that existed in the particular churches with which Paul was associated. Not until some time passed after Paul's death were these letters circulated among the churches and read along with the Old Testament Scriptures as a part of regular worship services. Still later, they came to be regarded as inspired writings comparable to the sacred Scriptures of Judaism.

To understand the contents of these letters, it is necessary to know something about the man who wrote them, as well as about the particular circumstances under which they were written. Fortunately for us, considerable information along these lines is available within the letters themselves and can be supplemented by biographical accounts written by Luke, who was a companion of Paul, and included in the Book of Acts.

Paul was a native of Tarsus, a city of considerable importance in the Greco-Roman world. He was a descendant of the Hebrew tribe of Benjamin and originally was named Saul, after Israel's first king. Raised in a Jewish home, he was taught the Old Testament Scriptures and brought up in strict accordance with the beliefs and practices of the Pharisee sect. As he grew older, he was sent to the city of Jerusalem, where he studied under Gamaliel, one of the leading Jewish rabbis of that day. Later, he returned to Tarsus and probably attended the Greek university located in that city, although we have no direct information about this.

A crucial turning point in Paul's career came after he returned to Jerusalem and began studies in preparation for becoming a rabbi. As a devoted and loyal Jew of the Pharisee sect, his attention was given primarily to a detailed analysis of the requirements set forth in the Mosaic Law. He became familiar not only with the Law itself but with the explanations and commentaries made by the leading rabbis of the Jewish faith. In harmony with one of the basic doctrines of Judaism, he believed that salvation could be obtained only by obedience to all of the laws that God had given to his people. But as Paul pursued his studies, he became conscious of the fact that a mere knowledge concerning what one ought to do does not produce the desire to do it. Furthermore, he realized that desires give rise to actions, but the Law is unable to give one the desires that are necessary to meet its requirements. In fact, the situation is even worse than that, for the knowledge that one ought *not* to do certain things often acts as a stimulus creating the desire to do it. This conflict between duty and desire became an intolerable situation for Paul; because of it, he gave up his plans for becoming a rabbi. To compensate for his failure to carry out his original plans, he was anxious to find something of real merit that he might do, which he believed he found in the need for suppressing a new religious movement that he regarded as both dangerous and heretical—Christianity.

This new religious movement was promulgated by a group of people who claimed to be followers of Jesus, a man who had been crucified but who, they now believed, had risen from the dead, ascended to heaven, and would return to earth in power and great glory. Putting an end to this movement was what Paul now devoted himself to with the utmost zeal. He hunted down the members of this group, had them committed to prison, and threatened them with death. But as he did so, he could not help but be impressed by the way in which the Christians met the persecutions inflicted upon them.

The stoning of Stephen was one of these incidents. With perfect calm and an inner peace of mind, Stephen knelt down and prayed that those who were casting the stones might be forgiven. It was perfectly evident that these Christians possessed that which Paul desired more than anything else: the peace of mind that comes with a clear conscience and a deep conviction that they are living in harmony with the will of God. Paul came to realize that there must be some connection between these persons' faith in Jesus and their manner of living. No doubt this conviction was growing upon him for some time, but the climactic turning point in his career came while he was journeying to Damascus. Convinced now that Jesus was a righteous man and that his death on the cross was not the just punishment of a criminal but rather that of a martyr who died for a noble cause, Paul was ready to give himself to that same cause, which was more alive than it had been before Jesus' crucifixion and which pointed the way to a salvation that could not be achieved by obedience to a set of laws that were contrary to human desires.

Paul's decision to cast his lot with the members of the Christian community did not make him a missionary all at once, for about fourteen years passed before his work as a leader in the movement received any general recognition. During this time, Paul had ample opportunity to rethink his religious conceptions, systematize his understanding of the meaning of Jesus' career on earth, and formulate plans for spreading Christianity throughout the world. Eventually, he was invited by Barnabas to come to the church at Antioch and assist in the work being done there. After serving this church for a brief period, Paul began a series of missionary journeys to spread the news of salvation offered through Jesus' physical death. While engaged in these missionary activities, he wrote the letters that are preserved in the New Testament.

GALATIANS

Summary

The occasion for this letter was a controversy that developed among the churches in Galatia, and especially the one in Antioch, concerning the matter of requiring Gentile Christians to obey the Mosaic Law. One law very much in question concerned circumcision, a religious rite that meant for Jews much the same thing as baptism came to mean for Christians of a later period. The Christians whose background had been in Judaism could see no reason why this rite should not be required of all Christians, as it was for Jews. As they understood it, the laws given by God through Moses were binding for all time and could never be set aside by human beings or by any set of circumstances that might arise.

When people with a Gentile background became followers of Jesus and sought admission to the Christian churches, they saw no particular value in the observance of the rite of circumcision and wanted to be excused from it. Paul, invited to work with the Gentile element in the church, was sympathetic to their position. The experiences that he encountered with the Mosaic Law prior to his conversion convinced him that no one could ever be saved by mere obedience to a set of external laws. His own conversion to the Christian faith was brought about by the conviction that the spirit manifested in the life of Jesus took possession of the hearts and minds of individuals and enabled them to be saved. Accordingly, if Gentile Christians were possessed by this spirit, which for Paul was the true meaning of faith, it made little or no difference at all whether they conformed to the letter of the Mosaic Law. So long as Paul remained with these churches, the Jewish and Gentile elements seemed to get along without any serious trouble, each group following the dictates of its individual conscience. But after Paul left on one of his missionary tours, trouble began when prominent officials of the church in Jerusalem visited the newly established churches in Galatia.

These church visitors insisted that the law concerning circumcision, as well as the other requirements of the Mosaic Law, was binding on all Christians, including those coming from a Gentile background. Furthermore, they launched a vicious attack on Paul because of his attitude about this matter. They even went so far as to charge that he was an impostor and was guilty of misleading the membership of the churches. In response to these charges, Paul wrote the Epistle to the Galatians.

At the beginning of the letter, Paul expresses astonishment at what has taken place during his absence from the Galatians. Surprised at the attitude taken by the so-called leaders of the Jerusalem church, he is deeply disappointed when the people among whom he labored are persuaded by these visiting brethren to turn from the message that he proclaimed and accept as obligatory the requirements characteristic of Jewish legalism. Replying to the accusation that he is not a qualified leader of the Christian community, Paul defends his apostleship by declaring that Jesus Christ—not men—called him to that office. In support of this claim, he reviews the experiences that led to his conversion and the circumstances under which he carried on his work among the churches. He describes his relationship with the so-called "pillars of the church" at Jerusalem, explaining both the purpose and the outcome of his conferences with them. Although he did not receive from them any directive concerning the content of the message he was to proclaim, they were fully informed about the work he was doing and gave their approval to it, specifying in particular that he should devote his main efforts toward working with people entering the church from a Gentile background.

Following this introduction, Paul proceeds to the main point of the letter: to explain and clarify his position concerning the Law, which he does by detailing both its uses and its limitations as a means of obtaining salvation. The Law, he maintains, lays bare the defects in a person's character. In this respect, its function is like that of a looking-glass, which reveals blemishes but does not remove them. He writes, "So the law was put in charge to lead us to Christ that we might be justified by faith." When this goal has been reached, the Law is no longer necessary: "Clearly no one is justified before God by the law." Only by faith in Christ are people justified. By faith, Paul means something more than a mere intellectual assent to a number of facts in connection with the earthly life of Jesus. He means a commitment on the part of an individual to the way of life exemplified in the person of Jesus. A person possessed by the same spirit present in Jesus will be saved from sin and the spiritual death that sin brings. That person's desires and whole nature will be so transformed that he will do what is right because he wants to act that way rather than because he thinks it is a duty to be performed in order to obtain a reward.

Paul presents a series of arguments in support of his position regarding the Law. For example, he refers to Abraham as the father of the faithful and insists that Abraham's righteousness could not have been obtained by obedience to Mosaic laws because those laws were not given until centuries after Abraham died. Hence, Abraham must have obtained righteousness by faith. But if Abraham's righteousness was achieved by faith, the same must be true for all of his spiritual descendants. When God made his great promise to Abraham, all of Abraham's descendants were included. Christians are, according to Paul, of Abraham's seed, for it is said, "If you belong to Christ, then you are Abraham's seed, and heirs according to the promise." This same point is elaborated somewhat further in the allegory of Abraham's two sons. One son, Ishmael, was born of a slave woman, but the other son, Isaac, was born of a free woman. Ishmael represents people who are under bondage to the Law, and Isaac represents people who are free in Christ: "It is for freedom that Christ has set us free. Stand firm, then, and do not let yourselves be burdened again by a yoke of slavery."

The Epistle to the Galatians concludes with a description of the kind of life that a person will live who is filled with the Spirit of God, a life that sharply contrasts to the kind of life a person will live who has carnal desires. The quality of living is determined by whether or not an individual is possessed by the Spirit of Christ.

Commentary

Galatians is important for several reasons. First of all, it is among the earliest, if not *the* earliest, of all the writings in the New Testament. The letter gives us an insight into the problems that arose in the Christian churches of the first century after Jesus' physical death, and most important of all, it reveals one of the most essential elements in Paul's conception of Christianity. The letter has sometimes been called "Paul's declaration of independence," a designation that means freedom from bondage to laws of any kind, whether human laws or divine laws. On this particular point, Paul made a definite break not only with Judaism but with those Christians of Jewish descent who thought of the new religion in terms of obedience both to the Mosaic Law and the laws enunciated by Jesus.

These two competing conceptions of Christianity generally were held respectively by the Jewish and the Gentile elements in the membership of the Christian church. Those with a Jewish background held what may be called a legalistic conception of religion; the Gentile element under the leadership of Paul believed in a mystical conception. According to the latter view, salvation can never be achieved by trying to obey the requirements of the Law. Human nature is so constituted that a person necessarily follows the desires of the heart, and so long as these desires are contrary to the requirements of the Law, the result will be disobedience and a sense of guilt.

When Paul speaks of salvation by faith, he means the situation in which desires have been changed so that what one wants to do will coincide with what one ought to do, a transformation that humanity cannot bring about by itself alone but that can take place only when the Spirit of God in Christ takes possession of hearts and minds. Salvation, the very essence of Christian mysticism, means a union, or oneness, of the individual and God. In other words, God dwells within the life of the individual, whose nature is thereby changed from that which is prone to do evil to that prone to do good. The earthly career of Jesus is significant because it illustrates what can happen to any human being who allows the Spirit of God to take full possession of him, an idea clearly expressed by Paul when he says, "I have been crucified with Christ and I no longer live, but Christ lives in me."

Paul's argument did not convince all members of the Christian community. Many members, especially those of a Jewish background and understanding, still held to the legalistic view. The conflict between the legalistic and the mystical interpretations of religion can be traced through all of the successive periods of Christian history and is still one of the vital issues in contemporary theology.

1 AND 2 THESSALONIANS

Summary

Two letters that Paul wrote to the church in Thessalonica are preserved in the New Testament. The first letter—1 Thessalonians—was written to a community of believers who had been Christians for only a short period of time, probably no more than a few months. We learn from the Book of Acts that during Paul's stay in the city of Thessalonica, he preached in a Jewish synagogue on three successive Sabbath days. He evidently stayed in the city for some time thereafter and continued his work among the Gentiles. Although his ministry was successful to the extent that he won converts to Christianity from both Jews and Gentiles, he did encounter opposition, especially from Jews who resented very much that he was able to win Jewish followers. Because of this opposition, Paul wisely left the city for fear that the newly formed Christian community would be persecuted as he had been. He regretted that he must leave the Christians before they were well established in the faith, but he hoped that he might visit them again in the near future. When sickness prevented him from returning, he sent his colleague Timothy to strengthen the group and then report back to Paul on the progress that had been made. When Timothy returned to Paul with the good news that the members of the church were standing firm in their new faith, Paul wrote the First Epistle to the Thessalonians.

Paul congratulates the Thessalonians on their fidelity to the gospel that he had proclaimed while among them and urges them to remain steadfast in the faith. He warns them against sensuality and various forms of self-seeking, which are contrary to the spirit of the Christian way of life. But the main purpose of Paul's letter is to deal with a special problem that developed after Paul left the city. Paul shared with the Christians at Thessalonica his belief that the end of the age would come in the very near future. In part an inheritance from Jewish apocalypticism, this belief held that the messianic kingdom would be ushered in by a sudden catastrophic event, at which time the heavenly Messiah would descend on the clouds of heaven with power and great glory. When the first Christians accepted the idea that the man who had died on the cross was the real Messiah, they were convinced that he must return to earth to complete the work that he had begun. The manner of his second coming was conceived in accordance with the apocalyptic conceptions. This belief was common among the early Christians, and Paul accepted it along with the rest. Although the Christians were quite insistent that no one knew the exact time when this second coming would take place, they felt sure that it would occur during the lifetime of those who were then members of the Christian community.

After Paul left Thessalonica, some of the people who belonged to the church died. Because Jesus had not returned, serious doubts arose in the minds of those Thessalonians who were still living, for they had been led to believe that Jesus the Messiah would return before any of them died. As they saw it, Paul was mistaken on this point, which then caused them to wonder whether he might also be mistaken on other points as well. Obviously, an explanation of some kind was in order, and this situation, more than any other single factor, prompted the writing of Paul's First Epistle to the Thessalonians.

In his statement regarding Jesus' second coming, Paul says that he has in no way abandoned his faith that the return of Jesus to this earth will take place in the near future. Concerning those who died or who might die before Jesus returns, he states that they will be raised from the dead and will share equally with those who are still living at that time: "For the Lord himself will come down from heaven, with a loud command, with the voice of the archangel and with the trumpet call of God, and the dead in Christ will rise first." To this statement, Paul adds, "After that, we who are still alive and are left will be caught up together with them in the clouds to meet the Lord in the air. And so we will be with the Lord forever." The letter closes with a reminder that the Day of the Lord will come as a thief in the night. No one knows just when it will come, but all are admonished to live in such a way that they will be ready for it at any moment.

Paul's Second Epistle to the Thessalonians is in one sense a follow-up to the first letter. Evidently, the first letter was well received. People were satisfied with Paul's explanation concerning those who died and were ready and willing to suffer persecution if need be in order to remain true to the gospel that Paul preached. However, some members of the Christian community were so overly zealous about Paul's teaching that the end of the age was near at hand that they stopped making any plans for the future. Indeed, some of them stopped doing any work at all, believing that in this way they were demonstrating their faith in the nearness of the great event. Those who did not work were a burden to those who did work, and this situation constituted a new problem. Paul addresses this concern in his second letter.

After commending the Thessalonians for their loyalty and assuring them that God will deal justly with their persecutors, Paul proceeds to the main point of the letter. Although the coming Day of the Lord is near, it is not as close as some people think. Concerning a report that had circulated among the people stating that the day had already come, Paul tells the Thessalonians not to be deceived on this matter, for the Day of the Lord will not arrive until after certain events have taken place, and these events have not occurred yet. The specific events to which Paul refers concern the coming of an Antichrist, someone in whom the power of Satan has become incarnate and who will establish himself in the Temple at Jerusalem, working with signs and wonders to deceive people. The basis for Paul's statement along this line is found in the Jewish apocalyptic writings, which were fairly well known to him. Concerning the coming of this lawless Antichrist, Paul says that the Antichrist's activities are already in operation and would be carried out more fully except that he is now being restrained. (Presumably, Paul means that the Roman government is restraining the Antichrist.) In due time, the Antichrist will be revealed, and "the Lord Jesus will overthrow [the Antichrist] with the breath of his mouth and destroy by the splendor of his coming." The letter closes with an admonition to the Thessalonians to continue their regular lines of work and not to wait in idleness for the return of Jesus.

Commentary

The two letters to the Thessalonians are of interest from a historical point of view because they reveal conditions that existed in the newly formed Christian communities. They are also of value in that they indicate something of the extent to which the early church was influenced by Jewish apocalypticism in its beliefs concerning the second coming of Christ and the setting up of the messianic kingdom. Jewish apocalypses taught that there would be a resurrection of the dead in connection with other events that would usher in the new age. Paul was able to make use of these apocalyptic conceptions in answering the questions that so troubled the Christians in Thessalonica.

Both of Paul's letters to the Thessalonians were addressed to this one church and were occasioned by the problems associated with that particular group of church members. It is quite unlikely that Paul anticipated any further use to be made of his letters. Little if anything in them throws much light on the theological issues involved in Paul's interpretation of Christianity. The letters do, however, indicate the type of instruction that Paul gave to newcomers in the Christian movement.

1 AND 2 CORINTHIANS

Summary

Paul wrote at least four different letters to the church at Corinth, three of which are included in the New Testament. In what is now called 1 Corinthians, there is a reference to a former letter in which instruction was given concerning the type of conduct that should not be tolerated in a Christian church. 2 Corinthians is made up of two different letters. Chapters 1-9 are written in a conciliatory tone that indicates that they were composed after Chapters 10-13 were received and accepted by the members of the church. Chapters 10-13 belong to what is often referred to as the "painful letter," in which Paul replies to the many false charges made concerning him and his work. The largest part of Paul's correspondence was with the church at Corinth, for the problems that he encountered in this place were more numerous than he had found in other cities, and if his message could be successful in Corinth, there was good reason to believe that it could have results that would be equally as good in any other place.

Corinth was an important city in Paul's day. Generally known as a city devoted to pleasure-seeking, it was a center for Greek culture and a busy commercial city with a cosmopolitan atmosphere that brought together people and customs from different parts of the world. Pagan religions with sexual rites and ceremonies existed, and both materialism and immorality were the accepted order of the day. In view of these conditions, no wonder Paul said he began his Corinthian mission with fear. However, his work was successful from the beginning. He was especially anxious to guide new Christian converts with reference to the many perplexing problems that were bound to arise. In other places, the Jewish element, with its legalistic tendencies, created difficulties, but in Corinth, the moral problem caused the greater anxiety. The Corinthian church's membership was composed of people from many different quarters, including those whose training and environment were foreign to the Hebrew standards of morality. Paul was deeply concerned that the Christian church in Corinth should make no compromise with the morality—or immorality—customary in a pagan society.

The longest of the letters written to the church at Corinth is known in the New Testament as 1 Corinthians. Containing sixteen chapters dealing with a wide variety of topics, the first topic mentioned is that of divisions within the church. Four distinct factions correspond to the four individuals whose teachings were followed by the respective groups: Paul, Apollos, Cephas, and Christ. Reportedly, the household of Chloe informed Paul that serious quarrels had taken place among these factions. The spirit of independent thinking emphasized so strongly by the Greeks evidently was influencing the Corinthian Christians. Paul's manner of dealing with the problem is noteworthy. He does not insist that all members of the community should think alike on every subject, nor does he advocate that someone with authority should tell others what to believe. What he does insist on is a unity of spirit and purpose that will allow each group to learn from the others.

On the subject of immorality within the membership of the church, Paul is very explicit. Any type of immoral conduct must not be tolerated among the believers. If any of their number persist in following the low moral standards of the pagans, they should be excluded from membership. Association with evildoers cannot be avoided so long as church members live in a wicked city, but it need not be permitted within the group that is called Christian. The function of the church is to set a high standard for the society in which it exists, which cannot be done by permitting low standards among their own members: "Don't you know that a little yeast works through the whole batch of dough? Get rid of the old yeast that you may be a new batch without yeast—as you really are."

Disputes arising among members of the Christian community should be settled peaceably without going to a civil court: "The very fact that you have lawsuits among you means you have been completely defeated already. Why not rather be wronged?" Paul refers to a popular Jewish belief that saints are to have a part in the judgment of the world. Certainly the Corinthians are not qualified to have a part in the judgment of the world if they are unable to settle difficulties among themselves.

Sexual morality was a real problem in the church at Corinth. Neither monogamy nor chastity was regarded as obligatory in the pagan society in which many of the church members were reared before becoming Christians. Paul's instruction regarding marriage must be considered in accordance with his belief concerning the imminence of the second coming of Christ, as well as with his desire to have the church at Corinth exemplify a high standard of living. The same can be said about his advice concerning the impropriety of women speaking in church. In the city of Corinth, prostitutes customarily spoke in public, and to protect the reputation of the women in the Christian church, Paul thought it would be wise for them to remain silent. He explains, however, that this is merely his personal opinion; he has received no direct revelation to this effect.

Regarding the eating of meat that has been obtained from animals sacrificed to idols, everyone should follow the dictates of their own consciences, the only condition being that each person should have respect for the conscience of the person who does not agree with him. One should refrain from needlessly offending another person, even though by doing so it is necessary to curb one's own appetite.

The Christian churches customarily commemorated the events associated with Jesus' death and resurrection by partaking of a common meal together. Some of the people at Corinth failed to see the significance of this meal and made it an occasion for feasting. Paul explains that the purpose of this meal is not for the enjoyment of eating and drinking together but rather for a renewed dedication to the spirit made manifest in the life and death of Jesus. In other words, each individual should examine his own heart and life and bring them into harmony with the Spirit of Christ. Any grievances that people have with one another should be set aside in preparation for the eating of the meal together.

Spiritual gifts among the various members of the church is another topic treated at some length in 1 Corinthians. Using the analogy of the human body, in which each organ has its special function to perform and no one of them can be regarded as more vital than another, the same principle applies within the church, which is the body of Christ. Some members have the gift of prophecy, others that of teaching, and still others that of offering help in carrying forward the work of the church. Those who are apostles or prophets are not to think of themselves as superior to those who exercise other gifts, for all gifts are necessary, and the church would not be complete if any of them were missing. To those who boast that they have the gift of tongues and are therefore in a position to exercise lordship over others, Paul writes that this particular gift, like all of the others, should be evaluated in terms of its usefulness in promoting the Christian way of life. He does not condemn this gift for those who might find it useful, but he says that so far as he is concerned, it is better to speak a few words that will be understood by others than to speak at great length in an unknown tongue that is quite unintelligible to those who might hear it.

Following the discussion of spiritual gifts is Paul's immortal hymn to Christian love, which is one of the great classics of Christian literature. The hymn makes love the foundation for all Christian conduct. What wisdom was for the Greeks, love is for Christians: "And now these three remain: faith, hope and love. But the greatest of these is love."

After the discourse on love, Paul discusses resurrection. For him, the subject is of primary importance, for he considers resurrection the basis upon which the whole structure of Christianity rests. If Christ is not risen, then our hope is in vain. Christ's resurrection is attested to by a large number of witnesses, of whom Paul counts himself one of the last. The significance of the resurrection, more than a vindication of the Messiahship of Jesus, assures us that what happened in the case of Jesus can and will happen to all those who believe in him. The resurrection of the righteous will be associated with the second coming of Christ: "For the perishable must clothe itself with the imperishable, and the mortal with immortality. When the perishable has been clothed with the imperishable, and the mortal with immortality, then the saying that is written will come true: 'Death has been swallowed up in victory.'" The letter closes with an appeal for a contribution to help provide for the poor among the Christians in Jerusalem. Paul will stop at Corinth on his way to Jerusalem and take the gift with him.

The so-called "painful letter," which is found in Chapters 10-13 of 2 Corinthians, contains Paul's defense of himself and of his work to the charges made against him by his enemies, including the Jewish legalists who said that Paul was an impostor who had not been authorized by the proper authorities to work among the churches. The legalists supported their charge by pointing out that Paul had a "thorn in [his] flesh," some physical defect that, according to ancient Jewish regulations, would have barred a man from the priesthood. They further maintained that Paul supported himself by doing manual labor rather than by accepting support from the members of the church. This labor, in their judgment, was an admission on his part that he was not qualified to be supported in the way that was customary for duly authorized missionaries. The legalists also accused Paul of cowardice on the grounds that he was bold so long as he was writing letters, but he was very mild when present with the legalists in person. Other charges of a similar nature were made in an all-out attempt to discredit the religious work that Paul was doing.

To all of these charges, Paul makes a vigorous reply. He shows wherein the charges are false, and he recounts for the people at Corinth the many trials and hardships that he suffered for their sake and for the sake of the gospel. Although he apologizes for seeming to boast of his own attainments, he explains the necessity for doing so. He indicates further that his greatest disappointment lies not in the fact that charges of this sort have been made against him but that the members of the Corinthian church have apparently been persuaded by them.

The first nine chapters of what is now called 2 Corinthians are a letter that appears to have been written some time after the "painful letter" was received and accepted by the church. This letter contains an expression of gratitude for the change that has taken place among the Corinthian believers. Paul rejoices that they are now on the right track again, and he summarizes for them the essential meaning of the gospel that he first proclaimed to them. Using the language of the Old Testament prophet Jeremiah, Paul tells them that the Christian gospel is none other than the New Covenant, written "not on tablets of stone but on tablets of human hearts." Toward the close of the letter, he again reminds them of the collection to be taken for the poor in Jerusalem.

Commentary

Although the Corinthian letters were addressed to a single church and were concerned primarily with local problems existing at that time, they are of special interest to readers of the New Testament. One reason for this interest is that the letters were written at an early date; therefore, they throw considerable light on the character of the Christian movement prior to the writing of any gospel account of Jesus' life. Paul's statements concerning the resurrection of Jesus constitute the earliest preserved record of that event. The same is true of his account of the institution of the Lord's Supper. His remarks concerning the gift of tongues, along with the other gifts of the spirit, help us to understand the way in which these manifestations were viewed by the early church. Finally, the many problems discussed in 1 Corinthians tell us a great deal about the conditions that prevailed at that time.

Paul's account of the resurrection enables us to see how his view differed from those of the ancient Greeks and also from the view found in certain portions of the Old Testament. The Greeks believed in the doctrine of the soul's immortality. According to this doctrine, souls do not have a beginning or an end. They are eternal realities capable of existing apart from the bodies in which they were incarnated. This view was contrary to the Hebrew conception, which viewed man as a single unit including body, soul, and spirit; the soul was not something that existed apart from the body. After death, all went down to Sheol, a cavern below the earth, but no memory or consciousness of any kind attended this state of existence.

In contrast to these views, Paul believed in a genuine resurrection from physical death in which a person's individuality and moral worth would be preserved. But this preservation was not to be a reanimation of the corpse and a continuation of life as it had been before. Flesh and blood, Paul tells us, will not inherit God's kingdom. The body that is raised will not be the natural body but rather a spiritual body. Paul does not tell us what this spiritual body will be like, but he is sure that it will be a body of some kind, for the personality includes body, soul, and spirit, and salvation is not achieved until all three have been transformed together. The Gnostics of Paul's day, who believed that only spirit is good and that all matter is evil, taught that Jesus did not possess a physical body but only appeared to do so. For Paul, this position was untenable: Unless Jesus possessed a body in common with other human beings, his triumph over evil would have no significance for humans. Jesus' resurrection means a triumph of the entire personality over the forces of evil; what it means for Jesus it also means for all those who put their trust in him.

ROMANS

Summary

Paul promised the church members at Corinth that he would visit them again as soon as he had the opportunity, and it was not long after sending his last letter to them that the opportunity came and he was able to spend several months with them. During this time, probably the latter part of the year 57 A.D., he wrote a letter to the church at Rome, the most ambitious of all his letters and the only one in which he presents a systematic account of his understanding of the gospel. Because he had not visited the church at Rome and was unfamiliar with their local problems, the letter is not written in the form that he used in his earlier correspondence with the other churches. Instead, it is a carefully prepared statement of what he regarded as the essential elements of the Christian religion. Paul wanted the gospel proclaimed throughout the then-known world, and it seemed most appropriate that he should not only visit the church at Rome but gain its full support for the missionary program that he envisioned. We do not know how the church at Rome was started, but it existed during Paul's life, and there were good reasons for believing that it would soon become one of the leading Christian churches of the world. Paul wanted the Roman church to have a firsthand knowledge of the gospel that he preached, but unable personally to visit its members in the immediate future, he set forth his convictions in a letter addressed to the Romans.

Parts of the sixteen chapters in the Epistle to the Romans are so detailed that a full explanation of Paul's meaning would require a large volume of commentary. The main substance of the letter can be summarized briefly by stating the answers given to a number of pertinent questions: What is the gospel? Who needs it? Why is it needed? What is the nature of salvation? How is it achieved? What difference does salvation make in an individual's life? What difference does it make with reference to society as a whole? Many other points are discussed in Romans, but these questions are sufficient to indicate the letter's general character.

The gospel, we are told, is the power of God unto salvation, for in it the "righteousness from God is revealed, a righteousness that is by faith." Man is a sinful creature who follows his own heart's desires and is powerless to change these desires by himself alone. Only through the power of God, working in cooperation with the human spirit, can these desires be changed and brought into harmony with the divine will. Jesus' life illustrates the way in which the power of God can work in and through a human life, thus enabling a person to overcome evil temptations, which are always present in the world. The same power that enabled Jesus to overcome temptations is also available to all those who have faith in him. The faith by which God's righteousness is revealed involves beliefs but also includes something that grips the entire personality and finds expression not only in what one thinks but in feelings, attitudes, and actions. The salvation of which Paul writes is salvation from the power of evil that entices man to sin against himself and God. Salvation means a transformation of one's nature so that what one wants to do will coincide with what ought to be done.

This salvation is needed by everyone, for all have sinned and come short of the glory of God. Salvation is just as necessary for the Jew as it is for the Gentile, and necessary even for those people who feel that they do not need it, for they may be the ones who need it most. How well people think of themselves is determined by the standard that they use in judging themselves. Anyone who measures himself by the righteousness of God will know that he falls short and is in need of improvement. The salvation of which Paul speaks is not something that will automatically make a person's character equal to the righteousness of God, but it will move the person in that direction and keep bringing him ever nearer to that goal. But, again, it is important to know that this salvation is available only to those who recognize their need for it and who are receptive to the divine power that is constantly being offered to them.

In his discussion of the way in which salvation is to be achieved, Paul presents the same arguments that he used in his Epistle to the Galatians. He emphasizes that salvation is not brought about by efforts on the part of the individual to observe the requirements of the Law. It makes no difference so far as this point is concerned whether the laws are human or divine in their origin. Laws of any kind are powerless to make people good, evidence of which can be seen in the state of society as it existed in Rome during Paul's life. The Romans boasted of the superior quality of their system of laws. Although their laws were among the best that the nations of the world had known up to that time, Roman society had become notoriously corrupt. The state of this corruption is indicated in the closing verses of the first chapter of Paul's Epistle to the Romans.

Concerning corruption, Paul argues that Jews are not better off than the Romans. The Romans have had their human laws, and Jews have had divine laws, but in neither case have the laws changed the desires of humans or transformed their natures from that which is evil into that which is good. Only by faith can a transformation of this kind occur. In this connection, Paul writes about justification by faith. Having pointed out that "no one will be justified in [God's] sight by observing the law; rather, through the law we become conscious of sin," he goes on to say that everyone is "justified freely by [God's] grace through the redemption that came by Jesus Christ." And again, he says, "For we maintain that a man is justified by faith apart from observing the law." People are in need of justification because they are estranged from God. They are not living in harmony with their own best interests, which is equivalent to saying that they are not in harmony with the divine will. Justification is that which overcomes the estrangement and puts people on the right track, a process that happens when the Spirit of God takes possession of one's heart and life. A person's desires are changed, and a "new creature" emerges, which is what Paul means by salvation.

Having developed his argument concerning the means of salvation, Paul supports his position by referring to Abraham, as he did in his letter to the Galatians. Abraham's faith was "credited to him as righteousness"; by faith, those who are his spiritual descendants can be saved. Jesus is the supreme example of faith in that he was a human being in whom the Spirit of God was manifested more completely than in any other person. In this respect, Paul thinks of Jesus as the ideal man in the same way that Adam was regarded as the symbol of the human race. Just as in Adam we all died, so in Christ are we all made alive. Adam's disobedience illustrates what happens in the lives of all human beings, and Jesus' triumph over the forces of evil illustrates what can happen when the

Spirit takes possession of a person's entire nature. This point, Paul insists, is the true meaning of Christian baptism and symbolizes the death and burial of one's sinful nature and a resurrection into a new quality of living.

Paul's own experience with the Law when he was studying to become a rabbi is described at some length to demonstrate again the impotence of the Law in contrast with the power of faith to transform one's nature. Trying to achieve salvation through obedience to the Law was indeed a miserable type of existence, comparable to having a dead person strapped to one's own body. In this state of affairs, a person is a slave to sin, as Paul notes: "I do not understand what I do. For what I want to do I do not do, but what I hate I do." And again, "Now if I do what I do not want to do, it is no longer I who do it, but it is sin living in me that does it." Under these conditions, Paul cries out in the name of humanity, "What a wretched man I am! Who will rescue me from this body of death?" The answer is that deliverance comes through faith in Jesus Christ: "Therefore, there is now no condemnation for those who are in Christ Jesus, because through Christ Jesus the law of the Spirit of life set me free from the law of sin and death."

The effects of salvation will be manifest first in the changed life of the individual and then, as this salvation takes place in increasing numbers, in society. The life of the Spirit that frees one from bondage to the Law does not give one the license to sin, nor can laws legitimately be violated just because they conflict with one's immediate desires. The Christian will be a law-abiding citizen whose freedom consists in the fact that he no longer wants to act contrary to laws. He will do what is right because he desires to act that way, not because he does it from a pure sense of duty or as a means of gaining a reward.

With reference to the future of the Jewish people, Paul expresses the hope that they, too, will be included with those who are saved through the gospel. Since the gospel is of divine origin and the great heroes of Israel achieved righteousness through faith, that the Jews would reject the gospel seems strange. When they refused to accept it, the opportunity was extended to the Gentiles. But Paul does not envision a complete break between Judaism and Christianity. He believes that the Jews eventually will come to accept the gospel since God is not willing that any person should perish but that all might be saved.

The closing part of Paul's Epistle to the Romans contains instruction in the manner of living. Paul tells the Christians in Rome to have respect for the civil government: "The authorities that exist have been established by God." He does not mean that Christians should obey the civil laws when these laws conflict with the laws of God but rather that Christians should not attempt to hide their conduct from the rulers nor escape the punishment that the state inflicts. Earthly governments are not perfect, and some laws are bound to be unjust. Nevertheless, laws preserve order in society, and Christians should abide by them. As in the other letters to different churches, Paul asks the Christians at Rome to contribute to the fund that he is gathering for the relief of the poor in Jerusalem.

Commentary

In no portion of the New Testament is the dynamic and universal character of Christianity set forth more clearly than in Paul's Epistle to the Romans, evidence of which can be seen in the fact that so many of the revival and reform movements in the course of Christian history have been started and promulgated by a restudy of this portion of the New Testament. For example, in the sixteenth century, Martin Luther's commentary on Romans was an important factor in the promotion of the Protestant Reformation, and in the twentieth century, when Karl Barth published his analysis of Romans, a new era was introduced in the contemporary interpretations of Christianity. Paul's letter to the church in Rome is without question one of the great documents in Christian literature. It has furnished the inspiration and guidance for many of the important developments that have taken place in the life of the church during the past and in all likelihood will continue to do so in the future.

The dynamic character of the gospel as Paul understands it is illustrated in the introductory portions of his letter, where Paul refers to the gospel as something that is powerful: "the power of God for the salvation of everyone who believes." The gospel is more than the acceptance of a set of speculative ideas, even though these are not necessarily excluded; it is the righteousness of God, an active force operating in the lives of people who are ready and willing to receive it. Available to all those who recognize their need for it regardless of their religious backgrounds, the gospel does for those persons who are willing to accept it something that they are wholly unable to do for themselves: produce within them a changed nature so that the desires of their hearts will coincide with what they ought to do.

The universality of the gospel is exemplified in the way in which it completely transcends all distinctions between Jew and Gentile. Among the early Christians, as well as in other communities, certain people believed that salvation was only for the Jews. Paul's letter to the Romans addresses a church whose membership is composed of people from both Jewish and Gentile backgrounds, and he wants to set forth the meaning of the gospel in terms that will be intelligible to all of them. Because he is familiar with both Judaism and Hellenistic culture, he uses concepts drawn from each of these sources to communicate his version of Christianity. Thus we find him using the terminology of Jewish eschatology and apocalypticism, as well as the language of the mystery cults and other forms of Gentile religion, to explain his conception of the real significance of the life, death, and resurrection of Jesus. His use of terms drawn from such different sources was not without its dangers: His readers might very well interpret these terms in a manner that was other than he intended. He did not want to convey the idea that the use of these terms in connection with the Christian religion was exactly like what either the Jews or the Gentiles had been taught. Rather, he used them to distinguish similarities that would aid in their proper understanding.

Salvation, as this term was used by the Jews of Paul's day, primarily refers to a future event when the kingdoms of this earth will be brought to an end and the new age identified as the kingdom of God will be established. The saved will be those who are not destroyed at that time but who will be permitted to live under the new order of things. Although Paul does not reject this view entirely, he couples with it the idea that salvation is something to be achieved here and now, as well as in the future. Being saved from yielding to evil temptations is achieved not by conformity or obedience to laws but by faith in the righteousness of God, manifested in the life of Jesus the Christ. In support of this conviction, Paul quotes the Old Testament prophet Habakkuk, who said that "the righteous will live by his faith." Paul's use of the word "faith" is somewhat different from that of the ancient prophet, for Habakkuk was speaking about his belief concerning the future that was in store for those who lived in obedience to the Law, or commands, of God; Paul is discussing a salvation that is apart from the Law. Thus we see how Paul uses a familiar Hebrew term to communicate to his readers a concept that was in some respects new to them.

In his discussion of the need for salvation, Paul implies what has often been called the doctrine of original sin. The Adam of the Genesis story is generally interpreted as a reference to all humanity. The same tendency toward evil present in Adam is also present in every human being. Yielding to these temptations brings about an estrangement between an individual and God. To explain the way in which this estrangement can be overcome, Paul draws analogies from customary court procedures and from concepts used in the mystery cults. He shows how all humans are guilty before God, and in this connection he speaks of justification and redemption. When the sinner acknowledges his guilt, he is accepted by God, and past sins are no longer held against him. Justified in the sense that the estrangement has been overcome, the former sinner is now in accord with the divine will, which does not mean that he will never sin again, but he will continually be aware of his need for improvement and will seek divine aid for its accomplishment. To explain the change that takes place in life when a person experiences justification and possesses the same spirit present in Jesus, Paul uses the language of the mystery cults. Just as the heroic redeemer of these cults experienced a death, burial, and resurrection, so Christian baptism means a death of one's old nature, a burial, and a resurrection in which one walks in a newness of life.

LETTERS WRITTEN IN CAPTIVITY

Summary

When Paul wrote his Epistle to the Romans, he expressed hope that he would visit the church in that city as soon as arrangements could be made following his journey to the city of Jerusalem. The visit to Rome was delayed for about three years, but when he finally reached the city, he arrived as a prisoner awaiting trial before the court of the emperor. While in Jerusalem, he was arrested on the charge of causing a riot in the Temple. After being held in prison in Caesarea for about two years, he was transferred to Rome at his own request to be tried. After spending about three years as a prisoner in Rome, he was tried and convicted.

Seven letters in the New Testament initially were credited to Paul on the assumption that he wrote them while a prisoner in Rome. However, three of these letters—1 and 2 Timothy, and Titus—now are generally recognized as belonging to a period somewhat later than Paul's death, and many New Testament scholars believe the same is true of the Epistle to the Ephesians, but the authorship question is in no way a completely settled issue. However, in all four of these letters, Paul's influence is recognizable; possibly they were written by disciples of Paul who wrote in accordance with the instruction that they believed he would have given. Three other letters—Philippians, Philemon, and Colossians—are still regarded as genuine letters of Paul, although some question remains about where they were written, for no conclusive evidence indicates whether it was Rome or Ephesus, in both of which Paul was a prisoner.

PHILIPPIANS

The Epistle to the Philippians is an informal correspondence that Paul sent in response to a gift he received from the church at Philippi. Knowing that Paul was in prison and probably in need of material benefits, the Philippian church sent one of its members, Epaphroditus, with a gift of money and the intention of staying with Paul to assist him in any way that Epaphroditus could. However, Epaphroditus became ill and was forced to return home, and Paul sent this letter to the church of Philippi with him.

The letter begins with an expression of thanks for the gift and a prayer for the well-being of the church. With reference to his own personal experience, Paul says that his only desire is to be free from prison so that he might be of greater service to the church. Regarding it a great privilege to be counted worthy to suffer for the cause of Christ, he writes a famous hymn concerning Jesus, "who, being in very nature God, did not consider equality with God something to be grasped, but made himself nothing, taking the very nature of a servant, being made in human likeness." Paul commends this spirit of humility and service to the church at Philippi, urging that its members be of the same mind as that which was manifest in Jesus.

Paul tells the church members that Timothy will visit them in the near future and asks that they receive him with kindness. Interrupting the main course of his letter to warn against the propaganda being circulated by Jewish legalists, he reviews his own experiences with Judaism and his conversion to the Christian faith. With a few practical admonitions and a prayer for God's blessing on the Philippian church, Paul closes the letter.

PHILEMON

The Epistle to Philemon, a very short letter dealing with only one topic, certainly was written by Paul. Onesimus, Philemon's runaway slave, had in some way contacted Paul and come under the influence of the Christian gospel. For Paul, the situation was in some respects threatening: For a slave to desert his master was considered a very serious offense legally punishable by death, and anyone who apprehended a runaway slave was to return the slave immediately to the slave's master. How long Paul knew about Onesimus we are not told, but evidently it was long enough for Onesimus to receive instruction concerning the meaning of the gospel. Once Onesimus accepted the Christian gospel, Paul insisted that the slave return to his master.

Paul's purpose in writing this letter is to request that Philemon not only take back Onesimus as his slave but that he treat him as a brother in Christ. The letter is written in a most tactful manner, for Paul knows that Philemon has a legal right to put Onesimus to death. Paul therefore appeals to Philemon's conscience as a Christian brother to recognize that Onesimus is not only a slave but also a child of God. In the eyes of the Roman government, Onesimus is a criminal deserving of death, but as Christians, both he and his master are brothers in Christ.

COLOSSIANS

The Epistle to the Colossians is addressed to a church that Paul did not visit. Epaphras, a visitor from Colossae, came to see Paul and brought news and greetings from the Christians in that city. Following a series of conversations with this visitor, Paul wrote his letter to the Colossian church. One of the main purposes of the letter is to warn the church members about a certain dangerous philosophy that was making inroads in that community. The particular doctrine that Paul apparently had in mind was a form of Gnosticism, a mixture of both philosophical and religious ideas. Believing that matter is evil and only spirit is good, the Gnostics held that the physical world was not created by a supreme being because a perfect deity would not have direct contact with an evil world. The world came into existence through the action of a series of intermediary beings whose worship was a necessary means toward human salvation. Paul writes that in Jesus there dwells all the fullness of the Godhead; there is no need for the worship of these intermediary powers. Furthermore, he rejects the asceticism and the sensual indulgence associated with the Gnostic conceptions of salvation.

Commentary

The letters that Paul wrote while a prisoner either in Ephesus or in Rome are the latest writings of his that are preserved in the New Testament. They represent his most mature thought concerning the meaning of Christianity and are of special value for that reason. Although he has some things to say with reference to particular problems in local churches, he mainly discusses the significance of Jesus' life in relation to both the salvation of human beings and its place in the scheme of the universe as a whole. The letters are also of interest because they reveal the changes that took place in Paul's own thinking during the years following his conversion to Christianity. Perhaps the most significant change that can be noted in these later writings lies in the fact that Paul no longer talks about the end of the age in terms of Jewish apocalypticism. His teaching emphasizes the quality of living that is made possible when a person's life is transformed by the indwelling presence of the Spirit of Christ.

Some critics maintain that in Paul's later years, he speaks less about the historic Jesus and more about the cosmic Christ. This criticism can be misleading if it suggests that, for Paul, the earthly life of Jesus was unimportant or did not provide the foundation on which Christianity is built. On the other hand, in Paul's judgment, the power of the one and only God of the universe, working in Jesus, makes Jesus' life significant and thus brings to all humanity an opportunity to see how the redemption of humanity can be achieved.

THE SYNOPTIC GOSPELS AND ACTS

The earliest Christians did not have any written records of the life and teachings of Jesus. During the course of Jesus' public ministry, no one felt the need to make a written account of what Jesus did or what he said. Those who were close to him could pass to others what they remembered about him. Those who looked upon him as the Messiah believed that he would soon inaugurate a new kingdom; all that was necessary to know about him could be remembered until that time. They were, of course, sorely disappointed when he was put to death on the cross, for it seemed as though his cause was lost. Afterward, they were convinced that despite his death, he really was the Messiah. With this recognition on their part, there was now a new reason for remembering the events of his earthly life. What he had done before his death took on a new meaning in relationship to what happened since that time. Evidence was needed that would convince unbelievers that Jesus was the Messiah, and the faith of those who already believed in him needed to be confirmed and strengthened. The early Christians believed that Jesus would soon return to earth and complete the work of preparing for the coming kingdom. An authentic record of his life on earth would be a great help to those who were expecting his return, and with the passing of the years, the need for such a record was greatly increased.

That the Gospels were not written until nearly forty years after Jesus' death often raises questions concerning their reliability. The situation is complicated also by the fact that the Gospels are not all alike, nor is it possible to harmonize completely all of the materials contained in them. They agree on many points but disagree on others. What has been called the "synoptic problem" concerns finding some hypothesis that addresses the origin of the Gospels and that accounts both for their agreements and for their differences. Many different solutions have been proposed, but no one of them is fully accepted by all New Testament scholars. The most widely held view maintains that the Gospels, in their present form, are based very largely on older source materials in existence at a time not far removed from the events that they record. If the authors of the Gospels used the same sources, the similarities between the Gospels would be explained; likewise, that other sources were used by only one of the authors would explain the differences that we find when comparing the different accounts. That the earliest source materials were written by people who were contemporaries of Jesus and his disciples adds considerable weight to their historical reliability.

The Gospel of Mark is generally agreed to be the oldest of the three Synoptic Gospels—Matthew, Mark, and Luke—and was used as one of the sources for each of the other two. The outline of events as they occur in Mark is followed by each of the other biographers, and about two thirds of the material found in Mark is also present in both Matthew and Luke. This similarity suggests very strongly, although it does not prove, that the authors of Matthew and Luke took their materials from Mark. There is also reason to believe that both Matthew and Luke had another source in common. Both of them report a considerable amount of Jesus' teachings in addition to what is contained in Mark. To account for this extra material, it is assumed that a document composed of Jesus' sayings was in existence and was another source for Matthew and Luke. Scholars refer to this other source with the letter *Q*, the first letter of the German word *Quelle*, which in English means *source*. Because there is some unique material in Matthew, possibly its author used still another source *M*, which was not used in any of the other Gospels. The same holds true for the Gospel of Luke, and scholars use the letter *L* to refer to his special source. This hypothesis concerning the origin of the Synoptic Gospels appears to be confirmed by the introductory paragraph found in the Gospel of Luke, which states that several lives of Jesus have been written and that Luke's author's purpose is to write a definitive biography about Jesus.

THE GOSPEL OF MARK

Summary

From a historical point of view, Mark, being the oldest of the Gospels, is the most reliable, the reason for which is not merely that it is closer in point of time to the events that it records but that less interpretation concerns the meaning of these events than in the other Gospels. The author of Mark was a Christian named John Mark, a relatively obscure person so far as New Testament records indicate. Believed to have been a relative of Barnabas, who was one of the leaders of the church in Antioch, Mark accompanied Paul and Barnabas on one of their missionary journeys and was a companion of Peter during the time when that disciple spent his last years in the city of Rome.

The Gospel of Mark records with as much accuracy as possible the main events of the life and teachings of Jesus. A record of this kind furnished evidence to support the belief that Jesus was the true Messiah; by believing in Jesus, people could obtain salvation. That this gospel has been preserved in the form in which we have it today testifies to the importance attached to it from its beginning. A relatively short gospel, most of the material contained in it is reproduced in the Gospels that were written later. The authors of both Matthew and Luke appear to have included in each of their gospels all that was necessary to be remembered from Mark, in which case the oldest of the Gospels would be replaced by later and more complete accounts. That Mark survived these attempts to replace it is probably due to the fact that its origin was regarded as more authentic than the others and that it was highly prized by the church at Rome, which was destined to become one of the leading churches in the entire Christian movement.

Although the Gospel of Mark became one of the main sources for the writings of Matthew and Luke, it, too, was based on older source materials. One of these, according to a well-authenticated tradition, was an oral source. Papias, an early church father writing about 140 A.D., tells us that Mark obtained much of the material for his gospel from stories related to him by Peter, one of Jesus' disciples. This statement by Papias has been accepted as reliable by most New Testament scholars, for it very reasonably explains the contents found in the first half of Mark. This portion of the gospel consists of a series of relatively independent stories assembled without reference to the particular time and place of each occurrence or the chronological order of the events. The particular sequence in which the stories are recorded is evidently due to Mark's arrangement of them. The second half of this gospel contains a fairly detailed account of the day-to-day happenings that occurred in or near the city of Jerusalem during the brief period that preceded the arrest, trial, and crucifixion of Jesus.

The Gospel of Mark begins with a brief account of the work of John the Baptist, who is referred to as the forerunner of the coming Messiah. During these days, Jesus came from Nazareth in Galilee and was baptized by John in the Jordan River. Following Jesus' baptism, the Spirit of God rested upon Jesus, and from that time forward Jesus dedicated his life to the work of preparing people for the coming of God's kingdom. His public ministry was preceded by a period of temptation in the wilderness. Soon after the arrest of John the Baptist, Jesus appeared in Galilee, preaching the gospel and saying "The kingdom of God is near. Repent and believe the good news!" After choosing his disciples, he began a vigorous program of evangelism by preaching to the people and healing the sick who were brought to him.

Mark was apparently more impressed by the mighty works that Jesus performed than by the content of Jesus' teaching. More than half of Mark's gospel is devoted to giving an account of the remarkable deeds that Jesus performed. Many of these deeds dealt with healing the sick. For example, Mark tells of the healing of Simon's mother-in-law, who was afflicted with a severe fever. A paralytic who was lowered through a hole in the roof was healed and made to walk again. A man with a withered hand was made whole when he encountered Jesus in a synagogue. Unclean spirits were driven out of the Gerasene demoniacs. Jairus' daughter, who was at the point of death, was made well again. A woman suffering from a hemorrhage was healed, and a boy who was possessed by an unclean spirit since early childhood was restored to health in the presence of his father. In addition to these miracles of healing, Mark reports such incidents as the stilling of the storm on the Sea of Galilee, the feeding of the five thousand, the cursing of the fig tree, and other significant events. Most of the miracle stories furnish the occasion for discourses on various themes. For example, the parable of the sower is related together with the interpretation that Jesus made concerning it. Although Jesus made considerable use of parables in his teaching, Mark does not relate very many of them.

As Jesus continued his work in the cities and villages of Galilee, many of the common people gladly heard him. But Jesus' plain-spoken messages aroused opposition on the part of Jewish elders and rulers, some of whom took issue with what Jesus was saying and sought to entrap him with clever arguments. Mark reports several of these clashes between Jesus and members of the Pharisee and Sadducee sects. In connection with these encounters, Jesus expressed some of his most important teachings. Following the opposition to his work that developed in the region of Galilee, he journeyed with his disciples into the northwest sections of the country, where Tyre and Sidon were located. Returning to Galilee, they passed through Caesarea Philippi, where the disciples raised the question of Jesus' Messiahship. Jesus revealed to them that he was the Messiah but told them to say nothing concerning this revelation. After a brief return to his home country, he announced to his disciples that he was going to carry his mission to the Jewish headquarters in the city of Jerusalem. When he told them what would likely happen to him at the hands of the chief priests and rulers of the nation, the disciples were shocked, for they did not believe that such violent harm could possibly happen to the Messiah. They were still hopeful that the time was at hand when Jesus and his followers would enter the promised kingdom.

In close connection with the journey to Jerusalem, Mark reports a number of Jesus' discourses, including Jesus' interview with a rich, young ruler, his reply to James and John when they asked for a prominent place in the new kingdom, the discourse given when the money-changers were driven from the Temple, the discussion about paying taxes to the Roman government, Jesus' foretelling of the coming destruction of Jerusalem, and his instruction to the disciples when he ate the Passover meal with them.

Jesus' entrance into the city of Jerusalem was a joyous occasion for those who believed that Jesus was about to establish a new kingdom. But this joy was of short duration, for the priests and rulers decided that Jesus was an enemy of their cause and determined to get rid of him. Mark reports the experience in the Garden of Gethsemane, the betrayal by Judas, Peter's three denials, the trial before Pilate, and the story of the crucifixion. The Gospel of Mark concludes with a brief account of the women who went to the tomb where Jesus' body was placed and discovered that Jesus had risen from the dead.

Commentary

The Gospel of Mark has several unique characteristics. It reports nothing concerning Jesus' birth, his childhood, or his activities prior to the time when he was baptized by John. This absence is remarkable in view of the beliefs that many early Christians held concerning the manner of Jesus' birth and the way in which his birth was announced in advance. If these beliefs were fairly common among Christians at the time when Mark wrote, he evidently did not think of them as having sufficient importance to be included in his gospel. For him, the real significance of Jesus' career began at the time of Jesus' baptism and his decision to devote his life to the work of God's kingdom. Throughout the gospel, Mark particularly emphasizes Jesus' humanity. For example, when Jesus becomes weary from his many activities, some people question whether he is behaving in a normal manner. At one point during the early ministry in Galilee, his friends are greatly disturbed because of the way he attracts attention, and even the members of his own family suspect that he is ill. However, Jesus never claims any greatness for himself over that of other people. When an ardent admirer calls him "Good teacher," Jesus promptly rebukes him, saying that no one should call him good since that quality belongs only to God.

Jesus never claimed to have any special power that was not available to others. The miracles that he performed were not meant to display any power of his own but rather to show how the power of God could be used in and through human lives. Jesus instructed his disciples that the works that he performed they would do also. He even told them they would perform greater works than he had done. Further evidence that his miraculous works were not done in order to attract attention to himself can be seen in the fact that after he healed someone, he would caution that person to say nothing about the healing. For example, a leper once came to Jesus pleading for help. Jesus, after healing the leper, said to him, "See that you don't tell this to anyone. But go, show yourself to the priest," according to the Law of Moses. In the synagogue at Capernaum, Jesus healed a man with an unclean spirit. When the man cried out that Jesus was the "Holy One of God," Jesus told the man to keep silent.

In the Gospel of Mark, Jesus does not reveal his Messiahship to his disciples until they reach Caesarea Philippi. This event was shortly before they began the journey to Jerusalem, and even then he cautioned them not to say anything about it. Whether Jesus was conscious of his Messiahship from the beginning of his ministry or it was revealed gradually in his own mind is not made entirely clear. Mark undoubtedly wrote with as much objectivity as possible, but viewing the events of Jesus' life from the perspective of what the Christians of thirty or forty years after Jesus' death believed about Jesus, Mark could not refrain from reporting some events in such a manner that they would agree with these later beliefs. An example of this kind can be seen in the explanation that Jesus gives for the failure of so many people to be convinced by the message he preached and the deeds he performed. To account for these disbelievers' attitude, Jesus refers to a statement used by the prophet Isaiah when the prophet attributed the Israelite people's failure to listen to the words of Yahweh to the fact that their eyes had been so darkened that they could not see the light and their ears had been made so dull that they could not understand. To Mark, nothing less than blindness and deafness could have caused people to reject Jesus' mission, which was so obviously in harmony with the divine will. But again, it was quite impossible for Mark to refrain from interpreting many of Jesus' sayings in view of what had occurred since Jesus' death, burial, and resurrection.

Mark gives a rather full account of Jesus' teachings and activities during the days preceding Jesus' trial and crucifixion. He tells about the women's visit to the tomb and their surprise at finding Jesus risen from the dead. We do not know what else Mark may have said concerning the appearances of Jesus after the resurrection, for the original ending of his gospel has been lost. The last twelve verses of the gospel as it now appears in the New Testament were not part of the earliest manuscripts. Even in later manuscripts, these verses are not the same. Evidently, they were added by an editor who recognized that something was lacking in the manuscript copy and therefore attempted to complete it. That the original ending of Mark's gospel has been lost is a serious handicap to readers of the New Testament, for when we omit the verses that were added, the account of the resurrection breaks off in the middle of the story. In fact, it breaks off in the middle of a sentence. Having the remainder of the story would furnish valuable information since it would be the oldest gospel account of this most important event, but we do not know what happened to the original ending of the manuscript.

THE GOSPEL OF MATTHEW

Summary

Although the Gospel of Matthew was not the first gospel written, it is generally regarded as the most important and was placed first in the collection of writings that constitute the New Testament. In addition to materials found in the Gospel of Mark, the Gospel of Matthew contains a large number of Jesus' sayings and discourses and also a group of stories not found in any of the other Gospels. Matthew contains an extensive account of Jesus' teachings and as such is considered the most authentic and fundamental doctrine of the Christian religion. Readers of the gospel are impressed with certain general characteristics that distinguish it from other writings in the New Testament, one of which is the systematic way in which the contents of the gospel have been arranged. For example, the document as a whole falls into five distinct divisions, with an introductory section preceding the first division and a concluding section following the last. Each of the five divisions is composed of a portion of the narrative concerning Jesus' activities, together with a group of his teachings. The words "When Jesus had finished saying these things" end each division. This five fold division of the Gospel of Matthew corresponds in a general way to the divisions found in various parts of the Old Testament.

The sayings and discourses of Jesus are apparently taken in large part from an older document known as "The Sayings of

Jesus," or the *Q* source, and are combined with the narrative found in Mark in the following manner: The author of Matthew uses the same sequence of events that are recorded in Mark, but at appropriate intervals he interrupts the narrative and inserts a group of sayings. One example of this kind is usually referred to as the Sermon on the Mount. The materials included in this sermon also can be found in the Gospel of Luke, but they are scattered throughout Luke instead of being grouped together. When Matthew reaches that place in the Marcan narrative where Jesus teaches the people, he inserts this group of sayings. The organization of these sayings into a single sermon thus appears to be the result of Matthew's arrangement.

Another rather striking characteristic of the Gospel of Matthew is its high regard for the teachings of the Old Testament. There are approximately fifteen instances in which Matthew interprets some event in the life of Jesus as a fulfillment of a prophecy in the Old Testament. Evidently the author of Matthew did not think of Christianity as something that involved a definite break with the Jewish religion. Instead, he considered Christianity as a continuation and fulfillment of that which had been set forth in the literature of the Old Testament. Not for a moment did he think that Jesus changed or set aside the requirements of the Mosaic Law. Rather, Matthew supplements and interprets the requirements in a manner that accords with their original purpose. In his zeal to show a close relationship between Jesus and the Old Testament, Matthew appears at times to make references to incidents in the life of Jesus for no other reason than to document them as fulfilling Old Testament prophecy.

A third characteristic of the Gospel of Matthew is its interest in ecclesiastical affairs. As the only gospel that makes a direct mention of the church, much of the instruction recorded in Matthew is especially appropriate for particular situations that arose in the Christian churches of the first century.

Matthew begins with a genealogy of Jesus that traces his ancestry as far back as Abraham. The ancestry is traced on the side of Joseph, although the author later definitively states that Joseph was not Jesus' father. Following the genealogy is an account of the wise men's visit to Jesus' birth site, Herod's attempt to destroy the newborn child, and the flight into Egypt for the child's protection.

After the death of Herod, the family returned and settled in the Galilee town of Nazareth, which, according to Matthew, fulfilled another Old Testament prophecy.

Following these introductory stories, Matthew continues his gospel by narrating the events in Jesus' public career in the same sequence as they are found in Mark. As mentioned before, this sequence is interrupted at appropriate intervals for the insertion of discourses that Jesus delivered on various occasions. This scheme enables Matthew to combine Jesus' teachings and events in one continuous narrative. While the author of the Gospel of Mark seems to have been impressed most of all with the wonderful deeds that Jesus *performed*, Matthew places the major emphasis on the marvelous things that Jesus *taught*. Some of the teachings were spoken directly to the inner group of disciples, but at different times and places Jesus addressed the multitudes, among whom were many who gladly heard him. Often Jesus spoke in parables, for in this way he could communicate his ideas concerning the kingdom of heaven in language that the people could understand because the parables were drawn from people's own experiences.

One of the important issues in the early history of the church was the attitude that Christians should have concerning the laws that are recorded in the Old Testament. Paul insisted that salvation is obtained by faith and not by obedience to laws. This insistence led some Christians to believe that whether or not these laws should be obeyed was a matter to be decided by an individual's own conscience. Many Jewish Christians did not agree with this individualistic attitude. The author of the Gospel of Matthew appears to have been one of them. According to his version of Jesus' Sermon on the Mount, Jesus stated, "I tell you the truth, until heaven and earth disappear, not the smallest letter, not the least stroke of a pen, will by any means disappear from the Law until everything is accomplished." And he also said, "Anyone who breaks one of the least of these commandments and teaches others to do the same will be called least in the kingdom of heaven." Some scholars maintain that this last passage directly refers to Paul and his followers. Of this we cannot be sure, but evidently Matthew was far more sympathetic toward the religion of Judaism than was true of other writers. In the story of the Canaanite woman who comes to Jesus imploring help for her daughter, who is possessed by a demon, Jesus says to the woman, "I was sent only to the lost sheep of Israel." When the woman responds, "Yes, Lord, but even the dogs eat the crumbs that fall from their master's table," Jesus commends her for her faith and heals her daughter.

This narrative of the woman and her daughter represents only one aspect of the Gospel of Matthew. Many other passages indicate that the gospel was intended for all people and not merely for Jews. In the parable of the householder who plants a vineyard, rents it to tenants, and leaves his servants in charge of the rent collection while he travels to another country, we have a clear indication that the scope of the gospel is inclusive of Gentiles. In this parable, the servants are beaten, stoned, and even put to death by the tenants. Then the householder sends his son to collect the rent, but when the tenants see the son, they cast him out of the vineyard and kill him, clearly a reference to the fact that Jesus was put to death because of his Jewish enemies. The parable concludes with the words, "Therefore I tell you that the kingdom of God will be taken away from you and given to a people who will produce its fruit."

While Matthew insists that the laws of God are eternal and that Christians and Jews are obligated to observe them, he recognizes that formal obedience in itself is not enough. This recognition is discussed in various parts of the Sermon on the Mount, as indicated by use of the expression "You have heard that it was said. . . . But I tell you. . . ." The point of the contrast in each instance is that not only the overt act but the *motive* that lies behind the act is of primary importance. This point is emphasized again in many of the discussions that Jesus held with the Scribes and Pharisees. Replying to their insistence about following certain regulations concerning eating and drinking, Jesus made it clear that the inner motives of the heart and mind are of far greater importance than following customs regarding table etiquette.

The early church seems to have entertained two different views concerning the coming of the kingdom of God. One view held that it was strictly a future event, to be established at the end of the age but not until after the earthly kingdoms had been destroyed; the other view held that the kingdom was already present insofar as right principles and motives were established in human hearts. In the Gospel of Matthew, certain passages support each view. Perhaps the author felt that these two opposing beliefs could be harmonized by regarding the kingdom within as a kind of preparation for a more complete establishment in the world without at some future time. In the chapter in which the sayings of Jesus concerning the coming destruction of the city of Jerusalem are identified as predictions concerning the second coming of Christ and the end of the world, we find a group of statements that discuss the signs that will portend when Jesus' return to this earth is near at hand. These signs include wars and rumors of wars, and famines and earthquakes in various places. The sun will be darkened, as will the moon, and the stars will fall from the sky. The gospel will be preached in all the world, and then the end will come. Jesus will descend to earth on the clouds of heaven in power and great glory. Then the kingdom of God will be established, of which there will be no end.

Matthew's gospel closes with accounts of Jesus' resurrection and his appearance to the disciples. Early in the morning of the first day of the week, Mary Magdalene and another Mary came to the tomb where Jesus' body was placed. They were met by an angel, who told them that Jesus was risen and asked them to look where Jesus' body had been. The women were commissioned to go and tell Jesus' disciples that Jesus would meet the disciples in Galilee. Because Judas, who had betrayed Jesus, was dead, there were only eleven disciples left. The disciples met with Jesus in Galilee as they had been directed to do, and there Jesus instructed them, "Therefore go and make disciples of all nations. . . . And surely I am with you always, to the very end of the age."

Commentary

According to a very old tradition, the author of the Gospel of Matthew was one of the twelve disciples of Jesus. This view was expressed by Papias toward the middle of the second century, but what basis he had for this view we do not know. That Jesus did have a disciple who had been a tax-collector is evident from the accounts given in the different Gospels. In Mark, the name of this tax-gatherer is Levi, but in the Gospel of Matthew, he is called Matthew. However, most New Testament scholars agree that the Gospel of Matthew was not written by one of Jesus' disciples, although it is quite possible that Matthew the Apostle may have had something to do with one or more of the sources that were used. One of the main reasons for rejecting the traditional view concerning the author is that several passages in the gospel itself indicate quite clearly that the gospel was not written until after the destruction of the city of Jerusalem. The date of its composition is generally regarded as somewhere between the years 80 and 85 A.D.

The Gospel of Matthew, like the others in the New Testament, evidently is based on sources that were in existence for some time. The two sources on which most of the material is based are Mark and the *Logia*. The latter is sometimes called "The Sayings of Jesus" and is often referred to as the *Q* source. In addition to these materials, another source, sometimes called *M*, seems to be necessary to account for the unique portions of the gospel. The introductory section, for example, contains several stories that are not found in any of the other Gospels. These stories include an account of the birth of Jesus, the visit of the wise men from the East, the meeting of these men with King Herod, Herod's decree calling for the death of male infants, the flight into Egypt, and the settlement in Galilee. Whether these stories were based on oral or written sources is unknown, but they are not found in either Mark or the *Logia*.

All that ancient Israel had looked for with hope and high expectation is now to be fulfilled in the Christian church. Ancient Israel was given the Law through Moses, and now the new Israel has received another and even higher law in the teachings of Jesus. The basis for membership in the new Israel is neither race nor color nor nationality nor anything other than the character of individuals who believe in Jesus and put their trust in him. Believers will come from both Jews and Gentiles and from all parts of the world.

In his selection and use of source materials for the writing of his gospel, Matthew represents different points of view. Some critics have argued that he was pro-Jewish in his outlook, but others have insisted that he was pro-Gentile. Some scholars regard him as a thorough-going legalist, while others find a strong element of mysticism in his writings. He was, according to some accounts, a disciple of Jewish apocalypticism, but others see him as one who believes that the kingdom of God will be established gradually in the lives of people. These different interpretations do not constitute evidence that Matthew was confused in his thinking or that he contradicted himself on these various topics; rather, they indicate that he tried to be fair with each of the different points of view, recognizing that there was truth to be gained from each of them. The result is the composition of a gospel that presents a balance between opposing conceptions and does so without destroying the element of harmony that brings them all together.

THE GOSPEL OF LUKE

Summary

The Gospel of Luke and the Book of Acts are closely related. Written by the same author and for the same purpose, both were addressed to a Christian named Theophilus and were designed for the purpose of presenting to him a complete and well-authenticated narrative of the early history of the Christian movement. In the introductory paragraph of the gospel, Luke tells us that many lives of Jesus were written on the basis of eyewitness reports. He does not find these narratives satisfactory in all respects and so has set himself the task of examining the records and writing a new account that will establish for all interested parties the certainty of the things about which Christians were instructed.

The first paragraph in Luke's gospel is especially informative to readers of the New Testament, for it describes the way in which the two narratives attributed to Luke came to be written. Luke evaluated the materials he wanted to use and then supplemented them in whatever manner seemed to him to be the most appropriate. In writing his gospel, he did not simply piece together bits of information that he gathered from different sources; rather, his own contributions include selecting and organizing these materials, along with whatever interpretation was necessary to make a complete and unified narrative.

We can be quite certain that Luke made use of at least three different sources: the Gospel of Mark, the Q source, or "The Sayings of Jesus," and a third source that is usually designated as L to distinguish it from other biographies. The Gospel of Matthew may have existed by the time Luke wrote his account, but nothing indicates that Luke knew anything about Matthew or made any use of it. Luke was a companion of Paul, and he was quite familiar with the different interpretations of the life of Jesus held by different groups within the Christian community. His purpose was to minimize the differences between the various groups and thus promote harmony within the church. He was aware, too, of the criticisms concerning Christianity that were being made by people who were outside the church, and he especially wanted to make an effective reply to those who claimed that Jesus was a revolutionist and hence an enemy of the Roman government. By giving to his readers an authentic account of the life and teachings of Jesus, Luke could show that the charges made against Jesus were false. He was quite sure that if people knew of the kind and sympathetic way in which Jesus met individuals, they would be won by the attractive power of Jesus' wonderful personality. Luke possessed rare ability as a writer, and it has often been said that his gospel is the most appealing of all those in the New Testament.

In the opening chapters of the gospel, Luke relates a number of stories having to do with the birth and childhood of Jesus, including the announcements made to Zechariah and to Mary concerning the births of John and of Jesus, and the story of the shepherds watching their flocks at night who came to worship the newborn child. We also have accounts of the journey of Joseph and Mary to Bethlehem and of the child being wrapped in swaddling clothes and placed in a manger "because there was no room for them in the inn." After eight days, the child was circumcised, and later he was blessed by Simeon and by Anna. These stories are not reported in the other Gospels, and we cannot be sure whether Luke learned about them from an older source or from oral traditions. Luke also recorded the only story we have in the New Testament about Jesus' boyhood. When Jesus was twelve years old, he went to Jerusalem with his parents to attend the Feast of Passover. On the way home, when his parents discovered that he was not with them, they returned to the Temple and found him involved in a profound discussion with prominent Jewish rabbis.

After the introductory chapters, Luke follows the outline of events as they are recorded in the Gospel of Mark. However, he does not follow Mark's narrative as closely as Matthew does. Occasionally, he leaves out some material and substitutes an item of his own. For example, he substitutes an illustration of Jesus' preaching in the synagogue at Nazareth in place of Jesus' proclamation at the beginning of his Galilean ministry.

Luke includes a considerable number of Jesus' teachings that are not recorded in the other Gospels. If he and Matthew both used the same source Q, evidently Luke used more material from it than did Matthew. In Luke alone we find the parables of the Good Samaritan, the Publican and the Pharisee who went to the Temple to pray, the rich man and Lazarus, the lost coin, the prodigal son, the unjust steward, the rich fool who would tear down his barns and build greater barns in order that he might store his goods, and the story of Zacchaeus, who climbed a tree in order that he might see Jesus. Each of these parables and stories illustrates what Luke regards as an essential characteristic of Jesus' work. Jesus was not trying to raise opposition to the Roman government, nor was he lacking in sympathy or understanding of those whom the Jews regarded as foreigners. He places the highest value on good character regardless of a person's race or nationality. For example, although many Jews looked with disfavor on the Samaritans, Luke emphasizes that of the ten lepers whom Jesus healed, only the one who was a Samaritan expressed his gratitude for what Jesus had done. And again in the parable of the man who fell among thieves on the road to Jericho, a Samaritan befriended the man and saw to it that he was given proper care.

Throughout his gospel, Luke emphasizes the fact that Jesus was a friend not only to Jews but to Samaritans and to so-called outcasts from different races and nationalities. Chapters 9-18 are often referred to as Luke's "long insertion," for in them he departs from the sequence of events in Mark and introduces a section that includes much of the most valued portions of Jesus' teachings. Here, we have a report of Jesus sending out the "seventy" to carry the message of the kingdom to different places. The number "seventy" is especially significant: In the Jewish Torah, the number refers to all the nations of the earth. Luke wants to make it clear that Jesus' mission is for all humankind and not just for the Jews. In the story that describes the conversation between Jesus and Zacchaeus, we have the statement "For the Son of Man came to seek and to save what was lost." And in the introductory chapters of the gospel where Luke, like Matthew, traces the genealogy of

Jesus, we find the same emphasis on the universality of Jesus' mission. Matthew traces the ancestry back to Abraham, who is regarded as the father of the Hebrew people; Luke traces it back to Adam, the father of all humanity.

In reporting Jesus' discourses with his disciples concerning the destruction of Jerusalem and the end of the world, Luke does not emphasize the nearness of the event as the other evangelists do. Toward the end of the gospel, he describes the events leading up to the crucifixion, stressing the point of Jesus' innocence of any wrongdoing toward either Jews or the Roman government. Pilate, the Roman governor, declares Jesus innocent of any crime, and a Roman centurion protests Jesus' execution with the words, "Surely this was a righteous man."

The gospel closes with an account of the resurrection and the subsequent meetings of Jesus with the disciples and others. As two men are walking to the village of Emmaus, Jesus joins them, but the men do not recognize Jesus until he sits at a table with them and blesses the food that they are about to eat. Later, Jesus meets with the eleven disciples in Jerusalem and overcomes their suspicions by showing his hands and feet to them. They cook some fish, and Jesus partakes of the food with them. Then follows a farewell discourse to the disciples, during which Jesus gives them instruction concerning what they should do. Afterward, they go together as far as Bethany, and after blessing the disciples, Jesus departs from them.

Commentary

If the Gospel of Matthew could be called the Jewish gospel because of its leanings toward ideas that were typically Jewish, there is an equal amount of evidence for calling the Gospel of Luke the Gentile gospel. Actually, neither gospel is purely Jewish or purely Gentile in its account of the life and teachings of Jesus, but it is fairly obvious in the case of each of them that the authors were influenced by the point of view with which they were associated.

Luke was a companion of Paul, who came to be known in Christian circles as the Apostle to the Gentiles. Paul's interpretation of Christianity as a universal religion did much to eliminate the barriers between Jews and Gentiles. He emphasized the idea that all humans are sinners and in need of salvation. Jesus was, for him, the supreme example of what the power of God can do in a human life. This point of view evidently made a deep impression on Luke and is reflected throughout the various parts of his gospel. One sees it first of all in Luke's account of the genealogy of Jesus, which is traced to Adam rather than to Abraham, thus indicating that Jesus was representative of the entire human race rather than simply a member of the Hebrew race, and it is seen in the attitude taken by Jesus toward the Samaritans, the Romans, and others outside the Jewish fold.

When Jews and Gentiles are contrasted in Luke, often the Gentiles are presented in the more favorable light. For example, in the story of the Publican and the Pharisee, both of whom go to the Temple to pray, only the Publican is commended for the attitude that he expresses. Following his journey into the northwest country, Jesus pronounces woes on Capernaum and other Jewish communities and states, "But it will be more bearable for Tyre and Sidon at the judgment than for you." This saying does not mean that Luke rejects the Jewish people but that membership in the kingdom of God is dependent on the quality of a person's life rather than on racial or religious backgrounds.

Paul has often been referred to as a Christian mystic because of his conviction that salvation comes only by a union of an individual and God. When the Spirit of God dwells in the human heart and mind, as it did in the person of Jesus, then a person belongs to God's kingdom. But Jewish apocalypticism regarded the coming of the kingdom as a future event, when the Son of Man would descend from heaven. In the Gospel of Luke, we find a blending of these two ideas. Luke, like Matthew, makes use of the apocalyptic section in Mark's gospel but with certain modifications. The nearness of the event is not stressed as much, and Luke recognizes that there is a sense in which the kingdom is already present. When Jesus was accused of casting out demons because he was exercising the power of a greater demon, he replied, "But if I drive out demons by the finger of God, then the kingdom of God has come to you." In the story concerning Jesus and Zacchaeus, the coming of the kingdom is portrayed in a similar manner. When Zacchaeus stands up and says, "Look, Lord! Here and now I give half of my possessions to the poor, and if I have cheated anybody out of anything, I will pay it back four times the amount," Jesus replies, "Today salvation has come to this house." These passages, as well as many others that might be mentioned, indicate that Luke was sympathetic to Paul's mystical conception of the Christ who lives and abides in human hearts. Luke does not abandon the apocalyptic conception of the coming of the age's end, but he emphasizes the quality of living that alone can prepare one for the coming of the future event.

As nearly as we can determine, the Gospel of Luke was written toward the end of the first century, probably between the years 85-90 A.D. By this time, Christianity was fast becoming a worldwide movement. Starting in Jerusalem, it spread to the surrounding territory and reached as far west as the city of Rome. With the increasing numbers of Christians, the movement not only attracted attention but encountered opposition from several different quarters. Rumors circulated to the effect that the founder of the movement was a dangerous character who was trying to overthrow the Roman government. Luke was a peacemaker, and he was anxious to show that Jesus was not the type of person that these critics supposed Jesus to be. Therefore, Luke takes particular pains to point out that Jesus had no quarrel at all with the Roman government. Pilate finds no fault in Jesus, and a Roman centurion declares Jesus innocent. Although Pilate finally consents to Jesus' crucifixion, it is not until he is pressured by Jews that he does so. Jesus' whole ministry was conducted in a quiet and peaceful manner. He was the friend of the poor and the outcast and had no political ambitions of his own and no intention of trying to interfere with the orderly processes of government.

Writing from the point of view of the Christian church toward the end of the first century, Luke is convinced that the characteristics of the movement that were then being emphasized had been present from the movement's very beginning. He shows, for example, that the opposition to Jesus and his work was present during Jesus' early ministry in Galilee and was demonstrated in people's reactions to the sermon Jesus preached in the synagogue at Nazareth. Those who opposed Jesus continued their harassment throughout Jesus' entire public career, and the cause of this harassment was their resentment of the criticisms that Jesus made of their formalism and hypocrisy. Determined to silence

Jesus' criticisms, they invented false charges concerning his disloyalty to the government.

Luke shows the broad humanitarian character of Jesus' work that was manifested from the first in Jesus' attitude toward the Samaritans and others whom the Jews regarded as their enemies. Jesus never failed to commend those who had a humble and contrite heart, and it made no difference whether they were Jews or Gentiles. At the time of Luke's writing, the Spirit of Christ was regarded as the guiding factor in the life of the Christian church. That this guiding factor was only a continuation of what had been present all along is shown by Jesus' repeated references to the Spirit of God throughout the period of his public ministry. What Jesus taught was now accepted to be in harmony with what the church believed. Many of the statements attributed to Jesus were now interpreted in light of what had happened already, implying that at least some of his statements were intended as definite predictions of what was going to occur.

ACTS

Summary

The Book of Acts, which continues the narrative that Luke began in his gospel, is especially important because it was the first written history of the Christian church. Acts concerns the very vital period in Christian history between the resurrection of Jesus and the death of the apostle Paul, the time when Christian ideas and beliefs were being formulated and when the organization of the church into a worldwide movement was being developed. Only with knowledge of this background can we understand the writing of the Gospels, as well as the other New Testament literature that followed.

The book has been called "The Acts of the Apostles," really a misnomer because Acts has very little to say concerning most of the original Twelve Apostles. Peter's activities are described at some length, and John and Philip are mentioned, but more than half of the book is about Paul and his connection with the Christian movement. Scholars are somewhat divided in their opinions concerning the book's authorship. There can be no question about Luke being the author of parts of the book, but the inclusion of what has been called the "we sections" raises some question about the persons to whom the pronoun "we" refers. Was someone other than Luke also involved in the reports that are made? While no definite answer can be given to this question, it seems highly probable that Luke was the author of the original book, but the work of editors and redactors was added before the text reached the final form in which we have it today.

The Book of Acts contains twenty-eight chapters. Of these, the first twelve report events between the time of Jesus' last meeting with his disciples and the beginning of Paul's work as a Christian missionary. The remaining sixteen chapters describe Paul's activities, beginning with his mission to the church at Antioch and ending with an account of his residence in Rome as a prisoner of the Roman government. The events recorded in the first section of the book include such topics as the ascension of Jesus into heaven, the choosing of a disciple to replace Judas, who had betrayed Jesus, the Feast of Pentecost and the so-called gift of tongues, Peter's sermon delivered on that occasion, the arrest of Peter and John in the Temple at Jerusalem, the sin of Ananias and Sapphira, the stoning of Stephen, Philip's meeting with the eunuch and the baptism that followed, the story of Paul's conversion on the road to Damascus, and Peter's visit with Cornelius, the centurion. In addition to giving us some insight concerning the early activities of the Christian community, these accounts are especially valuable in that they tell us about the beliefs that Christians held concerning Jesus prior to the writing of the Gospels.

Paul's letter to the church at Corinth is the earliest written summary of the Christian faith. Paul mentions that he received no direct revelation concerning the facts pertaining to the life of Jesus and their significance for the Christian faith, but he is passing on to the members of that church what has been related to him by others. From this statement, we can infer that the essential beliefs of the Christian community about Jesus were already formulated and were included in the preaching that took place prior to that time. The first section of the Book of Acts reports several different sermons that give us definite information about these beliefs. These sermons constitute the kerygma, or the primitive gospel that was proclaimed by early Christians before any written records were made. For example, we are told of Peter's sermon to a group of about one hundred and twenty people, another sermon that he delivered on the day of Pentecost, and a third one that he preached in Jerusalem, standing on Solomon's porch in front of the Temple. Stephen's sermon at the time of his stoning is reported at considerable length, and we are told of Philip's instruction to the eunuch whom he baptized and again of Peter's discourse with Cornelius and his report to the Christian leaders at Jerusalem. In the last section of Acts, a number of Paul's sermons are recorded in considerable detail. From these records, it is possible to reconstruct with a fair degree of accuracy the main contents of the kerygma, or earliest preaching of the Christian church.

The story of the stoning of Stephen throws some light on those factors in Paul's experience that led to his conversion on the road to Damascus. From Chapter 13 to the end of the book, we have a somewhat detailed account of Paul's missionary journeys and his experiences with different churches. In Chapter 15, we have a report concerning the Jerusalem council in which the issue concerning circumcision was discussed. The account that Luke gives with reference to the results of this meeting does not agree in all details with the account of the same meeting given in Paul's Epistle to the Galatians. Since Paul was a participant in the council and Luke was giving what might be called a secondhand account, the preference must be given to the one in the Galatian letter. Luke was a strong believer in Christian unity, and in this instance, as well as in others that might be mentioned, he was anxious to minimize the differences between conflicting views. To him, the question had to be settled in a manner that was satisfactory to everyone.

The remainder of the Book of Acts describes Paul's visit to Macedonia. While in the city of Philippi, Paul and his companion, Silas, were thrown into prison. After an earthquake shook the prison, they were released and at Paul's insistence were given a police guard until they were safely out of the city. Paul's experiences at Athens and at Corinth are related, as is his work at Ephesus, where he stayed for a considerable period of time, probably from two to three years. The occasion for Paul's last visit to the city of Jerusalem was the collection of gifts from the various churches that he wished to give for the relief of poor Christians in that city.

Trouble broke out while he was there, and he was accused of starting a riot in the Temple. Paul spoke at some length in his own defense. Forty men entered into a plot to kill Paul, but a friend warned Paul of the plot, and Paul appealed to a Roman officer for protection. The officer heeded his request, and Paul was given asylum at Caesarea, a seat of the Roman government. In Caesarea, hearings were held before Felix and Agrippa, to each of whom Paul was given an opportunity to speak in his own defense. At his request, he was permitted to go to Rome in order that his case might be tried in Caesar's court. On the voyage to Rome, he was shipwrecked but eventually did get to Rome, where he was accorded a considerable amount of liberty even though he was still a prisoner. After a time, he was tried, convicted, and executed.

Commentary

In writing the Book of Acts, Luke traces the expansion of the Christian movement from its earliest beginnings to the time when it reached worldwide proportions. Luke was keenly aware of the way in which Christianity was being attacked by enemies of the movement, and he wanted to present the story of its development in a most favorable light. Although it was quite impossible to write a complete history of the movement, he selected those events that he regarded as the more important ones, sufficient to characterize the movement as a whole. Having been a companion of Paul, he was more familiar with Paul's work than he was with the activities of other Christian leaders. Then, too, he was an admirer of Paul and realized the significance of Paul's work in bringing the gospel to various cities. He deeply appreciated the points of view held by Jewish Christians, who conceived of Christianity as a further development of Judaism instead of as an entirely separate movement. He wanted to emphasize the agreements rather than the differences among those groups whose ideas frequently clashed with one another. In this respect, he was a kind of troubleshooter of the early Christian movement.

We do not know what source materials Luke used for writing Acts. Some things he observed himself, and quite possibly he may have kept a diary from which he extracted materials that were useful for his narrative. Presumably he had access to other manuscripts, and some of what he reported was obtained by direct conversation with others. Many things were omitted, and Luke was not completely unbiased in all that he wrote, but given these limitations, Luke produced a remarkable piece of work whose inclusion in the New Testament contributes a great deal toward a better understanding of the entire work.

The early Christian sermons that Luke summarized and recorded form to a very great extent the basis for a reconstruction of the kerygma, and from this point of view, the gospel records were made. Luke's account of how Christianity made its way among Gentiles without discarding the more vital points of Judaism did much toward establishing unity. The account of Paul's arrest in the city of Jerusalem and the trials that followed clearly vindicate Paul in the eyes of any impartial reader. The end of the book is somewhat disappointing because one would expect to read about Paul's trial in Caesar's court, but the account ends rather abruptly. Some people think that Luke intended to write a third volume of his history but was unable to do so. Of this we cannot be certain. However, we are indebted to Luke in no small measure for the two accounts of Christianity that he did write.

THE PASTORAL LETTERS

Summary

Three short letters in the New Testament are addressed to Christian pastors. Traditionally, these letters were attributed to Paul on the assumption that he wrote them while he was a prisoner in Rome. Two are addressed to Timothy, a young man whose parents became Christians prior to the time when Paul visited them in the town of Lystra, in Asia Minor. Timothy joined Paul in his missionary activities and continued to minister to the churches after Paul became a prisoner in Rome. The third letter is addressed to Titus, a young man born of Gentile parents who became a Christian and who was one of the delegates sent by the church at Antioch to accompany Paul and Barnabas when they went to Jerusalem for a meeting of the council. Nothing is said in either of the letters to Timothy about the occasion for writing, but the Epistle to Titus mentions that Paul is in prison.

New Testament scholars generally do not agree whether or not these letters, at least in their present form, were written by Paul. The reasons for not believing that Paul is the author are based partly on the letters' style and vocabulary, which are quite different from what we find in the older letters that Paul wrote. The theological conceptions that Paul used so frequently are absent, but the major reason why some scholars believe that Paul did not write these letters is that the ecclesiastical order that these letters presuppose did not exist in Paul's day. Perhaps the letters were written by someone who was an admirer of Paul and who wrote the kind of instruction of which he believed Paul would approve.

1 AND 2 TIMOTHY

1 Timothy. 1 Timothy was written to give instructions in worship and in church administration, and to warn against false teachings in the churches. Certain forms of worship should be observed, and certain types of conduct should be strictly avoided. Because both bishops and deacons were necessarily appointed in the churches, it was highly important that these offices be respected and that careful attention be given to the selection of men to fill them. The bishop must be above reproach, temperate, dignified, of a peaceful disposition, and not a lover of money. The deacons, too, must be men of serious mind, free from greed, and conscientious in all of their activities. They should be tested first, and only those who are blameless should be permitted to serve in that office.

The letter contains a special warning against the false beliefs and practices that were associated with Gnosticism. For example, the author specifies the asceticism that was advocated by some Gnostics in their efforts to overcome the demands of the physical body, and the opposite method that was urged by others who taught that indulgence in various forms of sensuality would accomplish the same purpose. Both asceticism and over-indulgence were based on the Gnostic conception that matter is evil; only that which is spirit is good. Christians are also warned against being misled by the godless myths that formed a part of the special kind of knowledge that Gnostics regarded as essential for salvation. The letter expresses reproof toward those who try to make a profit out of religion, and it contains instructions concerning the attitude that

Christians should hold in their dealings with widows, presbyters, and slaves.

2 Timothy. Written by an experienced missionary, 2 Timothy urges Timothy to recognize that endurance is one of the main qualities essential for a successful preacher of the gospel. Evidently, situations developed within the churches that were especially difficult for Christian pastors. Timothy must stand firm and rekindle the gift of God that is within him. He must be willing to bear hardships when necessary and to conduct himself as a good soldier for God. He needs both courage and humility to perform the tasks that have been assigned to him. In combating false doctrine, he must refrain from all that is ignoble and must show that he can differentiate words of truth from false doctrine. He can draw help and inspiration from the example of Paul, who is now at the end of his career and about to receive a crown of righteousness. The letter closes with personal greetings to the members of the church.

TITUS

The Epistle to Titus contains three chapters. Similar in content to 1 Timothy, it specifies the qualifications for the office of bishop and gives instruction for the appointment of church elders. Because the bishop is God's steward, he must be blameless, hospitable, and able to control his temper, and he must not be arrogant, self-indulgent, or intemperate. He must have a firm grasp of the word of God and give instruction in sound doctrine. In dealing with the men and women who are members of the church, the bishop or elder in charge must train the congregation to be serious, temperate, sensible, and sound in faith, love, and steadfastness. Women are to be instructed to love their husbands and children. Younger men are to be taught to control themselves. Slaves should be taught obedience to their masters, and Christians must avoid hatred and wrangling. They should be encouraged to manifest meekness, gentleness, and courtesy, which are made possible by God's mercy in Christ.

EPHESIANS

The Epistle to the Ephesians can scarcely be called a pastoral letter since it was not addressed to a particular church leader. We have no proof that Paul wrote the letter, although it was supposed for a long time that he did. The evidence contained in the letter itself suggests very strongly that the letter was written after Paul's death, probably by one of his disciples who may have wanted it to appear that Paul wrote the letter because of the added prestige that his authorship would give to it. Although Paul was with the church in Ephesus for a period of about three years and would certainly have formed some close personal friendships, the letter does not contain personal greetings to particular individuals.

No mention is made of the Jewish controversy over legalism, which is found in nearly all of Paul's letters. The most convincing argument of all that Paul did not write the letter is the fact that reference is made to the apostles and prophets as the foundation of the church; Paul always insisted that the church had no foundation other than Jesus Christ. The letter was evidently written for the churches at a time when church organization had proceeded quite beyond the point it reached while Paul was still living.

Two main themes are expounded in the letter: the unity of all things in Christ and the Christian church as the visible symbol here on earth of that unity. The author of the letter asserts that Jesus' life reveals the divine purpose that has existed since the creation of the world. The centuries-old disunity is due to humanity's sin. The Spirit of God made manifest in the life of Jesus here on this earth has shown how this disunity can be overcome and the original harmony restored. Overcoming evil in the lives of human beings achieves a unity not only between humans and God but a cosmic unity that unites all things on earth and in heaven. Therefore, there is no need for any worship of powers that are intermediary between heaven and earth, as was taught by Gnostics.

Unity has been achieved between Jews and Gentiles through the person of Christ. The Gentiles, who at one time were separated from the people of God and who were in bondage to the evil powers of the universe, are now offered salvation and have been made one with the children of God through Jesus Christ. A new household of God has been created through the preaching of the apostles and the Christian prophets. The church has been called into being to bear witness to the divine purpose and to knit together people from all races and nations into a single community in which God dwells through his Spirit. The letter closes with ethical instructions for the members of the church from which this unity may be achieved. Because the church is the visible body of Christ, it must grow strong in the bonds of love as it fulfills its mission in the world.

Commentary

Although the pastoral letters can scarcely be attributed directly to Paul, they do contain passages that have every indication of Pauline authorship. Paul's influence can be seen in certain passages, even though such passages are now combined with other material that seemed appropriate for the conditions that existed in the churches at the time when the letters were written. The letters are especially valuable from a historical point of view since they reveal the beginnings of the type of church organization that, with modifications, has persisted even to this day.

From a religious point of view, the letters are inferior to those written by Paul. The chief difference lies in the fact that the pastoral letters do not show the close connection between Christian faith and Christian living that is so characteristic of Paul's writings. Paul never failed to point out that the fruits of the spirit would always be expressed in the quality of one's daily living. Faith was something that gripped the entire personality, and the results could be seen in one's actions, as well as in one's attitudes and beliefs. The pastoral letters emphasize two duties that are incumbent on all Christians: to believe certain things and to do certain things. However, the way in which these duties are related is not set forth in the manner that Paul so clearly made in his letters to the churches.

Despite this weakness, the letters set forth a high standard for Christian living. They contain practical instruction for meeting the problems that arise in daily life, and their message can be understood even by those who are not theologically inclined.

OPEN LETTERS TO THE CHURCHES

Summary

The era that immediately followed the death of the apostles is usually designated as the early post-apostolic period. It was a critical time in the history of the Christian church, for the church's membership had spread to various parts of the world, and in both size and influence the movement was growing. Because the early pioneers of the movement were no longer living, leadership was necessarily recruited from among newer members. Problems constantly arose, and there was need for guidance in dealing with them. For the purpose of helping meet this need, relatively short documents were produced and distributed among the churches. Because the problems with which these texts were concerned were not confined to any one local community, the documents were written for the church at large. For this reason, they have sometimes been designated as the Catholic Epistles. Although most of them have been credited either to one of the apostles or to someone closely associated with the apostles, evidence indicates that all of the documents belong to the post-apostolic period. When they first appeared, they were anonymous, but in later years they were attributed to individuals who were prominent in the beginnings of the Christian movement, which gave added prestige to the documents. This group of writings includes one letter attributed to James, two to the apostle Peter, three to John, the disciple of Jesus, and one to a Christian named Jude.

1 PETER

1 Peter is one of the more important letters in this group of open letters. Like the Book of Revelation, 1 Peter was written primarily for the benefit of Christians who were suffering severe persecution at the hands of the Roman government. However, Revelation was addressed to the seven churches in Asia Minor because it was in that locality that emperor worship was threatening to destroy all those who refused obedience to its demands. When 1 Peter was written, this type of "fiery ordeal" had become worldwide, and Christians, wherever they might be living, were called

upon in the name of the government to renounce their allegiance to Christ. Even to be called a Christian was considered sufficient grounds for condemnation. This situation did not exist prior to the reign of Emperor Domitian (81-96 A.D.) or during the last decade of the first century, which is one of the main reasons for assigning the letter to a period that came after the death of Peter the Apostle.

Although there is relatively little of a theological nature in this letter, it sets forth a very high standard of Christian living. In contrast with the Book of Revelation and all of its bitter condemnations of the Roman Empire, 1 Peter urges Christians to take a different attitude toward their suffering. The trials and afflictions that have come upon them are for the purpose of testing their faith. Christian character is not developed by living under conditions of ease and comfort. Only by meeting difficult situations and conquering them can Christians become spiritually strong, for they must be challenged in order to bring about the perfection of their character. Besides this, Christians have the example of Jesus to follow, and they should consider it a privilege to be counted worthy to suffer as Jesus did for the glory of God. To endure with patience even to the end is a goal worthy of attainment. However, Christians should be encouraged because they know that their suffering will last for only a short time; they have the hope of a glorious future, of which there will be no end.

One interesting passage in 1 Peter refers to the time when Jesus preached to "those who are now dead." Since Christians believed and taught that faith in Jesus the Christ is essential for salvation, the question arose concerning the fate of those who died without having the opportunity to know or even hear of Jesus. Could they be saved? If they could not, then the justice of God would be brought into question; if they could, then faith in Jesus would not be essential for salvation. In order to meet this dilemma, the idea to which this passage refers was developed.

According to this conception, Jesus, between the time of his death and his resurrection, descended to Sheol, where, according to ancient Hebrew tradition, all persons go after death. There, Jesus preached to all those who had died, thus giving to them a chance to accept or to reject his message. The influence of this idea can be recognized in that portion of the Apostles' Creed that reads, "He descended into hell."

2 PETER

2 Peter is attributed in its superscription to Simon Peter, the disciple of Jesus. Because 2 Peter contains many indications of authorship later than the death of the apostle, the superscription assumedly was used to give authority to the letter as a whole. The letter warns against those persons who are skeptical concerning the coming of the Day of the Lord. The churches are encouraged to hold fast the faith they have received, for as it was in the days of Noah, so it will be again when the Son of Man shall come. The Day of the Lord will come as a thief in the night. Therefore, all Christians should live in readiness for it.

JAMES

James' letter appears to have been written at a time near the close of the first century. The letter is traditionally attributed to James, who was the brother of Jesus, but the contents of the letter raise some doubts if this James is the real author, for the letter contains a conception of religion quite different from the one that James, who later was the head of the Jerusalem council, supported. Perhaps, then, the letter was written by yet another James, who had a message that he regarded as appropriate for the churches of his time.

Paul emphasized the importance of faith as the means of salvation and disparaged those who believed that salvation could be obtained by obedience to the laws of God. Many interpreters of Paul's comments understood his message to mean that nothing matters so long as a person believes that Jesus is the Christ. The Law was no longer binding, and Christians could follow their own inclinations in matters of conduct. To correct this notion, the letter of James was written.

The author defines "pure and faultless" religion strictly in terms of ethical conduct. As he sees it, the actions of individuals are far more important than the mere content of their intellectual beliefs. He insists that "faith by itself, if it is not accompanied by action, is dead." Furthermore, the standard of goodness is obedience to the laws of God. In obeying what the author calls "the perfect law that gives freedom," individuals gain their true freedom.

Anyone who breaks one of the commandments is guilty of all. However, evidently the writer has the moral rather than the ritualistic commandments in mind, for he sees no virtue in mere formalism. Helping the poor and the needy and maintaining a humble attitude exemplify the Christian religion. The writer also has much to say about the harm that may arise from gossip and careless use of the tongue. The rich, too, are severely criticized for hoarding their wealth instead of using it to meet the needs of their fellow humans. The letter ends rather abruptly but emphasizes the type of ethical conduct that should always characterize the life of a true Christian.

THE JOHANNINE LETTERS

1 John. A short homily written by a Christian elder, 1 John instructs the churches concerning a problem that was becoming more serious. Christians were taught that after Jesus left this earth, the Spirit of God would guide and direct the Christian movement. The spirit that was present in Jesus would speak through the apostles, and once the apostles were gone, the spirit would continue to speak through other individuals. As a result of this belief, many people claimed to be the medium through which God's truth was revealed to the churches. All sorts of ideas were advanced by individuals who insisted that the Spirit of God revealed to them whatever it was that they were advocating. Unless some restraint was placed on individuals who made such claims, the situation soon would become chaotic. This letter proposes that two tests be applied before accepting anyone who claims to have been informed by the Spirit of God.

One of these tests is doctrinal in character. It states that anyone who denies that Jesus Christ has come in the flesh is not of God. This test was directed especially against a form of Gnostic philosophy known as Doceticism. Docetists accepted the idea of Jesus' divinity, but they denied his humanity, insisting that Jesus only *appeared* to have a physical body.

The other test is an ethical one. People who claim to be possessed by the Spirit of God must be examined before being accepted in the church. If their conduct does not harmonize with the ethical teachings of Jesus, they are not to be received into church fellowship. The church is warned against the many false prophets and teachers who have arisen, and the church is urged to apply the test of brotherly love, as well as that of obedience to the commandments of God.

2 John. 2 John is a very short letter written by the same elder to a sister church that he designates as the "chosen lady." The letter indicates that the false teachers who deny that Jesus Christ was present in the flesh have made inroads in the church and are causing a serious schism. The church is warned concerning these deceivers and told to show no hospitality toward them.

3 John. In this letter from the same elder, the church is commended for receiving Gaius, who performed important services for the congregation. Also, the church is warned about a certain man named Diotrephes, who has spoken slanderously about the elder and tried to have him thrown out of the church.

JUDE

This writing of Jude, who speaks of himself as a servant of Jesus Christ and a brother of James, contains a single chapter, whose purpose is similar to that of 2 Peter. In fact, some scholars maintain that this letter was written before 2 Peter and that parts of it were copied and expanded by the author of 2 Peter. A polemical tract written to warn the churches against false doctrines that were gradually making inroads within the membership of the churches, it is directed primarily against Gnosticism and its teaching concerning a strange kind of wisdom expressed in mysterious language. The Gnostics' dualistic conception of good mind but evil body is out of line with Christian doctrine and should be rejected, and the same holds for their conception of Jesus as one who only *appeared* to have a human body. The author quotes from the Book of Enoch, which is one of the Jewish apocalypses included in the Pseudepigrapha of the Old Testament.

Commentary

The open letters to the churches are valuable as source materials for reconstructing the history of the early church. They tell us about the theological and practical problems with which the church contended. Some of these letters—especially 2 and 3 John,

2 Peter, and Jude—have little value apart from this history. But something more can be said for the other three. 1 Peter sets forth a conception of the Christian life that is attractive and ennobling. It tells how the hardships and trials of human life may become a means toward the development of Christian character, and it sets before Christians a glorious hope that may serve as a guide and inspiration. James' letter will always be remembered for its ethical conception of religion at its best. It serves, too, to correct the faulty notion that Christian faith is merely a matter of intellectual belief, and it shows that true faith in the Christian gospel will be expressed both in actions and in what one thinks. 1 John, which presents a conception of Christianity that has much in common with the Gospel of John, makes love the central element in the Christian life.

THE LETTER TO THE HEBREWS

Summary

After the Christian community had existed for a few decades, the enthusiasm that characterized its earlier years began to wane. The expected return of Jesus had not taken place, opposition to the movement had developed from different quarters, and doubts were beginning to arise concerning any permanent significance that Christianity might have over other religious sects and parties. To counteract these tendencies and to strengthen the faith of Christians who were associated with the new movement are the chief purposes of this letter. The author is unknown, but many guesses have been made concerning his identity. Authorship has been attributed to the apostle Paul; in many editions of the New Testament, this idea is expressed in the title given to the letter. However, the contents of the letter indicate that Pauline authorship is not likely. The ideas set forth in the letter are unlike those found in the genuine letters of Paul. In fact, Hebrews' interpretation of Christianity in many respects is foreign to the thought and work of the apostle.

Whoever the author may have been, we can be certain that he was someone who believed that Christianity was something more than just another religious movement. Convinced that

Christianity is the only true religion, he wanted to show its superiority over all the religions that were competing with it, and he was especially anxious to show its superiority over Judaism. To do this, he makes a series of comparisons between conceptions that he finds in the Old Testament and corresponding ideas in his interpretation of Christianity. In each of his comparisons, the Christian view is presented as the more advantageous of the two.

Hebrews begins with the statement that God, who in ancient times revealed himself through the prophets, has in these last days revealed himself through the life and teachings of a Son. This Son, who is identified with the person known as Jesus of Nazareth, is said to be greater than Moses or any of the prophets. He is superior even to the angels of heaven, for no one of them has ever been called a Son, nor did any of them have a part in the creation of the world. Because the messages delivered by angels have been valid and any transgression with reference to them has been justly punished, it is all the more important that people should heed what has been delivered to them by the Son. Calling Jesus the Son of God does not, for the author of this letter, constitute a denial of Jesus' humanity. On this point he is quite emphatic: "Since the children have flesh and blood, he too shared in their humanity." And again, "For this reason he had to be made like his brothers in every way." It is because of Jesus' humanity that it can be said of Jesus, "Because he himself suffered when he was tempted, he is able to help those who are being tempted."

Throughout the letter, Jesus is referred to as the great high priest whose ministry exceeds in importance the services performed by the priests of ancient Israel. The greatness of the priesthood of Jesus is emphasized in a number of different ways, one of which concerns the priesthood of Melchizedek. The author refers to a story in the Book of Genesis in which Abraham encounters Melchizedek, who was a priest and the king of Salem. Abraham, returning from a battle, received a blessing from Melchizedek, to whom he paid a tithe of all the spoils he had obtained from the battle. This is the substance of the story as reported in Genesis, but from this meager account a number of conclusions can be drawn. One conclusion is that what happened to Abraham in this encounter affected the entire Levitical priesthood since the priests were all present in the loins of Abraham, the father of the Hebrew people. Asserting that the lesser is always blessed by the better, the author infers that the Levitical priesthood is necessarily inferior to the priesthood of Melchizedek; because Jesus is a high priest after the order of Melchizedek, he is therefore greater than any of the priests of the Old Testament. Quoting from Psalms 110, the author assumes that it was Jesus about whom the statement was made, "You are a priest forever, in the order of Melchizedek."

Although Jesus is believed to have been a human being with actual flesh and blood, he is also the Son of God insofar as he is the incarnation of the divine Logos, or Spirit of God. This aspect of Jesus' nature is eternal and has neither beginning nor end in the processes of time. The author of Hebrews draws another comparison between Jesus and the priests of the Old Testament: The narrative in Genesis says nothing concerning the parentage of Melchizedek, and from this silence the author draws the conclusion that Melchizedek had no father or mother. In other words, he was an eternal rather than a temporal being. All of the Levitical priests were men who were born and who died, but Jesus, who was a priest after the order of Melchizedek, had eternal life. In addition, the work that Jesus performed as a priest exceeded in importance that which was done by the men who ministered under the Levitical priesthood. One of the reasons given to support this claim of Jesus' priestly superiority is that the priests of the tribe of Levi had to perform their services at repeated intervals. Even the sacrifice made on the great day of atonement had to be performed once every year. In contrast, Jesus as high priest offered the sacrifice of himself, which was done only once, but this one sacrifice was sufficient not only for all time to come but even for those who had died prior to the time when the sacrifice was made.

The real significance of Jesus' sacrifice rests not merely on the fact that it was made once rather than repeated at regular intervals, but that it was qualitatively different from the ones made by the Levitical priests. The priests' sacrifices involved merely the blood of bulls and of goats, but Jesus' sacrifice was that of his own blood. By insisting on this difference, the author of Hebrews does not mean to infer that the priests' sacrifices offered in ancient times had no value at all, for they did mean something to the people of Israel. His point is that the sacrifice made by Jesus has even greater value, not only for Jews but for all humans insofar as they believe in Jesus Christ. In fact, the real significance of the entire sacrificial system as set forth in the Old Testament stands in a very definite relation to the death of Jesus on the cross. As the Hebrews writer sees it, these sacrificial offerings were but shadows that pointed toward another and greater sacrifice to be made in the future and apart from which all of the Old Testament services would have been in vain.

Pursuing the subject of Jesus' priesthood still further, the author of Hebrews gives his own explanations concerning the necessity for a new type of priesthood to replace the older one associated with the tribe of Levi. Again he regards the question of duration as important. The office of priest was hereditary among the Levites; when a priest died, it was necessary for him to be replaced by another, whose right to the office was determined by whether he was a descendant from that particular tribe. Because it was generally recognized that Jesus came from the tribe of Judah, one that was not designated as a tribe from which the priests were chosen, it could be inferred that Jesus' right to the priesthood was based not on physical descent but "by the power of an endless life." Furthermore, we are told that Jesus' appointment to the priesthood was confirmed by an oath, whereas no such oath was used in the appointment of any of the Levitical priests. The author finds support in his interpretation of a passage from Psalms 110, which reads, "The Lord has sworn and will not change his mind: 'You are a priest forever.'" Assuming that the psalmist was referring to Jesus, the statement gives added support to the author's conviction concerning the superiority of the Christian priesthood of Jesus.

This conviction is illustrated again in the assertion that the services performed by the Levitical priests were a part of the system referred to as the Old Covenant. In contrast, the priesthood of Jesus belongs to the New Covenant. Mention of these two covenants is made in a reference to the passage in the Book of Jeremiah in which the prophet contrasts the idea of obedience to a set of external laws with the type of conduct that is motivated by the right desires and purposes within an individual. The former constitutes the basis of the Old Covenant, the latter the basis for the New Covenant. The author of Hebrews tells us that the imperfections of the Levitical priesthood were due, at least in part, to the attempt made to regulate conduct according to the requirements of the Mosaic Law. The failure of this attempt was one of the reasons that made a new and different type of priesthood necessary, which, the author holds, was accomplished in the priesthood of Jesus in accordance with which Jesus became a minister of the New Covenant.

The work of Jesus the high priest is further elaborated in the author's conception of the heavenly sanctuary. The writer holds that the tabernacle made by Moses and used by the Israelites during their wanderings in the wilderness was a kind of miniature copy of the true tabernacle, or sanctuary, that exists in heaven. He bases this belief on a statement found in the Book of Exodus describing the instruction that God gave to Moses concerning the construction of the tabernacle. The statement reads, "Then have them make a sanctuary for me, and I will dwell among them. Make this tabernacle and all its furnishings exactly like the pattern I will show you." The most important service performed by the Levitical high priest in the ancient tabernacle took place on the day of atonement, the time when the priest entered the most holy place and sprinkled blood upon the mercy seat of the ark in order to obtain forgiveness for the sins that people had committed throughout the year. The Hebrews author, believing that these services were intended to foreshadow things to come, contends that the work of Jesus as high priest is now declared to be the reality that fulfills the meaning intended by the ancient services. Following his resurrection and ascension to heaven, Jesus enters into the most holy place in the heavenly sanctuary and offers his own blood in atonement for the sins of humanity.

These references to the Old Testament in Hebrews are significant because they indicate the author's belief that in the events associated with the life, death, and resurrection of Jesus, the stories related in the Old Testament find their true meaning, especially with reference to those portions of the Old Testament that deal with the priests and the sacrificial system of which they were a part. The discussion concerning faith, toward the close of Hebrews, is in harmony with this same point of view. Enumerating a long list of Israel's heroes, the author maintains that it was by faith that all of these heroes' mighty works were accomplished. His conception of faith is then identified with a belief on the heroes' part that at some future time, Christ would appear and do those things that have now been accomplished.

Commentary

Hebrews holds a unique place in the literature of the New Testament. It presents interpretations of Jesus and of the entire Christian movement that are decidedly different from those found in other writings. The letter's author sees Jesus as the great high priest of the Christian religion performing services analogous to the ones carried out by the Levitical priests of the Old Testament. In other portions of the New Testament, Jesus is regarded as a prophet, but only in this letter is he considered a priest. This designation is significant: The prophets usually represented a point of view that in many respects was the very opposite of that of the priests. The prophets were the great social reformers; the priests, whose work occupied a very prominent place in the lives of people whose religious heritage was in Judaism, attended to the offering of sacrifices and the performing of ritualistic requirements that were necessary in order to obtain forgiveness of sins. With the destruction of the Temple in Jerusalem and the cessation of priestly activities, it seems probable that some individuals felt the need for something to be substituted for the priests' activities. Perhaps considerations of this kind influenced the author of this letter. At any rate, he interprets Jesus' death on the cross in a manner that not only meets the requirements of Judaism but goes beyond them.

The use of the Old Testament in Hebrews has led some people to refer to the letter as the classical example of the New Testament interpretation of the Old Testament. Such a reference illustrates the tendency on the part of some Christians to read their own ideas back into the literature of the ancient people of Israel. Having arrived at certain convictions concerning the meaning and significance of the life of Jesus, they assume that these same ideas were present in the minds of those who wrote the Old Testament, for it becomes a fairly easy task to find in the Old Testament writings the very ideas for which they are looking, which the author of Hebrews apparently did in many instances in his writing, and especially in his references to the sacrificial system of the Levitical priests and in the passages that refer to the priesthood of Melchizedek.

In the Synoptic Gospels, as well as in other portions of the New Testament, reference is made to the messianic prophecies of the Old Testament. In Hebrews, no reference is made to these prophecies. Instead, the sacrificial offerings made by the priests anticipated the coming of Jesus and his death on the cross. This way of looking at the Old Testament has had an important bearing on the development of Christian doctrine and has led in some instances to the view that the Old Testament is really a Christian rather than a Jewish book. The people for whom the Old Testament was written did not understand it, and only through Christian beliefs can its true meaning be discerned. The most extreme statement of this position is expressed in the words of one Christian writer who maintained that "the Old Testament is but the New Testament concealed, and the New Testament is the Old Testament revealed."

The influence of Hebrews is reflected in many of the generally accepted teachings of the Christian church, one of which is the doctrine of the blood atonement, or the idea that the blood of Jesus atones for or pays the penalty for human transgressions. Likewise, the interpretation of the faith by which people are saved as being identical with the mere belief that Jesus died for the sins of the world has sometimes been supported by quotations from this letter. This suggestion does not mean that the author of the letter believed that Christian faith involved no more than this belief, but rather that some of the specific things he did say have in many instances suggested this interpretation.

Aside from these peculiarities, several other ideas must be taken into account in evaluating the value of the letter as a whole. The statement "The Son is the radiance of God's glory and the exact representation of his being, sustaining all things by his powerful word" explains the relationship between Jesus and God the Father in a most meaningful way. The humanity of Jesus is emphasized in the assertion that he "suffered when he was tempted," and again that he was made "perfect through suffering." Because the letter was addressed to Christians who were becoming discouraged and growing weak in the faith, the messages that Hebrews conveys were both comforting and reassuring.

THE BOOK OF REVELATION

Summary

In the Book of Revelation, the apocalyptic hopes of the early Christian community find their clearest and most complete expression. Apocalypticism was not a new phenomenon among Christians; it was a well-established belief among Jews, who held that the coming of the kingdom of God would not be brought about by a gradual transformation but by a sudden intervention, when God would end the present age and establish his kingdom in the world made new. This conception of coming events is associated with the belief that prior to this future time, the struggle between the forces of good and evil will become more intense. As the evil powers grow stronger, they will inflict persecution and in some instances even death upon those who follow a course of righteousness. The struggle will eventually reach a climax, at which time God will intervene, destroy the forces of evil, and set up a new order in which the righteous will live for all time to come. The appearance of the Messiah will coincide with the coming of these events.

When the members of the Christian community affirmed their belief that the crucified Jesus was the long-awaited Messiah, they necessarily revised their understanding concerning the work Jesus was to do and especially the way in which his work would be completed. Because they were convinced that the work of the Messiah must end in triumph and glory, they believed that this end could be accomplished only by a return of Jesus back to this earth from the heaven to which he had ascended. This second coming, occurring at the time when all the events connected with the apocalyptic program will take place, will inaugurate the coming of the new age, as well as the final destruction of all the forces of evil.

As time passed, many Christians—especially those who were suffering persecution at the hands of the Roman government—became deeply concerned about how long it would be before these events would take place. Toward the end of the first century of the Christian era, emperor worship was fairly well established, not only in the city of Rome but in the outlying regions that formed a part of the empire. When Christians refused to worship the emperor, they were accused of all sorts of crimes and subjected to the most severe penalties. Some of them suffered martyrdom rather than deny their faith. It was a critical time for the entire Christian movement, and many of its members wondered whether the persecution would ever end, while others were perplexed about the course they should follow. Some were even tempted to abandon their faith or at least to make concessions to Rome sufficient to enable them to save their lives.

Under these conditions, a Christian named John wrote Revelation, addressing it to the seven churches that were in Asia Minor. The purpose of the book was to strengthen the faith of the members of these churches by giving to them the assurance that deliverance from the evil powers arrayed against them was close at hand. John was confident that the great day of divine intervention would occur within a comparatively short time, but in accordance with the apocalyptic literature with which Jewish Christians were familiar, he knew that many terrifying events would take place first. He wanted to warn his fellow Christians concerning these events and thus prepare them for the time when their faith would be put to a more severe test than anything that they had experienced thus far.

In writing Revelation, John follows the pattern that was used in such older apocalyptic writings as the Book of Daniel in the Old Testament, 1 Esdras in the Apocrypha, the Book of Enoch in the Pseudepigrapha, the Assumption of Moses, and many other well-known writings, including sections of the Book of Ezekiel and portions of the Synoptic Gospels. In all of these writings, events appear as though they were predicted long before they actually took place. The revelations are usually through dreams or visions in which coming events are symbolized by strange figures, the meanings of which are sometimes disclosed by an angelic messenger who was sent for that particular purpose. The apocalypses were produced in times of crises, and they were written for the benefit of people who were suffering hardship and privation at the particular time when the writing was done.

At the beginning of Revelation, John tells us that while he was on the Isle of Patmos, where he was banished because of his religious faith, he heard a loud voice telling him to write what he saw and then to send the writing to the seven churches in Asia.

The voice was that of Jesus Christ, who had been raised from the dead and who had ascended to heaven. Christ's messages are addressed to seven angels, each one of which is the guardian for a particular church: Ephesus, Smyrna, Thyatira, Pergamum, Sardis, Philadelphia, and Laodicea. Christ commends these churches for the good works that they have performed, but for five of them, he also sends a message of warning and reproof. He is especially critical of those who tolerate the doctrines of the Nicolaitans, whose teachings he considers a real menace to the Christian community because they approve of the practice of eating meat obtained from animals that have been used as sacrifices to idols. Although the apostle Paul and other Christians maintained that this practice was not a matter of vital importance and that everyone should be permitted to follow the dictates of their own consciences, apparently John did not share this attitude. As he understands it, the crucial test for all Christians, as it is for Jews, is strict obedience to all laws, and the rules pertaining to forbidden food are no exception. Although it might appear to be relatively unimportant, people's attitudes toward matters of this kind indicate the way in which they will behave toward weightier matters.

Christ commends those churches whose members have endured persecution and, in some instances, even death rather than declare their allegiance to Roman rulers, who proclaimed their own divinity and demanded that they should be worshipped along with the other gods of the empire. He refers to Pergamum as Satan's home inasmuch as it was in this place that the cult of emperor worship was particularly strong.

Christ warns Christians to expect that their persecutions will be even more severe in the immediate future. Nevertheless, they are to remain faithful and regard these afflictions as tests of their character. Those who remain loyal will be delivered from the hands of their enemies, and in the new order of things soon to be established, they will be given a crown of life and the assurance that the new order will last forever. The persecutions that are now taking place will last for only a short time, for the hour of God's judgment is close at hand.

Following Christ's messages to the seven churches, John describes the seven seals, scrolls on which is written an account of the events that are about to take place. The risen Christ, who is referred to as the Lamb of God, is said to be the only one who is accounted worthy to open the seals. When the first seal is opened, there appears a white horse, whose rider goes forth to conquer. Other seals are opened, and three more horses—a red one, a black one, and a pale one—appear in rapid succession. These four horses and their respective riders symbolize the conflicts that will mark the beginning of the final destruction of the Roman Empire. When the fifth seal is opened, John is permitted to look upon the souls of those who, in the midst of their distress, cry out, "How long, Sovereign Lord, holy and true, until you judge the inhabitants of the earth and avenge our blood?" They are told that the forces of destruction are about to be turned loose in the world, and they may have to endure even greater torment, but if they are faithful through it all, they will be among the redeemed whose names are written in the book of life.

Following John's vision of the impending disasters soon to be inflicted upon the world, the scene changes, and four angels representing the four winds of heaven are told to hold back these winds until the servants of God have had seals placed on their foreheads. John then reveals the number of those who are sealed. Drawing an analogy between the twelve tribes of ancient Israel and the Christian community regarded now as the new Israel, he gives the number of 144,000, or 12,000 from each of the tribes of Israel. Before the opening of the seals is completed, another series of disasters is revealed in the appearance of seven angels, each one carrying a trumpet. The blowing of these trumpets announces such physical catastrophes as the coming of a great earthquake, the turning of rivers into blood, and the darkening of the sun and the moon, as well as the falling of the stars from heaven. After these physical phenomena, which will indeed be appalling, the wrath of God will be visited more directly upon those who persecute members of the Christian community. Before describing the manner of this visitation, John identifies the power now vested in the Roman emperor with an evil being, who, through the centuries, has been at war against the forces of righteousness.

This evil being is none other than Satan, the archenemy of God, who is now putting forth a supreme effort to destroy the righteous from the face of the earth. He is the Dragon who launched a rebellion against God. John tells us that "there was war in heaven" as Michael and his angels fought against the Dragon and his angels. The result of the conflict was that the Dragon was cast out of heaven and one third of the angels were cast out with him. This same Dragon worked through King Herod in an attempt to destroy the Christ child as soon as he was born. His work has continued ever since, and according to John, he is now trying to accomplish his purpose by working through the Roman emperor. His evil character is manifest in the cruel persecutions that are being inflicted upon Christians.

In characterizing this power that now appears to be gaining mastery over the world, John resorts to imagery used in the Book of Daniel to describe the wicked ruler who tried to coerce the Jews into submission. The author of the Book of Daniel uses the symbol of a great and terrible beast that has seven heads and ten horns. In like manner, John uses a beast to represent the Roman emperor, whose image was stamped on the coins used in the empire. At one point, John is quite specific in his identification of the one symbolized by the beast. He says, "This calls for wisdom. If anyone has insight, let him calculate the number of the beast, for it is man's number. His number is 666." John is seemingly referring to the Roman emperor, but he is also personifying the forces of evil, and his condemnation of the emperor is due to the fact that John believes Satan is incarnate in the actions of the empire, for Satan and the empire are linked together for the achievement of a common purpose.

As John sees the end drawing near, he describes the angels of heaven crying with a loud voice. Three angels appear, the first one announcing that the hour of God's judgment has come, the second one crying out that Babylon, which is used as the symbol of Rome, is fallen, and the third one describing the terrible fate of those who worship the beast or its image. As a final punishment, these false worshippers are thrown into a lake of fire, where they will forever be destroyed. Seven more angels then appear, each one carrying a bowl, the content of which symbolizes the wrath of God about to be poured out in the form of the seven last plagues. The plagues will inflict the wicked of John's day, just as a series of plagues inflicted the ancient Egyptians prior to the time when the Israelites were delivered from their bondage. When the first angel pours out his bowl upon the earth, foul and evil sores grow on the men who bear the mark of the beast and who worship its image. When the second angel pours out his bowl on the sea, the sea turns to blood and everything living in it dies. Catastrophes of a similar nature follow when the remaining angels empty their bowls.

The great catastrophic events that bring an end to all the kingdoms of earth will also be the occasion for the return of Christ on the clouds of heaven. As Christ approaches the earth, the wicked people will be slain by the brightness of his coming. For a period of a thousand years, Satan will be bound, and the earth will be desolate. During this time, the righteous will be made safe in the city of God, which is the new Jerusalem. At the end of the thousand years, the city of God will descend to earth. Then the wicked will be raised from the dead, and after making an attempt to overthrow the city of God, they will be destroyed in what John tells us is the second death. The closing chapters of Revelation present a glowing description of the new Jerusalem with its streets of gold, its walls of jasper, its gates of pearl, and the river of life, which will flow eternally from the throne of God. In this heavenly abode, neither sorrow nor crying will exist, for God will wipe away all tears, and there will be no more death.

Commentary

The Revelation of John is the one book in the New Testament that claims John as its author. By the time the writings that are now included in the New Testament were assembled in their present form, three letters and one gospel were also attributed to John. But in the case of these writings, the name of the supposed author was added at a later date, and their respective contents indicate that they were not written by the same John who wrote Revelation.

The Book of Revelation often has been regarded as a mysterious book, quite beyond the comprehension of the average lay reader. Its many references to angelic beings, its elaborate description of Christ as he appears in the heavenly courts, its use of such mystic numbers as three, seven, twelve, and their multiples, the accounts of strange beasts, symbolic names, and definite time periods—all suggest some hidden and esoteric meaning that supposedly can be detected only by an expert. For these reasons, many

people have ignored the book, feeling that any attempt to understand it is futile. Other people have taken an opposite attitude and
have found in this book what they believe to be predictions of
whole series of events, many of which have already occurred and
the remainder of which are about to take place in the near future.
The basis for these views, many of which sound strange and fan-
tastic, is found in the elaborate symbolism used in the book. The
use of symbols has an important place in religious literature, for
there is no other way in which a person can talk or even think
about that which is beyond the realm of finite human experience.
But there is always a danger that the symbols may be interpreted
in a way that was not intended by the author who used them. Only
in regard to the content in which the symbols are used can we determine what the author meant.

One source of confusion has been the result of a failure to
distinguish between prophetic writing and apocalyptic writing.
The prophets used a particular literary form in which they expressed their messages; the apocalyptic writers used a different literary form, one that was better suited to the particular purpose
that they had in mind. To understand either group, one must interpret their writings by considering the respective literary form that
they used. The characteristics of apocalyptic writing are fairly well
known. In addition to the Book of Daniel and the Book of
Revelation, a wealth of apocalyptic writing exists in the Apocrypha
and the Pseudepigrapha of the Old Testament. A careful study of
these writings shows that they have a number of common characteristics: They were produced in times of crises; they describe the
conflict between the forces of good and evil; future events are
made known through dreams and visions; the end of the conflict is
to come shortly; and those who remain faithful through persecution and trial are promised a reward in the messianic kingdom
soon to be established. The messages are for the benefit of the persecuted and are usually conveyed by means of symbols that only
the faithful can understand.

Interpreted in light of these characteristics, the Revelation of
John is comparatively easy to understand. In many respects, it is
the least original of any of the New Testament writings. In its style
of writing, the number and kind of symbols that are used, and the
purpose for which it was written, the book closely follows the

precedent established in the older apocalyptic writings. The unique feature about Revelation is the particular occasion that caused it to be written. Toward the end of the first century of the Christian era, the attitude of the Roman government toward Christianity became especially hostile. Nero, the Roman emperor, charged that Christians were to blame for the burning of Rome. Although the charge was false, it was sufficient to cause many people to regard the new Christian movement with suspicion. Jews and Romans alike resented the fact that Christians condemned so many of the things they were doing, and they especially disliked the belief on the part of Christians that their religion was superior to the older faiths that had been honored for centuries. The Christians often held their meetings in secret places, and their critics imagined that they were doing all sorts of evil things. It was easy to circulate rumors of this kind, and along with other things, Christians were charged with plotting against the Roman government. As the opposition to Christianity became more intense, the followers of the new movement were asked to prove their loyalty to the Roman government by denouncing Christ and by worshipping the statue of the emperor. When they refused to do this, they were tortured and even put to death.

Under these conditions, the Revelation of John was written. It would be difficult to imagine anything more appropriate for the members of Christian churches at that time. They needed encouragement and the assurance that their trials would soon be over, that the evil powers of the earth would be destroyed, and that the triumph of righteousness would be established in the world. The message of Revelation was intended for this particular time and set of circumstances. Christians familiar with the older apocalyptic writings would understand the book's symbolism, for practically everything John said to his contemporaries was said before to people who suffered under similar circumstances. It is a mistake to suppose that John was predicting events that would take place in the later centuries of Christian history. Writing to the people of his own day about events that would happen while they were still living, he states that Christ will return while those who put him to death on the cross are still living. The permanent significance of Revelation lies in the author's conviction that right will ultimately triumph over evil.

THE GOSPEL OF JOHN

Summary

The Gospel of John is the latest-written of the four biographies of Jesus that have been preserved in the New Testament. Written by a Christian named John, the contents of the book indicate quite clearly that the author was not the John who was one of the twelve disciples of Jesus, for it contains no direct personal references of the type that one would expect from an intimate associate of Jesus. On the contrary, it presents an interpretation of Jesus that reflects ideas and situations that prevailed in the Christian community toward the end of the first century of the Christian era, a time when Christianity was under attack from several different quarters, including Jews, Romans, skeptics, and others making charges against it. The author of the Gospel of John was evidently aware of these attacks and knew that some of the accounts given in earlier gospels were interpreted in a manner that seemed to support these charges. Because he believed so firmly in the new Christian movement, he wanted to write a gospel that set forth its essential truth in the best possible manner. His hope was that he might write one that was not only true but that offered a presentation of the Christian faith that would overcome the objections of its critics and gain the respect of the educated and cultured people of his day. This objective helps us to understand many of the unique characteristics of John's gospel, especially the ones that sharply contrast the Synoptic Gospels. It explains the omission in the Gospel of John of many items found in the earlier accounts, and it also explains, at least in part, the different attitude about Jews, the allegorical interpretations of certain miracle stories, the absence of apocalypticism with reference to the second coming, the subordinate role of John the Baptist, and a new concept of the Messiah.

The purpose of this gospel, as stated by John himself, is to show that Jesus of Nazareth was Christ, the Son of God, and that believers in him might have eternal life. This purpose was one that John had in common with the men who wrote the Synoptic Gospels, but his method for achieving it distinguishes his gospel from the earlier ones. The central theme in the Synoptic Gospels is the coming of the kingdom of God, and it was in relation to this event that the accounts were given of the life and teachings of Jesus. The messianic character of Jesus' mission was described in terms of the miracles that he performed, his kindly attitude toward the poor and the oppressed, his power to cast out demons and to heal the sick, and his instructions concerning the way people should live in view of the imminence of the coming kingdom.

In the Gospel of John, the central theme is the divine Logos, the word that was with God and that was God. This Logos became flesh and dwelt among men in the person of Jesus of Nazareth. John says nothing of a supernatural birth. He regards Jesus as a human being who possessed actual flesh and blood, the same as other people. The most significant thing about Jesus is that the divine Logos was present in him, and all of the marvelous things that he accomplished were by virtue of the power of God. In this way, John conceives the relationship between the divine and the human. Because God was present in Jesus, it is appropriate to refer to Jesus as the Son of God, which is an example of what can happen in the life of anyone else in whom the power of God dwells. In this connection, John says, "Yet to all who received him, to those who believed in his name, he gave the right to become children of God."

John's account of the ministry of Jesus consists of two parts. The first twelve chapters describe Jesus' public ministry, beginning with his meeting John the Baptist and closing with the visit of the Greeks who came to worship at the Feast of Passover. The remaining chapters deal with the closing days of Jesus' earthly ministry, when he gave instruction to his disciples and explained the meaning of his life and approaching death in a number of lengthy discourses. This division of the gospel into two parts follows the pattern used by the Synoptic Gospels' writers, but the contents of the two sections differ widely from the earlier accounts. According to John, Jesus' public ministry can be summarized in connection with a number of miracles that John reports and then follows with interpretations that point to their spiritual significance.

John records only seven miracles, considerably less than the number reported in the Synoptic Gospels. But John's use of the miracle stories is different from that of his predecessors. John does not regard the stories' miraculous elements themselves as having great significance but rather the spiritual meanings that he finds implicit in them. The miracles are signs not of the imminence of the coming of God's kingdom as that term is used in the Synoptic Gospels but of the presence of the Logos, or the power of God, which brings about a transformation in people's lives.

The seven miracle stories recorded in John are, first, the turning of water into wine at a marriage feast in Cana; second, the healing of a nobleman's son who was at the point of death; third, the healing of a man at the sheep-gate pool; fourth, the walking on water; fifth, the feeding of five thousand; sixth, the healing of the man born blind; and seventh, the raising of Lazarus. Each of these stories is used as an introduction to a discourse concerning the significance of Jesus and his message in relation to the quality of a person's life. This use of the miracle stories for the purpose of teaching spiritual lessons is made possible by analogies and, in many instances, by allegorizing the materials found in the stories. For example, the story of Jesus' turning water into wine is interpreted to mean the contrast between the old and the new dispensations. The water symbolizes a cleansing, and the transformation that takes place when a person's life is filled with the spirit present in Jesus sharply contrasts with the rites and ceremonies performed in the Jewish Temple. This meaning of the story is given special emphasis in the narratives that follow. In one of these, Jesus drives out the buyers and sellers from the Temple. In the Synoptic Gospels, this event is placed toward the close of Jesus' ministry, but John situates it toward the beginning because to him it represents the goal of Jesus' entire earthly career. He quotes Jesus as saying, "Destroy this temple, and I will raise it again in three days," which is a reference to John's belief that Jesus' death and resurrection have brought about a new and more meaningful conception of salvation. The point is illustrated even further in the story of Jesus' conversation with Nicodemus, in which Jesus says that unless a person is born of the water and the spirit, that person cannot see the kingdom of God. The same point of view is expressed again in the account of Jesus' conversation with the woman at the Samarian well. In reply to her questions concerning the proper place and manner of worship, Jesus explains that external forms of worship are not as important as worshipping the Father "in spirit and truth."

The feeding of the five thousand appears to be taken from the Synoptic Gospels, which present the story as evidence that

Jesus is the Messiah because he worked miracles. John reports the story as it was customarily understood, but the use that he makes of it is quite different from that of the earlier writers. For John, the amount of physical food that came into existence was not of primary importance. Instead, the important meaning of the story is the spiritual food that alone can sustain the quality of living that characterizes true followers of Jesus. Accordingly, the account of the miracles is followed immediately by a discourse in which Jesus says, "I am the bread of life." In an obvious reference to the Christian practice of celebrating the Eucharist, or the Lord's Supper, John quotes Jesus as saying, "Whoever eats my flesh and drinks my blood remains in me, and I in him." It is the presence of the Logos, or Spirit of God, in human life that really nourishes the spiritual quality of a person's life. Just as Jesus, by virtue of this spirit, gives the living water that brings eternal life, so he gives the food that can bring a new quality of life to the world.

When Jesus heals a man who was born blind, his disciples inquire of him, "Rabbi, who sinned, this man or his parents, that he was born blind?" In reply, Jesus says, "Neither this man nor his parents sinned, but this happened so that the power of God might be displayed in his life." The discussion that follows this exchange makes clear that John's major concern in this narrative is not physical sight in place of physical blindness but rather the curing of men and women of their spiritual blindness. Those who fail to understand Jesus and the purpose of his mission in the world are spiritually blind. Only by coming under the influence of his spirit can we pass from darkness into light.

In the story of the resurrection of Lazarus, the brother of Mary and Martha, John's interpretation of the signs reaches its climax. Lazarus was dead for four days, and at the call of Jesus he came back to life. For John, an event of this kind is a most appropriate symbol of what happens to spiritually dead people when they are receptive to the power of God made manifest in the person of Jesus. That this story is found only in the Gospel of John raises some questions concerning the historicity of the event, for it does not seem at all probable that the authors of the Synoptic Gospels would have failed to relate an event as important as this one if they had known about it. Whether John was recording a popular tradition or writing a sequel to the story of the rich man

and Lazarus, recorded in the Gospel of Luke, we do not know. At
any rate, the story in Luke closes with the statement that those
who do not believe Moses and the prophets will not be convinced,
even if a person raised from the dead should speak to them. In
John's story, someone does come from the dead, and even then the
Jews are not persuaded by what he says and does. As John interprets the story, its deeper meaning is disclosed in a statement that
Jesus makes: "I am the resurrection and the life. He who believes
in me will live, even though he dies; and whoever lives and believes in me will never die." Lazarus is typical of all human beings.
Without the indwelling presence of the Spirit of God, all human
life is meaningless. When the Spirit of God enters into our lives, we
are no longer dead in a spiritual sense but are partakers of the life
that is everlasting.

The remaining portions of the Gospel of John record incidents closely related to the closing days of Jesus' earthly ministry.
Unlike the Gospel of Mark, the story of the anointing of Jesus by
Mary is placed before rather than after Jesus' triumphal entry into
Jerusalem, and the Passover meal with the disciples is said to have
taken place one day earlier than in the account given in the
Synoptic Gospels. These changes are quite in harmony with John's
conception of Jesus as "the Lamb of God, who takes away the sin
of the world!" Because the paschal lamb used as a sacrifice by the
ancient Jews was always slain on the day before the Passover, it
seemed most appropriate to John that the sacrifice of Jesus should
be in conformity with the ancient tradition.

The major emphasis in this part of John's gospel is found in
the discourses that are attributed to Jesus. Because John is interpreting the meaning of Jesus' earthly career from the perspective
of the post-resurrection experiences and beliefs of the Christian
community, these discourses are presented as though they were
made in anticipation of the events that followed. This narrative device is exemplified in the story of the foot-washing that precedes
the eating of the Passover meal. By performing the work of a servant, Jesus not only gives to his disciples an example of humility
that they are to follow, but the water used in the service is a symbol of that spiritual cleansing essential for all those who become
true followers of him. This symbolic washing is the meaning of
Jesus' statement made to Peter: "Unless I wash you, you have no

part with me." And when Jesus says to the group of disciples, "And you are clean, though not every one of you," he is referring to Judas, who betrays Jesus by contacting Jesus' enemies.

In one of the discourses, Jesus explains his relation to God the Father by using the parable of the vine and the branches. He shows in what sense it is true that the Son and the Father are one in spirit and in purpose without either of them losing their personal identities. The Father works through the Son for the redemption of the world, but the task must be continued after the earthly career of the Son has ended. In this connection, Jesus speaks of going to the Father in order that the Comforter or Spirit of God may be present in the hearts and minds of the believers and thus continue through the church the work that Jesus did while dwelling in their midst, which is John's version of the second coming. John replaces, at least in part, the apocalyptic expectations present in all three of the Synoptic Gospels. John, no less than the Synoptic Gospels' writers, believes that some day the forces of evil in this world will be overcome, and God's reign of righteousness finally will be established. But instead of being brought about by a sudden catastrophic event that will destroy the nations of the world and at which time Jesus will return to earth in power and great glory, John sees the return of Jesus whenever and wherever the Spirit of God enters into the lives of human beings. He believes that the function of the Christian church is to follow the guidance and direction of this spirit until the whole world has been transformed into a kingdom of God.

In a long and remarkable prayer that John attributes to Jesus, the meaning and significance of Jesus' entire career are neatly summarized. We may be sure that the language used is that of John rather than of Jesus, for it contains the same type of statements used throughout the Gospels, and there are places where Jesus is referred to in the third person, but this is a relatively unimportant item. What is important is that the prayer contains that which John believes to be implicit in the life and teachings of Jesus. It is a fitting resume, as John sees it, of what Jesus has done for the Christian community and indeed for all those who at any future time will become members of it. The Christian community, at the time when John wrote, was experiencing a great deal of opposition, not only from Jews but from Romans and others who were skeptical of the claims that Christians were making. At times, this opposition led to severe persecution, and some Christians wanted to withdraw from direct contact with the people of the world. It is to these Christians that Jesus' words to God are addressed: "My prayer is not that you take them out of the world but that you protect them from the evil one."

Following the prayer, John describes the events that culminate in the crucifixion of Jesus and reports the words that Jesus utters while on the cross. Jesus' last words—"It is finished"—carry a double meaning, for they indicate not only that Jesus is about to die but that the whole purpose of the incarnation is now complete. The gospel closes with an account of the post-resurrection experiences that took place both in Jerusalem and in Galilee.

Commentary

The importance of the Gospel of John can scarcely be overestimated. Throughout Christian history, it has been read and cherished far more than any of the other preserved accounts of Jesus' life. The genius of the gospel lies in the way in which John conceives of the relationship between the human and the divine. This relationship has always been a problem that has puzzled people. How can God, who is conceived as an eternal, omniscient, and omnipotent being, have any direct contact with that which is temporal, changing, and limited by the conditions of space and time? In other words, how can divinity ever be united with humanity unless one thereby becomes involved in a contradiction of terms? John's answer to this question is his statement, "The Word became flesh and made his dwelling among us." The Logos is identified with God and is the spirit that dwelt in the human being known as Jesus of Nazareth. This divine spirit motivated Jesus' activities and enabled him to meet triumphantly the temptations to which all human beings are subject. As John sees it, no human being using only his own strength can overcome the forces of evil. Only God can impart the power to human beings to do this. That it was done in the person of Jesus is all the evidence needed to assure that triumph over evil is a possibility for humans and that the ultimate overthrow of the forces of evil is something that has now been made certain.

Throughout John's gospel, Jesus appears in the role of a human being, which is especially important because it means that he is an example for other people to follow. As a typical human being, he possessed no extraordinary power that is not available to anyone else who asks for it and who meets the conditions for receiving it. Because Jesus' will is in complete harmony with the will of God, it is proper and right to refer to him as the Son of God; in this connection, we are to understand the statement "Yet to all who received him, to those who believed in his name, he gave the right to become children of God."

John's treatment of the miracle stories is especially significant. In the Synoptic Gospels, the purpose of the miracles appears to be that of presenting evidence to support the claim that Jesus is the true Messiah. The evidence for this claim rests on Jesus' ability to do that which ordinary human beings cannot do. In this case, the historical accuracy of an event as reported would be crucial. In John's gospel, only seven miracles are reported, and in no one of these instances is the real meaning of the story dependent on its historical accuracy, which is not to say that John has any doubts about the events' historical accuracy. He does not discuss historicity, for he has something else in mind that he regards as far more important: the spiritual lesson that he derives from the stories, whether the details are reported accurately or not. One of the advantages of the Gospel of John is that it presents the meaning of Christianity in a way that makes its validity dependent on neither scientific accuracy nor historical verification. This position is a fortunate one for modern readers since we have no adequate means for determining exactly what happened in regard to any of the reported events. All of the evidence we have is what the individuals who made the records believed to have happened.

The interpretation of Christianity set forth in the Gospel of John may be characterized as mystical in the same sense that Paul's letters are mystical. In both instances, the essence of salvation is the mystical union of the human and the divine. The presence of God in the life of Jesus of Nazareth enabled Jesus to overcome the temptations that arise from contact with the flesh and the world, and this same presence can enter into the heart and life of any individual who allows this spirit to become the motivating life force. Paul expresses this conception in the words "I have been crucified with Christ and I no longer live, but Christ lives in me." John says that just as the branch cannot bear fruit except that the fruit abides in the vine, so a Christian cannot live the good life unless Christ abides within that person. This type of mysticism unites the believer with God, yet it does so without destroying the individuality of either. In this respect, Christian mysticism differs from those types in which individual personality is destroyed by becoming wholly absorbed in the deity.